"In this unique edited volume, readers will find a hydrofeminist cornucopia of oceanic contemplations, and reflections on highly creative eco- and art-activist practices, and Indigenous-centred methodologies. Using South Africa as a lens to Global South epistemologies, contributors ask: How to rethink haunting colonial histories, as well as resist post-apartheid inequalities, and extractive capitalism's violent exploitations of environments and local communities through hydrofeminist approaches? This book is a 'must' for everyone wanting to engage with the question: What does it mean for environmental and social justice-to-come to shift for a thinking- and sensing-with oceans, sea critters, and ancestral knowledges of watery interconnections?"

Nina Lykke, *Professor Emerita, Gender Studies, Linköping University Sweden, and Aarhus University, Denmark*

"Take your thoughts on a wild swim and a free dive with this finger-on-the-pulse collection. Drawing together an impressive range of contemporary hydro-related theories, the volume refracts these from a global south and feminist perspective, re-exploring South Africa's haunted histories via its coasts, shorelines and beaches. Exploring a range of media forms, this collection will be welcomed by anyone with an interest in oceans, climate change and social justice."

Isabel Hofmeyr, *Professor Emeritus, University of the Witwatersrand*

"As the seas rise, watery thinking is coming into view. This experimental collection of essays and provocations brings together many ways of thinking and being with oceanic environments. Through distinctive contributions enabled by South Africa's historical, political, and physical conditions, these authors advance innovative practices, eco-theories, and visions for social and environmental justice."

Steve Mentz, *St. John's University, USA, Author of* An Introduction to the Blue Humanities *(Routledge, 2023)*

"This exciting multi-disciplinary text is at the forefront of new thinking on blue environmental justice. Immersed in the under-explored bathymetric setting of South Africa, the book draws from a depth of activist voices, perspectives and knowledges that caution us on how important past, present and future blue care is for all communities that live by, on, in and under the water."

Ronan Foley, *Associate Professor, University of Maynooth, Ireland*

"This rich, transdisciplinary, and beautifully composed edited collection offers readers spaces for critical and ethical scholarship, promoting hopefulness for a justice to come. Hydrofeminist thinking is creatively shaped by storytelling inspired by art, literature, and activism, such as memories, poetry, photography, theatre, and swimming, writing, walking, and conversation. The multiplicity of local stories of Ocean/s and beaches in the South African geopolitical context in this book inspired me to slow and diffractive reading to read and read again, see, and see again, listen, and listen again, from different and entangled stories, wordings, and images. There is much to learn for international readers from this edited collection about how we become locally situated watery selves and the political and scholarly possibilities of hydrofeminist thinking for pedagogical creativity and environmental justice."

Mona B. Livholts, *Professor of Social Work, University of Helsinki, Finland, Author of* The Body Politics of Glocal Social Work: Essays on the Post-Anthropocentric Condition *(Routledge 2023)*

HYDROFEMINIST THINKING WITH OCEANS

Hydrofeminist Thinking with Oceans brings together authors who are thinking in, with and through the spaces of ocean/s and beaches in South African contexts to make alternative knowledges towards a justice-to-come and flourishing at a planetary level. Primary scholarly locations for this work include feminist new materialist and post-humanist thinking, and specifically locates itself within hydrofeminist thinking.

Together with a foreword by Astrida Neimanis, the chapters in this book explore both land and water with oceans as powerfully political spaces, globally and locally entangled in the violences of settler colonialism, land dispossession, slavery, transnational labour exploitation, extractivism and omnicides. South Africa is a productive space to engage in such scholarship. While there is a growing body of literature that works within and across disciplines on the sea and bodies of water to think critically about the damages of centuries of colonisation and continued extractivist capitalism, there remains little work that explores this burgeoning thinking in global Southern, and more particularly South African contexts. South African histories of colonisation, slavery and more recently apartheid, which are saturated in the oceans, are only recently being explored through oceanic logics. This volume offers valuable Southern contributions and rich situated narratives to such hydrofeminist thinking. It also brings diverse and more marginal knowledges to bear on the project of generating imaginative alternatives to hegemonic colonial and patriarchal logics in the academy and elsewhere. While primarily located in a South African context, the volume speaks well to globalised concerns for justice and environmental challenges both in human societies and in relation to other species and planetary crises.

The chapters, which will be of interest to scholars, activists and other civil society stakeholders, share inspiring, rich examples of diverse scholarship, activism and art in these contexts, extending international scholarship that thinks in/on/with ocean/s, littoral zones and bodies of water. The book offers ethico-political perspectives on the role of research in ocean governance, policy development and collective decision-making for ecological justice. This book is suitable for students and scholars of post-qualitative, feminist, new materialist, embodied, arts-based and hydrofeminist methods in education, environmental humanities and the social sciences.

Tamara Shefer is Professor of Women's and Gender Studies, Faculty of Arts and Humanities, University of the Western Cape, Cape Town, South Africa. She primarily writes about young people, gender and sexualities. She currently focuses on post-qualitative, feminist, decolonial scholarship, including thinking with oceans for alternative knowledge and ethical living.

Vivienne Bozalek is Emerita Professor of Women's and Gender Studies, Faculty of Arts and Humanities, University of the Western Cape, Cape Town, South Africa, and an Honorary Professor at the Centre for Higher Education Research, Teaching and Learning (CHERTL) at Rhodes University, Grahamstown, South Africa. She currently focuses on post-qualitative feminist, new materialist and post-humanist scholarship.

Nike Romano teaches history and theory of design at the Cape Peninsula University of Technology, Cape Town, South Africa. Her artistic research interests explore the relationship between thinking, making and doing through a post-humanist and feminist new materialist frame.

Postqualitative, New Materialist and Critical Posthumanist Research

Editor in Chief: Karin Murris (Universities of Oulu, Finland, and Cape Town, South Africa)
Editors: *Vivienne Bozalek* (University of the Western Cape and Rhodes University, South Africa)
Asilia Franklin-Phipps (State University of New York at New Paltz, USA)
Simone Fullagar (Griffith University, Australia)
Candace R. Kuby (University of Missouri, USA)
Karen Malone (Swinburne University of Technology, Australia)
Carol A. Taylor (University of Bath, United Kingdom)
Weili Zhao (Hangzhou Normal University, China)

This cutting-edge series is designed to assist established researchers, academics, postgraduate/graduate students and their supervisors across higher education faculties and departments to incorporate novel, postqualitative, new materialist, and critical posthumanist approaches in their research projects and their academic writing. In addition to these substantive foci, books within the series are inter-, multi- or transdisciplinary and are in dialogue with perspectives such as Black feminisms and Indigenous knowledges, decolonial, African, Eastern and young children's philosophies. Although the series' primary aim is accessibility, its scope makes it attractive to established academics already working with postqualitative approaches.

This series is unique in providing short, user-friendly, affordable books that support postgraduate students and academics across disciplines and faculties in higher education. The series is supported by its own website with videos, images and other forms of 3D transmodal expression of ideas–provocations for research courses.

More resources for the books in the series are available on the series website, www.postqualitativeresearch.com.

If you are interested in submitting a proposal for the series, please write to the Chief Editor, Professor Karin Murris: karin.murris@oulu.fi; karin.murris@uct.ac.za.

Other volumes in this series include:

Invisible Education
Posthuman Explorations of Everyday Learning
Jocey Quinn

HYDROFEMINIST THINKING WITH OCEANS

Political and Scholarly Possibilities

Edited by Tamara Shefer, Vivienne Bozalek and Nike Romano

Routledge
Taylor & Francis Group

LONDON AND NEW YORK

Designed cover image: Cover Artwork by Lauren Hermann

First published 2024
by Routledge
4 Park Square, Milton Park, Abingdon, Oxon OX14 4RN

and by Routledge
605 Third Avenue, New York, NY 10158

Routledge is an imprint of the Taylor & Francis Group, an informa business

British Library Cataloguing-in-Publication Data
A catalogue record for this book is available from the British Library

ISBN: 9781032408972 (hbk)
ISBN: 9781032408996 (pbk)
ISBN: 9781003355199 (ebk)

DOI: 10.4324/9781003355199

Typeset in Times New Roman
by Newgen Publishing UK

CONTENTS

FIGURES

ABOUT THE CONTRIBUTORS

Vivienne Bozalek is Honorary Professor in the Centre for Higher Education Research, Teaching and Learning (CHERTL) at Rhodes University and Emerita Professor in Women's and Gender Studies, Faculty of Arts and Humanities, University of the Western Cape. Her research interests and publications include the political ethics of care and social justice, posthumanism and feminist new materialisms, innovative pedagogical practices in higher education, post-qualitative and participatory methodologies. Her most recent co-edited books include *Posthuman and Political Care Ethics for Reconfiguring Higher Education* with Michalinos Zembylas and Joan Tronto (Routledge, 2021), *Post-Anthropocentric Social Work: Critical Posthuman and New Materialist Perspectives*, with Bob Pease (Routledge, 2021), *Higher education hauntologies: Living with ghosts for a justice-to-come* with Michalinos Zembylas, Siddique Motala and Dorothee Hölscher (Routledge, 2021) and *In conversation with Karen Barad: Doings of agential realism* with Karin Murris (Routledge 2023). She is the editor-in-chief of the open-source online journal *Critical Studies in Teaching and Learning*.

Delphi Carstens is a lecturer at the University of the Western Cape and a member of the Orphan Drift collective. His research interests include animal studies, the new synthesis in biology, feminist new materialisms, Deleuze–Guattarian theory, uncanny science–fictions and figurations of the Anthropocene/Capitalocence in contemporary culture. He has published widely on the relevance of these matters to HE (higher education) pedagogy, most recently in the edited volume *A Human Pedagogy* (Palgrave) and the journals, *Religion, Ethics & Social Welfare* (with Viv Bozalek), *CriStal*. Vol.8 (SI) and *Somatechnics 10*(1).

Adrienne van Eeden-Wharton is an artist-researcher who is passionate about finding ways of restorying fraught and entangled terraqueous, multispecies relatings. Her praxis focuses on intra-oceanic environmental histories, and she dreams of working in the polar regions. Adrienne is a postdoctoral fellow at the University of Pretoria, South Africa, on the *Antarctica, Africa and the Arts* project, funded by the National Research Foundation (NRF) as part of the South African National Antarctic Programme (SANAP).

Buhle Francis is an environmental scholar-activist and a researcher based at Rhodes University, at the Faculty of Education at the Environmental Learning Research Centre, in a project funded by One Ocean Hub. Buhle Francis is involved in co-engaged research on coastal justice issues focusing on the ocean governance of small-scale fishers and the livelihoods of women.

Simone Fullagar (she/her) is Professor and Chair of the Sport and Gender Equity research hub and lead for the Inclusive Play theme in the Reimaging Disability, Griffith Inclusive Futures programme at Griffith University, Australia. She has published feminist, interdisciplinary sociological research using postqualitative approaches across sport, leisure and mental health fields. Simone collaborates with colleagues to produce theoretically informed research that explores gender relations and diverse forms of embodied movement. Simone is Fellow of the Academy of Social Sciences, UK.

Karen Graaff (she/her) is a gender studies scholar and general ocean enthusiast. She worked and published on masculinities and violence for over a decade and has more recently begun to focus on the spaces for activism and social change being created by queer surfers in the dominant heteronormative surf culture. She is currently working on a podcast project with Dr. Glen Thompson that aims to involve the surfing community and the wider public in academic conversations about surfing cultures in the global South. Her most recent publication was: The implications of a narrow understanding of gender-based violence. *Feminist Encounters*, 5(1): article 12. https://doi.org/10.20897/femenc/9749

Cheri Hugo is a storyteller, illustrator, figure drawing lecturer and a PhD candidate at the University of the Western Cape. Her academic interests revolve around transitions, in-between spaces, storytelling, poetry, visual methods and art-based methodologies. She employs feminist methodologies and theories to challenge traditional academic practices and create a more inclusive scholarly landscape. Cheri's work blends academic rigour with creative expression, using visual methods and art to uncover fresh perspectives and profound insights into human experiences. As a figure drawing lecturer, she seamlessly combines her artistic expertise with her academic pursuits, bridging the gap between academia and the world of visual arts.

Cheri is committed to swim methodologies, which offer alternative approaches to knowledge production and academic engagement. Through her photovoice essay and ongoing research, she aims to expand the boundaries of academia, encourage critical reflection and amplify marginalised voices.

Meghan Judge is an artist and researcher living in Johannesburg, South Africa. Judge works largely in the Southern African Indian Ocean world. She holds an MA (cum laude) from Wits School of the Arts and is currently a PhD scholar at Wits Institute for Economic Research (WiSER) in the Oceanic Humanities for the Global South project and the Wits School of the Arts. She is a founding member of the Africa|Nosy Art Exchange.

Zayaan Khan is a transdisciplinary artist using the local urban and ecological relationship/s to understand the elements that build ecosystems. Through curiosity, research, experimentation and engagement, her work finds a resting place through food as a means of understanding the world, particularly seed, land, sea and our collective heritage. Influenced by tradition, both inherited and the creation of new ones, reclaiming culture and reviving tradition through progressive interpretation in order to enact a listening of the future and steady present survivalism. Zayaan is currently completing her PhD entitled, 'From seed-as-object to seed-as-relation' through the Environmental Humanities South at the University of Cape Town.

Barry Lewis is the Director of UBU (Ubuhle Bakha Ubuhle/Beauty Builds Beauty), a company specifically focused on developing the technology of Sandbag housing in low-income communities in South Africa. Formally an architect from the United Kingdom, Barry arrived in Cape Town in 2009 and worked for The Warehouse Trust (NGO) before founding UBU in 2012, specifically working in an informal community called Sweet Home Farm in Philippi. UBU played the role of facilitator in the City of Cape Town's UISP (Upgrade of Informal Settlements Programme) project in the community whilst developing the idea of the Process House, an incremental model of housing utilising Sandbags and EcoBeams all built by members of the community over a 2.5-year period. UBU's mission is to activate and equip humans to self-build places of belonging in both formal and informal areas.

Aaniyah Martin focuses on work that connects people and nature. She has 15 years of experience in the conservation sector with a strong emphasis on finding the balance between what is good for the earth and good for the people. In 2021, she was selected as one of 20 African female conservationists to participate in the first cohort of *Women for the Environment in Africa* (WE Africa). Aaniyah is the founder and director of a non-profit organisation called *The Beach Co-op* and works part-time for WE Africa and *Homeward Bound* – the latter two organisations that focus on women's leadership in STEMM and the environment. She is a registered PhD student at the Environmental Learning Research Centre, Rhodes University.

Dylan McGarry is an educational sociologist and artist from Durban, South Africa. He is a Senior Researcher at the Environmental Learning Research Centre (ELRC) at the University currently known as Rhodes. As well as a co-director of the Global One Ocean Hub research network. Dylan is the co-founder of Empatheatre and a passionate artist and storyteller. He explores practice-based research into connective aesthetics, transgressive social learning, decolonisation, queer-eco pedagogy, immersive empathy and socio-ecological development in South Africa. His artwork and social praxis (which is closely related to his research) are particularly focused on empathy, and he primarily works with imagination, listening and intuition as actual sculptural materials in social settings to offer new ways to encourage personal, relational and collective agency. Dylan recently wrote, co-directed and produced the short animated film: "Indlela Yokuphila – the Soul's Journey", which was used as evidence in three court cases against Oil and Gas giant Shell – to show the intangible cultural connections some South Africans have with the ocean and is the focus of his contribution to this book.

Astrida Neimanis is a cultural theorist working at the intersection of feminism and environmental change. She is Associate Professor and Canada Research Chair in Feminist Environmental Humanities at the University of British Colombia – Okanagan Campus on unceded Syilx Okanagan territory in Canada. Her research focuses on bodies, water and weather and how they can help us reimagine justice, care, responsibility and relation in the time of climate catastrophe. Her most recent book, *Bodies of Water: Posthuman Feminist Phenomenology*, is a call for humans to examine our relationships to oceans, watersheds and other aquatic life forms from the perspective of our own primarily watery bodies and our ecological, poetic and political connections to other bodies of water. Additional research interests include theories and practice of interdisciplinarity, feminist epistemologies, intersectionality, multispecies justice and everyday militarism. Astrida's research practice includes collaborations with artists, writers, scientists, makers, educational institutions and communities, often in the form of experimental public pedagogies. Her writing can be found in numerous academic journals and edited collections, artistic exhibitions, catalogues and online media.

Joanne Peers is a PhD candidate at The University of Oulu in Finland, where she is pursuing relationality in education through thinking with bodies, water, time, memory and space. Her interest in justice and activism in the Global South brings watery ways of relating to oceans, environments and education. She is Head of Academics at The Centre for Creative Education in Cape Town, a nonprofit teacher education institution. Her unique position of working in higher education and fulfilling the role as a collaborator with resourced and under-resourced schools in Cape Town allows extensive worlding with theory and practice in education.

Mer Maggie Roberts is a London and Cape Town-based artist/educator. She is the co-founder of the Orphan Drift collective. Her practice explores different kinds of perception, proprioception and virtual and synthetic worlds with the intention of generating more multidimensional, imaginative and experimental versions of being human. She has exhibited artworks and contributed to symposia internationally for nearly three decades and is currently working with the Serpentine Gallery's Creative AI Lab and the Royal College of Art's Ai Design Lab. She taught critical studies on fine art in BA at Central St Martins and was a recent research fellow with visual cultures at Goldsmiths College, London.

Nike Romano teaches history and theory of design at the Cape Peninsula University of Technology. Her artistic research interests explore the relationship between thinking, making and doing through a Posthumanist and Feminist New Materialist frame. Her most recent publications include: Touching Text: Feeling My Way Through Research-Creation in *Qualitative Inquiry*, 29(1), 69–81, and Th/reading through Mull: Cutting a Fashion Theory Course Together-Apart, pp 158–171. In Murris, K. And Bozalek, V. (Eds), *In Conversation with Karen Barad (Postqualitative, New Materialist and Critical Posthumanist Research) 1st Edition.* Routledge.

Tamara Shefer is Professor of Women's and Gender Studies in the Faculty of Arts and Humanities at the University of the Western Cape, Cape Town. Her scholarship has been directed at intersectional gender and sexual justice, with particular emphasis on young people. She is currently engaged with re-conceptualising academic knowledge with an emphasis on embodied, affective, feminist and decolonial pedagogies and research, with emphasis on collaborations across art and activism and thinking with oceans and water. Most recent books include: *Knowledge, Power and Young Sexualities: A Transnational Feminist Engagement* (co-authored with J. Hearn, 2022, Routledge); *A feminist critique of sexuality education for gender justice in South African contexts* (co-authored with S. Ngabaza, 2023, CSA&G Pretoria University) and *Routledge International Handbook of Masculinity Studies* (co-edited with L. Gottzén & U. Mellström, 2020).

Kristy Stone is a practising artist and PhD candidate in the Department of History at the University of the Western Cape. From 2016 to 2020, she was an A.W. Mellon Doctoral Fellow at the Centre for Humanities Research (UWC). Her thesis is titled *Affect and art: Encounters with objects of power in South African museum and archival collections.* Kristy has a background in Fine Art (BA Hons.), Education and Heritage Studies (MA) from the University of the Witwatersrand. She has worked in museum education for several years and continues to write arts-based training materials for teachers and students.

Toni Giselle Stuart works as a poet, performer, writing teacher and creative mentor. Her work is rooted in the practice of listening for the stories that help us reclaim and remember our ancestral wisdom and gifts. Poetic works include *Krotoa-Eva's Suite – a cape jazz poem in three movements* with filmmaker Kurt Orderson; Poetry, Paramedics and Film with filmmaker/health researcher Leanne Brady (2018); What the Water Remembers at Woordfees (2020); forgetting and memory with vangile gantsho and Vusumzi Ngxande, at the Virtual National Arts Festival (2020). She has an MA writer/teacher (distinction) from Goldsmiths, University of London, where she was a 2014/2015 Chevening Scholar. Her poems have been published in *Poetry Magazine* and *Callaloo Journal*, among others. She was the founding curator of Poetica at the Open Book Festival.

INTRODUCTION TO THE SERIES

Postqualitative, New Materialist and Critical Posthumanist Research

Simone Fullagar
Series Co-editor

Hydrofeminist Thinking with Oceans: Political and Scholarly Possibilities makes a distinctive contribution to postqualitative scholarship through an expansive collection of chapters that invite us to immerse ourselves in feminist ways of thinking with oceans and question the seemingly solid ground of humanist thought. Readers and writers are brought together in a postqualitative conversation that connects the poetic and political through particular rhythms of inquiry, hauntings and worlding practices that move us to (un)learn. Reflecting the central aim of this book series, the editors and authors write to disrupt binaries and bring ideas into relation through South African scholarship that explores surfaces and depths, seen and unseen ocean ecologies facing threats of pollution-extraction-consumption. The specificity of this context offers readers a nuanced journey through the histories of exclusion that haunt the immediacy of sensory experience, and the awe produced by nonhuman nature that is an invitation to research *with* the affective powers of watery worlds. It is a collection of critical and generative practices born of listening deeply to the violence of historical power relations that produce bodies of water, and possibilities of de-colonising movement, freedom and justice-to-come.

The diverse enactments of postqualitative research in each chapter work to enliven our imaginations by entangling thinking with swimming-floating-drowning-drifting-attuning with creatures, othered bodies, pollution in the tidal spaces of learning, harvesting and bodily movement. The book importantly provides a provocation for exploring ways of knowing otherwise as oceans require different theory-method approaches that recognise porosity, intra-active flows and matter in movement. *Hydrofeminist Thinking with Oceans* is a creative endeavour as it crosses boundaries, mobilising images and language to connect readers with the multiplicity of ocean ecologies and what they can 'do' to move us towards different ways of knowing. The collection provides an invaluable resource for doctorate students as well as more established researchers working across disciplinary perspectives and cultural locales. Bringing feminist thought into a dynamic relation with postqualitative provocations, the contributors leave readers to ponder a pedagogical question concerning how the materiality of our knowledge practices becomes entangled in the process of learning by attuning to objects, spaces, bodies and the liveliness of watery worlds.

FOREWORD

Hydrofeminisms and the desire for a watery "we"

Astrida Neimanis, *Associate Professor and Canada Research Chair in Feminist Environmental Humanities, University of British Colombia Okanagan*

The trouble with "we"

We live in a watery world. More accurately, we are the watery world – metonymically, temporarily, partially and particularly. Water irrigates us, sustains us and comprises the bulk of our own soupy flesh. We are all adrift, afloat, swimming or sinking; flowing, floundering; trickling down, welling up, overflowing, rerouting, recharging. We are all bodies of water.

Yet it isn't easy to begin any kind of introduction with an invocation of a "we". In her influential 1985 essay, "Notes towards a politics of location", US lesbian feminist Jewish mother and poet, Adrienne Rich (1986, p. 217) wrote that "the problem was we did not know whom we meant when we said we". Attuned to the problems of universalism and the erasure of the experiences of different women (which we might now more inclusively speak about in terms of differently gendered people), Rich knew that "we" is a dangerous word.

This trouble with "we" is indeed a longstanding feminist preoccupation. As Australian-born queer feminist Sara Ahmed has recently put it:

> Feminist histories are histories of the difficulty of that "we", a history of those who have had to fight to be part of a feminist collective, or even had to fight against a feminist collective in order to take up a feminist cause.
>
> *(2017, p. 2)*

From suffrage, to reproductive justice, to equal pay and the second shift, to transnational struggles that have both crossed borders and created new ones, feminist victories have never been victories for any kind of unified "we" – neither locally, nor globally. Many feminists have long recognised the potential violence of the "we". This is a violence that is hidden by many of "our" calls to justice: *We* are all in this together. *We* have the right, *We* belong, *We* demand, *We* can do it: We, we, we, we, all the way home… Ironically, in its hasty pull to include everybody, the troubling exclusions of this mundane pronoun are exposed.

Now, in the shadow of the so-called Anthropocene, where run-of-the-mill racialised heteropatriarchy meets and amplifies climate crisis and environmental devastation, the question of "we" seems increasingly salient. The altogetherness that this pronoun summons is described by Michif pollution scientist Max Liboiron as something like a convenient myth that falsely redistributes both vulnerability and culpability. Instead, Liboiron insists that "there is no such thing as we". They continue:

> Terms like the Anthropocene or arguments that "we" are destroying the planet or "we" must all band together as One, miss forces like colonialism and other differences in how pollution, discarding, and extraction have continually benefited some types and groups of people and burdened others.
>
> *(2020, np)*

In one sense, Liboiron is right. We are all in this together, but who is waving, who is drowning? Solidarity – feminist or otherwise – is pretty cheap, when it can be simply proclaimed with a signature on a petition, or a blacked-out box on Instagram. The rubber hits the road when we start to consider whose body bears the burdens of "our" collectively rendered Age of Man. In this time of climate catastrophe – fuelled by centuries of colonialism, slavery and heteropatriachal mastery, and augmented by a global pandemic with its grotesquely uneven distribution of vulnerability – just who do "we" think "we" are?

Hydrofeminism

Hydrofeminism springs partly out of a desire to grapple with this problem of "we". As a kind of environmental feminism, hydrofeminism is interested in the false claims of universality that resonate not only across personal and political realms but planetary ones, too, as climate crisis escalates. But more than just an "add climate crisis and stir" mode of feminism, hydrofeminism is itself environmental, ecological, and watery. As a way through the paradox of the "we", hydrofeminism pays attention to water as it moves through the world. Hydrofeminism asks: What can water teach us?

Water's first lesson is that the "we" is in one sense unavoidable. We are – literally, factually, constitutively – all bodies of water. This pertains to other thoroughly watery humans, with whom this "we" invites a watery kinship: the baby you may have bathed into being upon your own amniotic seas, as well as the worker who sat beside you on the bus this morning, are bodies that are made mostly of water. This watery kinship gathers us across generations, including grandmothers (Francis & McGarry, this volume), ancestral presents (Martin, this volume) but also "disorderly ghostly matters" (Peers, this volume). This "we" connects us, moreover, to all of the more-than-human aqueous bodies into whom we leak and seep and spill: the eucalypt, the dung beetle, the kelp frond, the whale, all shimmering in their aliveness and haunting in their "multispecies death assemblages" (Van Eeden-Wharton, this volume). As bodies of water, our "we" expands also geologically and meteorologically to include airborne, rock-bound and sandy-bottomed bodies too: oceans, rivers, aquifers, subterranean streams, clouds, storms, swamps and soils – bodies that are all dripping, lifting and misting; bodies that are mineral and tidal and damp. We all circulate through one another in a multibeing,[1] more-than-human hydrocommons.

But while this watery abundance is certainly a beautiful idea, the risk here is that "we" all get swept up and swept away. This "oceanic feeling" is what anthropologist Elizabeth Povinelli refers to as an "absorptive, relations-erasing universalism" (Povinelli, 2022, p. 168). What kind of politics could a common wateriness offer if it were just dissolving us all into one amorphous puddle? We recall that in her "The Cyborg Manifesto", Donna Haraway rejected the easy lure of a "common language" (2010, p. 5), if this means that difference is simply incorporated and universalised. In other words, to understand our wateriness simply as a constitutive fact does not move us beyond the problem of "we". It simply moves this problem offshore. So what else can water teach us? What else do we notice?

Water is social. We feel this sociality in water's circulations. Even the stillest of puddles quivers with the approach of another body. As bodies of water, we are sensitive to the presence of others. We pool. This material sociality is not only spatial – two rivulets converging at a dip in the sand – but it tumbles in a temporal cascade, too: we drink the ghosts of bodies at the bottom of the ocean, condensing as clouds and precipitating into our open, cupped hands. We gift this water to the future with each breathy word that rises, with each bead of sweat that slides from our skin. We irrigate what comes next.

Water teaches us about the inalienable relation of all bodies, but if we pay attention, we will also notice that amongst all of this watery conviviality, water is always becoming different. As Charles Darwin once quipped, "our ancestor was an animal which breathed water, had a swim bladder, a great swimming tail, an imperfect skull, and was undoubtedly a hermaphrodite!" (cited in Zimmer, 1998, np). Darwin's "pleasant genealogy" reminds us of our evolutionary fishy beginnings, whereby all terrestrial life came from the sea, folding that marine habitat inside of ourselves as we learned to stand on our own two feet.

Water is responsive. Water does not know what comes next, so it learns to adapt, to shape-shift, to code-switch. Water's continual differentiation has been the name of the game for over four billion years. Our planet produces no water in addition to that which has always been here, yet it is not in spite of, but rather because of water's "closed" system that its embodiment in the world is so open. It is only because of difference that water continues to generate itself. Water is always seeking out difference, even as its brute materiality, one might say, seemingly repeats. It is water's sociality, its refusal of permanent containment, that invites difference to proliferate and grow. Water is not a common language; it is a language that swirls upon a billion different tongues, or none.[2]

When water leaves one body, it is already seeking out another. But in its proliferation of difference, water teaches us that difference also, paradoxically, returns. Or, from the perspective of a distant shore, we could say that water is already pulling itself back in. Perhaps this is water's own "practice for return" (Judge, this volume.) Although it may seem that water is always leaving, if we are all bodies of water, then we could also say that water is just finding its way back.

We are for water

For hydrofeminism, this means that we also must find our way back to water. Hydrofeminism is not only a feminism in the context of our contemporary water crises, nor even only a feminism that learns from water. Hydrofeminism must also be a feminism that gives back to the water from which it has learned so much. As Toni Stuart (this volume) reminds us, water shows us "an endless cycle of give and take / one we keep breaking / but have the power to repair." How can hydrofeminism guide us in this repair? Hydrofeminism is a nourishing idea, but it is also an action concept. It is accountability to water. Water wants to find its way back to us, and to itself; this is water's responsibility. Our responsibility is to help it do so.

As water crises escalate, we are tempted to turn away from these lessons. We feel divided in our vulnerability. We are suspicious of structures of power that still burden "us" unequally. "We" is both too easy and too hard. Are we all in this together? Maybe. But is there something less solid than solidarity, yet more confluent than the loneliness of separation?

Listen again to the water. When asked, *Are you this or that, with or against, here or there, now or then, North or South, in or out?* water's reply is simply: yes. Yes, and. We are all in this together, and we are all in this together, differently. Water is this kind of difference. Here swims the beautiful, difficult, irresolvable paradox of "we".

The "we" keeps coming back, because we can't let it go. Like water, it lures us in. To say we are all bodies of water, then, is also to say something about desire. Sara Ahmed recognises something like this when she writes:

> To build feminist dwellings we need to dismantle what has already been assembled; we need to ask what it is we are against, what it is we are for, knowing full well that this *we* is not a foundation but what we are working toward. By working out what we are for we are working *out* that we, that hopeful signifier of a feminist collectivity.

(2017, p. 2)

Might this be akin to Haraway's alternative to a common language – a wild and "infidel heteroglossia" (181)? What if hydrofeminism – a feminism always learning from and with water, a feminism responsible for and accountable to water– were the kind of blasphemous feminism that Haraway suggests can resist the pull of universalisation but still insist on "the need for community" (149)? Haraway was interested in the "tension of holding incompatible things together because both or all are necessary and true" (149). Yes, and.

Traveling concepts: Hydrofeminism as a methodology for specificity and connection

In other words, the hydrofeminist incantation "we are all bodies of water" is also prefigurative: hydrofeminism is *for* water, whatever it will become. "We" are for water. We are desiring a relationship of mutuality without sameness. This is a feminist desire, but one that is amplified against the existential shadow of planetary crises of hydrocolonialism (Hofmeyr, 2019), cis-heteropatriachy, global capitalism and the attendant necropolitics (Mbembe, 2019) of all of these structures of power. The stakes of inhabiting this desire have never been higher.

The offerings in this collection on hydrofeminism from a South African context are already grappling with these questions amongst themselves: "South Africa" is not one place; its waters are not one water. Its human languages are abundant and diverse, as are the languages it speaks in multibeing tongues: the scamper of a crab, the screech of a shorebird, the soft whisper of ocean spray on the rocks of tidal pools. This "infidel heteroglossia" also includes other multibeing forms of language such as poetry, weaving, theatre as evidence in legal procedures, walking or strandlooping, swimming – all forms of speaking to/as/with/from multibeing waters described in this volume, and activated to find new means of watery communication, in service of justice. As Megan Judge remarks in this book's Afterword, even as these offerings do not necessarily "sound in harmony", they find a way, in their differences, to "noise together". These heteroglossic swirlings extend tentacles beyond South Africa too – travelling across oceans that are both connecting and connected bodies, searching out new ways of configuring a useful and workable "we". These hydrofeminisms are specific, and expansive. Yes, and.

Resisting the non-specificity of an oceanic and amorphous universal "we", might we instead think of ourselves as leaky and porous, as sponging and sopping? These watery ways of being do not erase our borders and our differences but in fact call attention to them: transformation happens at the edges. Embodying hydrofeminism, we are sweaty – awkward and not always at home (see Peers, this volume), even as the world courses through us and we through it. Water asks us to be always a little bit in excess of ourselves, always willing to pass on our wateriness in service of somebody else. This collection is about these transformations, these gifts, and water's always-return – even, and especially, in its difference.

Notes

1 "Multibeing" is a term coined by oceans scholar Susan Reid to express not only a multiplicity of biological species but also ecologies of relation that include elements, the so-called non-living and the multiciplicity of being/body that also occurs across and through time (see Reid 2023).
2 This phrasing is a play on Yusoff (2018) and their rejection of calculable difference in favour of difference's incalculability.

References

Ahmed, Sara (2017) *Living a Feminist Life*. Duke University Press.

Haraway, Donna (1991) "The Cyborg Manifesto: Science, technology, and Socialist-Feminism in the Late Twentieth Century" in *Simians, Cyborgs, and Women: The Reinvention of Nature* (149–81). Routledge.

Hofmeyr, Isabel (2019). "Provisional Notes on Hydrocolonialism." *English Language Notes, 57*(1), 11–20.

Liboiron, Max (2020). "There's no such thing as 'We.'" *Discard Studies*. https://discardstudies.com/2020/10/12/theres-no-such-thing-as-we/

Mbembe, Achille (2019). *Necropolitics*. Duke University Press.

Povinelli, Elizabeth (2022.) *Routes/Worlds*. Sternberg Press.

Reid, Susan (2023). "Ocean Justice: Reckoning with Material Vulnerability." *Cultural Politics, 19*(1), 107–27.

Rich, Adrienne (1986). "Notes towards a Politics of Location" in *Blood, Bread and Poetry* (pp. 310–32). Norton.

Yusoff, Katherine (2018). *A Billion Black Anthropocenes or None*. University of Minnesota Press.

Zimmer, Carl (1998). *At the Water's Edge: Macroevolution and the Transformation of Life*. Free Press.

ACKNOWLEDGEMENTS

Editing this book has been a rich and rewarding experience, also a joyful one, particularly since the edition emerges from a community of practice and shared response-abilities and commitments to oceanic justice and doing academia differently. We have worked with inspiring authors who are researchers, artists and activists, and our book is not only a volume of separate chapters that are linked by shared foci; rather, the texts also gesture to our multiple and diverse entanglements with each other through embodied practices in and through the ocean and beaches. The book is just one product that has been carved out of a few years of swimming, reading, writing and thinking together. We have made this possible even during COVID-19 times of isolation, which also became an important source of comfort and community. We have held a number of swimming-writing retreats over this time where we have lived together, cooked together, thought together and shared our work while swimming and walking in and alongside our local oceans. At times, our engagements have extended to activist and artistic endeavours, too. We acknowledge the financial support of the National Research Foundation of South Africa for 'Doing academia differently' (Grant number 120845), which was a primary support for these activities; the Andrew W. Mellon Foundation funded project 'New imaginaries for an intersectional critical humanities project on gender and sexual justice' (Grant No. G-31700714) that assisted in hosting a number of our academic forums; and the SASUF funded project on ('Re)configuring scholarship in higher education' that allowed us to share our work further afield and swim in Swedish waters. We also acknowledge the constructive engagements of the reviewers who generously gave of their time to support the development of the book. Appreciation also to Karen Graaff for editorial assistance. Finally, a special thank you to all authors for their timeous submissions and their responsiveness to frequent requests for various details and also the generosity of those who wrote the foreword, Astrida Neimanis, and afterword, Meghan Judge, and those who gifted us with endorsements. We are deeply grateful for the watery care that flows through these pages.

OCEAN HOME

Toni Giselle Stuart

new moon
at low tide, the waves pull back, exposing
the rocky shore. bare feet step and scramble
slowly over ragged edges, and into pools.
eyes search the crevices and hidden wells
for straws, earbuds, chip packets, bottle tops,
sweet wrappers, fishing line, water bottles,
light sticks, carrier bags, lollipop sticks

these totems of our fast consumption, swimming
with starfish, and nudibranchs, growing
next to sea anemones, and feather duster worms

a dozen dirty lifetimes wash into the ocean's swell

first quarter moon
before dawn, the harbour hums
with engines switched on, ropes
whipped back and nets hurled on

fathers, uncles, husbands, brothers
throw silent prayers overboard
calling for the currents to run with

their nets, to fill their boats, to feed
their families, keep the lights on,

out in the deep water, the men remember

the stories of sea as living being,
who must be honoured for its provision

the men speak of a time when whale
was ancestor, just as cave was, and rain
and how rain begins in the ocean

a dance between sun and sea: evaporation
water in air cools its breath: condensation
clouds exhale to cleanse our skies: precipitation
rivers, soil, lakes, take the water back: collection

an endless cycle of give and take
one we keep breaking
but have the power to repair

full moon
this is False Bay
this is the bay of slavery and escape
this is the bay of railway lines
this is the bay of ship wrecks and fishermen
this is the bay of forced removals
this is the bay of tidal pools for "whites only"
this is the bay where Kwa Mata sleeps

this is Table Bay
this is the bay of Hoerikwaggo
this is the bay of canalised rivers
this is the bay of sweet waters
this is the bay of washerwomen at the river
this is the bay of trade and travel
this is the bay where our ancestors fought
this is the bay where our ancestors won

and deep below the surface
in the dark stillness we cannot see, phytoplankton
absorb carbon, release oxygen
creating clean air for us to breathe

third quarter moon
these tidal pools were fish traps
built by Khoe hands, stone for stone

now we swim with octopus and sea hare,
urchins and cuttlefish.

in the water, ordinary citizens
become scientists and the children,

of people forcibly removed,
return to learn again that

the sea is our home too. so with paper
and pencil, or an app on a phone

we record, collect data, as we clean
this shore that has fed us for generations

we swim, we dive and explore the world
below, and with each wade into shallow waters,

with each deep breath held long
we remember to ask: who walks with us,

who swims with us, who breathes with us?

Poem commissioned by Tongue Fu and Liv Torc for the Hot Poets Project, in collaboration with The Beach Co-op, Cape Town.

1

HYDROFEMINIST SCHOLARSHIP AND ACTIVISMS IN/ON/WITH SOUTH AFRICAN OCEANS AND SHORES

Tamara Shefer, Vivienne Bozalek and Nike Romano

Introduction

Ocean/s are powerfully political spaces, globally and locally entangled in the violences of settler colonialism, land dispossession, slavery, transnational labour exploitation, extractivism, omnicides and wars (Ghosh, 2021; Probyn, 2023; Sharpe, 2016). There is currently a proliferation of international writing on ocean/s, water, (wild) swimming and other sea engagements from multiple and diverse angles. Research and public interest have focused on physiological and therapeutic benefits of swimming, especially in natural, outdoor spaces and immersion in cold water (for example, Fitzmaurice, 2018; Foley, 2017; Foley & Kistemann, 2015; Liptrot, 2016; Wardley, 2017; Yfanti et al., 2014). Critical ocean studies and hydro-criticism are growing bodies of work within larger eco-critical emphases that speak to the impact of anthropocentric and colonial damages to the earth, humans and other species through an engagement with ocean and waters (Alaimo, 2016; Deloughrey, 2019; Duara, 2021; Green, 2020; Talbayev, 2023). A range of feminist and queer scholarship that unpacks the history and current contexts of swimming, oceans and bodies of water as entangled in feminist and justice projects is also emerging (for example, Chow & Urcaregui, 2023; Landreth, 2021; Neimanis, 2012, 2013, 2017a, 2017b; Tsui, 2021). Relatedly, there is a rich body of feminist decolonial, indigenous, Black, Black-indigenous, eco-critical, hauntological, new materialist and posthumanist work which engages with water and the ocean and ocean species for alternative environmental humanities (for example, Åsberg, 2020; Nxumalo & Villanueva, 2020; Chen et al., 2013; Deloughrey, 2019; Gumbs, 2020; McKittrick, 2006; Mohulatsi, 2023; Probyn, 2023; Pugliese, 2023; Sharpe, 2016; Stelder, 2023). Some scholarship also considers how thinking-writing with bodies of water contributes to doing academia and pedagogical practices

DOI: 10.4324/9781003355199-1

differently, often in dialogue with art, literature and activism (for example, Bailey-Charteris, 2020; Boon et al., 2018; Burnett, 2017, 2019, 2021; Wong & Christian, 2016; DeLoughrey, 2007, 2019; Hamilton Farris, 2019; Hessler, 2018; Ingersoll, 2016; Jue, 2020; Macura-Nnamdi & Sikora, 2023; McNight, 2016; Neimanis, 2012, 2013, 2017a, 2017b; Pratt et al., 2020; Probyn, 2016; Shefer & Bozalek, 2022; Shewry, 2015).

In South Africa, there is a welcomed growing focus on sea and water as part of a critical project on hydrocolonialism (for example, Green, 2020; Hofmeyr, 2019; Hofmeyer et al., 2022; Mennon et al., 2022; Mohulatsi, 2023), yet narratives and experiences from the Global South that are engaging the sea for justice scholarship have not been well represented in international spaces and writings.

This edited collection brings together authors who are thinking in, with and through the spaces of ocean/s and beaches in South African contexts to make alternative knowledges towards a justice-to-come and flourishing at a planetary level. Primary scholarly locations for this work include feminist new materialist and posthumanist thinking, specifically a hydrofeminist (Neimanis, 2012, 2013, 2017a, 2017b) framework and place-based, hauntological and indigenous knowledges. South Africa is arguably an important location to engage in hydrofeminism, at a local level with respect to undocumented and untheorised knowledges and with respect to the contributions it adds to transnational work on hydrofeminism. While there are some other edited and co-authored volumes on wild engagements with oceans and hydrofeminism (Boon et al., 2018; Chen et al., 2013; Wong & Christian, 2016), there are few that are specifically located in South Africa and that bring a queer, indigenous and decolonial feminist lens to bear on current injustices to humans, more-than-humans and the planet. Thus, while there is a growing body of literature that works within and across disciplines on the sea and bodies of water to think critically about the damages of centuries of colonisation and continued extractivist capitalism, there remains little work that explores this burgeoning thinking in Global South and more particularly South Africa contexts. South African histories of colonisation, slavery and more recent apartheid, which are saturated in the oceans, are only recently being explored through oceanic logics (see, for example, Mohulatsi, 2023). This volume offers valuable Global South contributions and rich situated narratives to such hydrofeminist thinking. It also brings diverse and more marginal knowledges to bear on the project of generating imaginative alternatives to hegemonic colonial and patriarchal logics in the academy and elsewhere.

On the other hand, while primarily located in a South African context, the book speaks to globalised concerns for justice and draws on and extends international scholarship that thinks in/on/with ocean/s, littoral zones and bodies of water.

Philosophical and methodological framings

This book and its chapters are located in a range of intersecting bodies of work that are directed at justice efforts in higher education and politics more broadly. Like the kelp that buoys us up and offers a place to hold to and rest, these strands of thinking are key to the project of thinking with the sea. They destabilise us while also offering a framework to think deeper and further about what we do in the academy and what we are doing (and have done) as humans to each other, other species and the planet. Here, we attempt to disentangle some of the key bodies of work that anchor this project of engaging with ocean, oceanic fauna and flora and liminal spaces of beach and place.

Hydrofeminism is one of the strongest threads that we are thinking with and that resonates strongly throughout this book project. The term was coined by Astrida Neimanis (2012, 2013, 2017a, 2017b), who is a lead scholar in this thinking that has been taken up in diverse geopolitical contexts. Deploying the figuration of 'bodies of water', Neimanis allows us to appreciate our watery selves and the permeable boundaries between each other, all living and non-living entities and the planet itself. Through such a figuration that connects us all, we are importantly reminded that we "reside within and as part of a fragile global hydrocommons, where water – the lifeblood of humans and all other bodies on this planet – is increasingly contaminated, commodified and dangerously reorganised" (Neimanis, 2013, pp. 27–28). Through locating ourselves within hydrofeminist thinking, the book is therefore an engagement with the question that Boon et al. (2018, p. 60) have asked: "What can we learn from water? How might an engagement with water inform our politics, our daily living, our selves?"

However, this ethico-onto-epistemological framing of hydrofeminism is also a part of and extends a larger movement in critical scholarship, that of the project to challenge the colonial, patriarchal and humanist university. Decolonial and feminist scholarship and activism directed at eurowestern dominance in the academy and in global capitalist material inequalities have been a key part of such efforts. Disrupting the Cartesian logics of the university which has excluded embodied, affective and other silenced knowledges have been central to this turn (Alaimo, 2016; Ferdinand, 2022; Ghosh, 2021; Glissant, 1990/2010; Mbembe, 2016; Shahjahan, 2011, 2016; Simpson, 2022; Stein & Andreotti, 2017; Yusoff, 2018).

Efforts to reconceptualise scholarly practices have further benefited from contemporary new feminist materialist and posthumanist framings of justice-to-come (Barad, 2010, 2017, 2019) towards radical revisioning of the logics of scholarship and its project of justice. A growing literature on alternative ways of doing scholarship, research and pedagogical practices differently has been evident globally. In South Africa, this has had a particular urgency given decades of post-apartheid efforts to transform the university, emphasised from 2015 by students' decolonial, feminist and queer calls. The global and local turn to alternative ethical and political ontological, epistemological and methodological practices in scholarship has opened up a wide range of scholarship in South African contexts of higher education that has been working with these calls for radical shifts in knowledge (for example, Bozalek et al., 2018c; Bozalek & Hölscher, 2022; Bozalek et al., 2021a, 2021b). Slow scholarship has provided ways of refusing the effects of colonial logics, neoliberalism and bureaucratic cultures on higher education, including writings on Slow wild swimming as ways of developing different sensibilities for reconfiguring academia (Bozalek, 2017, 2022; Shefer & Bozalek, 2022). Similarly, response-able pedagogies predicated on a relational ontology, where entities and humans come into being through relationships, have contributed to ways of rendering each other capable in higher education scholarship and pedagogies (Bozalek, 2017; Bozalek et al., 2018b; Bozalek & Zembylas, 2019, 2023). Thus, the book is also speaking to efforts to reconceptualise knowledge while also impacting on larger justice for humans, other species and the planet.

The collection of essays is further located in place-based methodologies (for example, Nxumalo, 2020; Simpson, 2022; Springgay & Truman, 2018, 2019). The book engages with temporalities, spacialities and mobilities, through a number of localised beach- and sea-situated studies to explore the way in which histories and their material aftermaths of colonial and apartheid violences shape past, current and future injustices and ecological crises, as well as how they might be resisted. Some of the specific contexts of South Africa's colonial and apartheid history are explored and unravelled through innovative watery thinking and generating place-based knowledges that speak to the many silenced histories of knowledges, peoples, animals, plants and land over centuries of colonial theft, plunder, slavery, exterminations as well as the more recent decades of apartheid that specifically entrenched racialised land segregation, resulting in the exclusion of the majority of South Africans from many beaches and seas.

Thus, a hauntological approach is also very key to the overall approach of this book. In a recent volume that engages hauntology for thinking about justice in the university, Zembylas et al. (2021, p. 25) argue that a hauntological decolonising framework involves an emphasis on "revealing the absences/presences of the there/then, here/now and effects of the past/present/future on people's lives and the environment". It also involves an engagement with "affective investments" and affect in general that are located in histories and presents of privilege and subjugation. This edited volume is strongly located in a marking of and engagement with hauntings of coloniality but also future hauntings shaped by anthropocentric and capitalist current and future exploitation of human, other species and planetary resources (see also Motala & Bozalek, 2022 on South African hauntings in District Six).

A further strong component of the book is the multiple and diverse engagements with arts-based and embodied and affective methodologies, including theatre, art, walking and swimming, for public and higher education-based sites of teaching and learning as well as for activism and advocacy (for example, Bailey-Charteris, 2020; Boon et al., 2018; Hamilton Farris, 2019; McKnight, 2016; Shefer & Bozalek, 2022). Post-qualitative methodologies and the disruption of disciplinary divides and academic ownership of knowledge are also evident in many of the chapters in this edited collection, which are transdisciplinary and which use post-qualitative inquiry to move away from traditional research approaches, experimenting with new sensibilities and "structures of intelligibility" (St. Pierre, 2021, p. 6) to create something new in academia.

This volume – a local focus on oceans/a watery genealogy

This book emerges from a set of ongoing concerns and individual and collective research projects. Some of the contributions are written papers originally presented at an online colloquium held in Cape Town on 19 August 2021 with a similar title. Further contributions are from other local scholars, activists and ocean people who are currently working on and concerned with various aspects of hydrofeminisms around the South African coastline and other watery places. While the chapters in this volume provide various instances of contemporary scholarly, artistic and activist engagements with ocean/s in South African contexts, they arguably hold global import, in ways that matter.

The book takes up three entangled thematics that run through all of the chapters, albeit through differing lenses and with varied emphases. These include the recognition and working with ocean/s as a political, haunted space with respect to the violent past of colonisation and apartheid and its remains in the present; a deep sensitivity and engagement with ocean/s and hauntings of the present and future of global environmental damages and challenges; and an appreciation of the ocean and beaches as spaces of possibility for individual and community healing, transformation, pedagogy, alternative scholarship, activism, justice and change.

The first theme deals with historical haunting of violences of colonisation, slavery, apartheid that need to be articulated, explored and spaces created for healing and revisioning. In South Africa, seas and littoral spaces are haunted sites where histories of colonisation and apartheid, characterised by segregation, exclusions and violence, bleed into the present, shaping current space-time-matterings. Oceans in South Africa have a specific haunted history. As already elaborated, seas and beaches are particular sites where histories of colonisation, racial capitalism and apartheid, characterised by segregation and exclusions, seep into the present, shaping current imaginaries of space and place (Hofmeyr, 2019; Shefer, 2021; Shefer & Bozalek, 2022). The volume takes up this thematic in multiple ways, through engagements with ocean waters and beaches.

For example, in the chapter entitled *Restless Remains and Untimely Returns*, Adrienne van Eeden-Wharton documents material-affective encounters along the shores of the Atlantic Ocean of the South African West Coast and adjacent islands as part of an ongoing praxis of walking, gathering, carrying and learning alongly – as an act of bearing witness to under acknowledged Indigenous histories and practices. The author tells a story in pieces that reckon with the hauntings of violent legacies, environmental exploitation through her encounters with multispecies death assemblages, toxic entanglements and overspill. Described as dirty slow work, which cannot be done at a distance, van Eeden-Wharton touches on issues of indebtedness and complicity, of breaking and being undone.

The book also explores this thematic through more human-focused engagements, such as the politics of ocean, beaches and water sports, interrogating the way in which sea and beaches were politicised through apartheid, serving the ends of this draconian system and continue to mirror these histories of inequality and reproduce exclusions. For example, Cheri Hugo's photo essay is an affective engagement with the ocean and the exclusion of Black people through White appropriation of beaches and seaside residential areas. The loss of confidence in ocean, indigenous beliefs and knowledges and sense of belonging is articulated through her narratives and artworks. But this body of work also serves to disrupt such exclusions as she illustrates the re-turn to the ocean.

Joanne Peers's chapter disentangles "the multiple temporalities that seep into my body through the watery memories of childhood, through my womb as a place of life and labour in my early twenties and into my salty hair" through her swimming in False Bay oceans. She documents her own experiences and inheritances of racism and questions which emerge in the waters of her research practice. She asks how we can learn to live with these ghosts of colonial violence, which have shaped losses, displacements and shape current memories and materialities of space. She uses the figuration of *Sea-Place* as a way of becoming response-able while becoming researcher. As a figuration, Peers's Sea-Place gestures to unboundedness and emphasises the porous nature of time, place, memory and research. In this way, it destabilises the assumed stable nature of research and unitary ways of imaging the world, which St. Pierre (2021) sees as a necessary precondition for post-qualitative inquiry. Arguing that colour continues to matter, the figuration is brown – a porous brown body in salty waters – since as she re-turns to the past and memories, her brown skin follows.

Karen Graaff takes up a further angle in this respect by researching surfing as one example of the way in which water sports in South Africa (and globally) have been shaped by gendered, raced and classed inequalities which continue in the present. She begins by noting that surfing has been and continues to be seen and represented as a predominantly male, White, cis-gendered, heteronormative, able-bodied and North-dominated sport. She cites well-known feminist queer surfing scholar lisahunter (2018), who argues that the sport's patriocolonial past impacts heavily on the current context globally, demanding assimilation from marginalised surfers, thus excluding alternative versions, line-ups and experiences. This chapter asks what surfing could be(come) if such spaces were created, both locally in South African seas and globally. Graaff does so by providing historical context for surfing's current norms, and then looking at examples of environmental, gender and social justice activism by surfers, focusing on community and individual resistances, which disrupt and offer alternative imaginaries for surfing and surfers. While located within a particular sport (and industry), the chapter speaks to larger contexts of watery engagement in South Africa and other seas and beaches.

Buhle Francis and Dylan McGarry, in their chapter entitled *Grandmothers of the Sea: Stories and lessons from five Xhosa Ocean elders*, explore an alternative perspective on the remains of the past and efforts to revision the current and future. They offer a reading of the nuanced and complex relationship of communities with the ocean and the politics of natural resource management, access, livelihoods, gendered labour and cultural connectivity with the ocean that is seldom seen or recognised in ocean decision-making or marine meaning-making. Working with first-hand accounts and stories, the chapter explores these entangled relationships that reveal how, despite having a deep connection and custodianship of the ocean, the women elderly respondents she worked with find themselves excluded from almost all decision-making in ocean governance.

The second key thematic in the book speaks to a haunting of the present and the future, that of the environmental impacts of racial capitalist extractivist human-centred engagements, also located in colonial histories, that we encounter in oceans and beaches. Mirroring more extensive planetary conditions, the ominous impacts of capitalist exploitation, such as extractivist oceanic mining, over-fishing, sewage spillage and other invasive practices, devastate the ocean/s and all life on earth. There is an emergence of eco-ethico-political thinking, practices, arts and activisms in contemporary South Africa. South Africa currently faces the ominous present and future of extractivist oceanic mining and the ever-increasing ramifications of capitalist, anthropocentric practices. At the edge of disaster, overfishing, sewage spillage and other invasive and toxic practices (see Green, 2020) are devastating the livelihoods and well-being of humans, animals and the living oceans and beaches, such as recent examples of polluted beaches and seas, malnourished dying seals and threats to kelp forest communities. It is not surprising that there is a groundswell of ethico-political thinking, practices, arts and activisms in contemporary South Africa. This edited collection extends such initiatives by applying a decolonial, relational, ethics of care and hydrofeminist lens to surface the injustices and violences of the colonial past, inextricably entwined with ongoing ecological damage (Alaimo, 2016; Ferdinand, 2022; Ghosh, 2021), through embodied engagements with ocean/s and other materialities.

Zayaan Khan's poetical essay is a collection of anecdotal Cape Town-based stories and memories of the ocean over what she calls a deep timeline, thinking of the ocean as "a place where prehistoric solution mixes and eddies with waters of the Anthropocene". In this respect, her essay speaks powerfully to the intersecting thematics of colonial and environmental hauntings. She surfaces the grief that the ocean holds and argues that the "compounding realities of colonial invasion, ecocide and capitalistic belittling of life has created a critical point in our collective healing". She reminds us that the ocean is a graveyard, holding innumerable bodies, yet it is also the origin of life and a place of life and healing. She traces, for example, a picture of Cape Town harbour and city which is built on 'reclaimed' land and therefore over billions of mummified animal and plant bodies. The deep timescale she offers through these stories is a call to listen to the ocean, to remember and witness what it holds, past, present and future, as the "original brine to ferment with, learning the nuances of salt to water and the oceanic spectrum of flavours – from delicious to uncomfortable".

Aaniyah Martin's chapter similarly works with histories and presents of ecological damage but also engages with a more material eco-activism, in this case, directed at community response-ability for cleaning beaches of litter. Martin's work is underpinned by the proposition that caring for our hydrocommons and our marine environment is critical for the health of the ocean, the planet and humans and more than humans. Arguing that while we all on the planet depend on the health of the oceans, we do not all share in our responsibility equally to care for this common resource. Her research focuses on humans' understanding of care for the marine environment and is directed at the development of a collaborative pedagogy of care and shared response-ability for our hydrocommons in South Africa. Noting that the legacy of apartheid continues to shape Black and Indigenous People of Colour (BIPOC) access or lack thereof to oceans and beach spaces, she proposes regenerative care practices that are culturally and historically sensitive. Her study is informed by the complementary frameworks of research-creation, transgressive learning, agential realism and decoloniality. These frameworks have led her to a creative and inspiring research methodology, which includes practices of 'strandlooping', swimming and collectively constructing and mending a hydro-rug, made of waste materials from the ocean.

Dylan McGarry's chapter, entitled *When ancestors are included in ocean decision and meaning-making*, shares some of the activism of One Ocean Hub, an organisation directed at collaboratively influencing decisions and practices related to the future of the ocean for justice and sustainability and the Coastal Justice Network, an eclectic group working in solidarity with Small Scale Fishers, customary rights holders and other ocean defenders. The chapter focuses on the role of public storytelling and what creative practice can offer in trying to raise public consciousness and impact on policy and practice. The chapter flags the way these groups have particularly focused on experimenting with diverse ways to bring 'intangible heritages' into decision-making, and even into courtrooms, "where ancestors can enter and be present and tangible collaborators".

The third theme that a range of chapters contribute to is the project of thinking differently, making alternative knowledges and knowledge practices in the university and elsewhere – thinking with ocean/s for justice scholarship and just ways of living. Following Melody Jue (2020), who thinks with swimming in the discipline of literary and media analysis, we are not only concerned here with thinking about the sea or oceans as objects of research, but as a modality to think with and to diffract knowledge of the ocean through other knowledge (Barad, 2007, 2017). Jue (2020, p. 6) calls for thinking in and through the ocean as a form of *radically situated knowledge*:

> thinking with the ocean productively estranges the terrestrially inflected ways of theorizing and thinking to which we have become habituated. Thinking with the ocean involves asking: *How would ways of speaking about (x) change if you*

were to displace or transport it to a different environmental context, like the ocean? (emphasis in original).

Within this thematic, there are diverse ways presented here of thinking with the sea and/or sea critters such as octopus, and sea flora such as kelp and land flora which take to the ocean (e.g. sea beans) as a way of making a difference to practices and logics of knowledge. As mentioned, the project of reconceptualising higher education is particularly directed towards disrupting the Cartesian logic of mind-body disengagement that is endemic to normative academic institutions and mainstream scholarship in general. This requires alternative ways of thinking, reading, and writing. In this respect, many of the chapters refuse the erasure of the author and their affects, rather working with embodiment and affect as bound up with intellectual knowledges.

The book and its chapters also refuse the depoliticisation and claims to 'scientific', neutral knowledge by showing up the politics of knowledge and actively engaging with politics in *what* they are writing about and *how* they are writing. Different chapters engage with thinking with the ocean differently; they may think with the watery fluidities that gesture to relationalities and response-abilities, as in the chapter by Shefer, Bozalek and Romano. They may think with oceanic flora as with the kelp forest thinking engaged with by Barry Lewis or with the sea bean that Kristy Stone follows in thinking about alternative justice in urban living. Others think with sea creatures, as Alexis Pauline Gumbs (2020) has done with her thinking about marine mammals. The poignant figuration of the octopus is taken up by Delphi Carstens and Mer Roberts, which they argue offers humans a wide range of alternative ways of ethical living and being in relation.

In *Diffracting forests: Making home in the (Post)Apartheid city*, Barry Lewis foregrounds the challenges that designers face within the dynamic ruin of homemaking in (post)apartheid Cape Town. Centred around informal settlements in which shacks are constructed with zinc, he notes how the zinc forest is constantly changing in an ongoing state of becoming as it takes root and grows. The chapter explores how thinking with the figurations of the zinc and kelp forests might contribute towards re-conceptualising and understanding the nature of place-making and forming a home in the face of histories and memories that refuse to go away.

Delphi Carstens and Mer Roberts' chapter Octopoid Aesthetics is a rich example of documenting an ongoing collaborative, immersive, experimental and cross-disciplinary multimedia project that draws from a series of Becoming Octopus Meditations that emerged from free-dives undertaken in the Cape Peninsula's underwater seascapes. Thinking with the Common Octopus and its distributed consciousness as informed by interspecies communication, marine biology, speculative fabulation and embodied ocean immersion, the authors explore the possibility of merging individual and collective ways of being, thinking and doing.

In so doing, they "re-conceptualise the role of speculative imagination and non-human cognition as propositions for pedagogies and artistic practices that aim to combat the destructiveness of the Anthropocene by concretizing a more inclusive more-than-human Chthulucene (Haraway, 2016)".

In their chapter entitled *Oceanic swimming-writing-thinking for justice-to-come scholarship*, Tamara Shefer, Vivienne Bozalek and Nike Romano document their swimming-writing-thinking together practice that emerged out of their engagements with re-conceptualising higher education in the context of South African post-apartheid challenges and within the larger project of justice and decolonial scholarship globally. In a move away from the normative practices of the neoliberal that repeat colonial, patriarchal and humanist logics, the authors embark on a "playful experimental Slow scholarly hydrofeminist praxis" that includes swimming, reading, image-making and writing together, while holding in mind the project of doing ethical scholarship for justice-to-come. The authors show how their becomings together, generate new thinkings as they take their thoughts for a swim and open up new possibilities for making knowledge.

Kristy Stone deploys an oceanic method, "as an alternative, embodied and affective scholarly practice", to think with the sea bean, *Ntindile* (or *Entada rheedii*), which are found throughout the Indian Ocean region and usually make their way to the sea where they can float for several years before washing up on near or distant shores. In many cultures, such beans were endowed with magical properties, categorised as 'charms' in the Iziko Social History Archive in Cape Town, South Africa, where Stone found the pair that she works with. Working towards an ontological justice project with museums and archives, Stone opens up an alternative way of engaging with these types of collections, which "continue to be discredited by the persistent use of colonial categorisations and bely a scientific arrogance which turns the metaphysical practices of Others into irrational 'beliefs' and superstitions". She illustrates how the sea beans speak directly to the idea of nomadacy, movement and exchange and thus "destabilise land-based notions of identity and indigeneity" and static, rigid colonial ideas of categorisation that is still normative in museums. The story of the sea bean within an oceanic method thus speaks to alternative history-making and knowledge in general, challenging "reductive biomedical sciences and outdated archival practices" while also opening up ontological conversations about healing, humanness, disease and human-plant relationships.

Concluding thoughts

This book brings together just a handful of some of the inspiring thinking and practices that many critical scholars, artists, educators, practitioners and activists are currently engaging in through heterogeneous encounters with oceanic, watery spaces and water edges. This collection speaks predominantly from the South African geopolitical landscape, its histories, currents and futures. However, we are aware that our experiences and contexts are by no means exceptional or unique and that the book is both informed by and resonates with diverse global and transnational contexts and temporalities. The book also in multiple ways speaks to the challenge of decolonising higher education and finding new and diverse ways of appreciating, making and sharing knowledge. We see it as an innovative and unique intervention to broaden an engagement with the growing field of blue oceanic studies informed by diverse other perspectives. We are grateful for the richness of thinking that is increasingly engaging with decolonial, indigenous, new materialist and posthumanist thinking and in this context the rich hydrofeminist work that provides such a meaningful conversation for our watery work to join. Our hope is that slowly, with Slow oceanic thinking, doing and making, we may contribute some small watery particles to the wave of relationality, justice and care that is building up locally and globally as we recognise our (urgent) response-abilities for our hydrocommons and planetary survival and flourishing.

References

Alaimo, S. (2016). *Exposed: Environmental politics and pleasures in posthuman times.* University of Minnesota Press.

Åsberg, C. (2020). A sea change in the Environmental Humanities. *Ecocene: Cappadocia Journal of Environmental Humanities 1*(1), 108–122. https://doi.org/10.46863/ecocene.2020.12

Bailey-Charteris, B. (2020). Precipitational learning in the hydrocene. Paper presented at ACUADS 2020 conference, Sydney. Retrieved February 16, 2020, from https://acuads.com.au/conference/article/precipitational-learning-in-the-hydrocene/

Barad, K. (2007). *Meeting the universe halfway: Quantum physics and the entanglement of matter and meaning.* Duke University Press.

Barad, K. (2010). Quantum entanglements and hauntological relations of inheritance: Dis/continuities, spacetime enfoldings, and justice-to-come. *Derrida Today, 3*(2), 240–268. https://doi.org/10.3366/drt.2010.0206

Barad, K. (2017). What flashes up: Theological-political-scientific fragments. In C. Keller & M-J. Rubenstein (Eds.), *Entangled worlds: Religion, science and new materialisms* (pp. 21–88). Fordham University Press.

Barad, K. (2019). After the end of the world: Entangled nuclear colonialisms, matters of force, and the material force of justice. *Theory & Event, 22*(3), 524–550.

Boon, S., Butler, L., & Jefferies, D. (2018). *Autoethnography and feminist theory at the water's edge: Unsettled islands.* Palgrave Macmillan.

Bozalek, V. (2017). Slow scholarship in writing retreats: A diffractive methodology for response-able pedagogies. *South African Journal of Higher Education, 31*(2), 40–57.

Bozalek, V. (2022). Slow scholarship: Propositions for the extended curriculum programme. *Education as Change, 25*, https://doi.org/10.25159/1947-9417/904

Bozalek, V., Braidotti, R., Shefer, T., & Zembylas, M. (Eds.) (2018a). *Socially just pedagogies in higher education: Critical posthumanist and new feminist materialist perspectives.* Bloomsbury.

Bozalek, V., & Hölscher, D. (2022). From imperialism to radical hospitality: Propositions for reconfiguring social work towards a justice-to-come. *Southern African Journal of Social Work and Social Development, 34*(1), 1–20.

Bozalek, V., Bayat, A., Gachago, D., Motala, S., & Mitchell, V. (2018b). A pedagogy of response-ability. In V. Bozalek, R. Braidotti, M. Zembylas, & T. Shefer (Eds.), *Socially just pedagogies in higher education: Critical posthumanist and new feminist materialist perspectives* (pp. 97–112). Bloomsbury.

Bozalek, V., Braidotti, R., Zembylas, M., & Shefer, T. (Eds.) (2018c). *Socially just pedagogies in higher education: Critical posthumanist and new feminist materialist perspectives.* Bloomsbury.

Bozalek, V., & Zembylas, M. (2019). Perceptions on socially just pedagogies in higher education. In G. Mare (Ed.), *Race in education* (pp. 5–40). Sun Press.

Bozalek, V., & Zemblyas, M. (2023). *Responsibility, privileged irresponsibility and response-ability: Higher education, coloniality and ecological damage.* Palgrave Macmillan.

Bozalek, V., Zembylas, M., & Tronto, J. C. (2021a). *Posthuman and political care ethics for reconfiguring higher education pedagogies.* Routledge.

Bozalek, V., Zembylas, M., Holscher, D., & Motala, S. (Eds.) (2021b). *Higher education hauntologies: Speaking with ghosts for a justice-to-come.* Routledge.

Burnett, E-J. (2017). *Swims.* Penned in the Margins.

Burnett, E-J. (2019). In the Dart the water is peaty; like downing a shot of neat whiskey. *The Guardian Weekly.* Saturday 10 August. Retrieved August 6, 2020, from www.theguardian.com/lifeandstyle/2019/aug/10/launch-naked-into-unknown-writers-joy-wild-swimming

Burnett, E-J. (2021) *Of sea.* Penned-in-the-Margins.

Chen, C., MacLeod, J., & Neimanis, A. (Eds.) (2013). *Thinking with water.* McGill-Queens University Press.

Chow, J., & Urcaregui, M. (2023). Just keep swimming? Queer pooling and hydropoetics. *Angelaki, 28*(1), 36–52, https://doi.org/10.1080/0969725X.2023.2167783

DeLoughrey, E. (2007). *Roots and routes.* University of Hawai'i Press.

DeLoughrey, E. (2019). *Allegories of the anthropocene.* Duke University Press.

Duara, P. (2021). Oceans as the paradigm of history. *Theory, Culture & Society, 38*(7–8), 143–166. https://doi.org/10.1177/0263276420984538

Ferdinand, M. (2022). *Decolonial ecology: Thinking from the Caribbean world* (A. P. Smith, Trans.). Polity.

Fitzmaurice, R. (2018). *I found my tribe: A memoir.* Vintage.

Foley, R. (2017). Swimming as an accretive practice in healthy blue space. *Emotion, Space and Society, 22*, 43–51.

Foley, R., & Kistemann, T. (2015). Blue space geographies: Enabling health in place. *Health & Place, 35*, 157–165.

Ghosh, A. (2021). *The nutmeg's curse: Parables for a planet in crisis.* The University of Chicago Press.

Glissant, E. (1990/2010). *Poetics of relation.* University of Michigan Press.

Green, L. (2020). *Rock/water/life: Ecology and humanities for a decolonial South Africa.* Duke University Press.

Gumbs, A. P. (2020). *Undrowned: Black feminist lessons from marine mammals.* AK Press.

Hamilton Faris, J. (2019). Sisters of ocean and ice: On the Hydro-feminism of Kathy Jetñil-Kijiner and Aka Niviâna's Rise: From One Island to Another. *Shima, 13*(2), 76–99. https://doi.org/10.21463/shima.13.2.08

Haraway, D. (2016). S*taying with the trouble. Making kin in the Chthulucene.* Duke University Press.

Hessler, S. (Ed.) (2018). *Tidalectics: Imagining an uceanic worldview through art and science.* MIT Press.

Hofmeyr, I. (2019). Provisional notes on hydrocolonialism. *English Language Notes, 57*(1), 11–20.

Hofmeyr, I., Nuttall, S., & Lavery, C. (2022). Reading for water. *Interventions, 24*(3), 303–322, https://doi.org/10.1080/1369801X.2021.2015711

Ingersoll, K. A. (2016). *Waves of knowing: A seascape epistemology.* Duke University Press.

Jue, M. (2020). *Wild blue media: Thinking through sea water.* Duke University Press.

Landreth, J. (2017). *Swell: A waterbiography.* Bloomsbury.

Liptrot, A. (2016). *The outrun: A memoir.* Canon Press.

lisahunter. (2018). The long and short of (performance) surfing: Tightening patriarchal threads in boardshorts and bikinis? *Sport in Society, 21*(9), 1382–1399. https://doi.org/10.1080/17430437.2017.1388789

Macura-Nnamdi, E., & Sikora, T. (2023). Water. *Angelaki, 28*(1), 3–8, https://doi.org/10.1080/0969725X.2023.2167778

Mbembe, A.J. (2016). Decolonizing the university: New directions. *Arts and Humanities in Higher Education, 15*(1), 29–45.

McKittrick, K. (2006). *Demonic grounds: Black women and the cartographies of struggle.* University of Minnesota Press.

McKnight, L. (2016). Swimming lessons: Learning, new materialisms, posthumanism, and post qualitative research emerge through a pool poem. *Journal of Curriculum and Pedagogy, 13*(3), 195–205. Retrieved August 6, 2020, from https://doi.org/10.1080/15505170.2016.1220875

Mennon, D.M., Zaidi, N., Malhotra, S., & Jappie, S. (2022). *Ocean as method: Thinking with the maritime.* Routledge.

Mohulatsi, M. (2023). Black aesthetics and deep water: Fish-people, mermaid art and slave memory in South Africa. *Journal of African Cultural Studies,* https://doi.org/10.1080/13696815.2023.2169909

Motala, S., & Bozalek, V. (2022). Haunted walks of District Six: Propositions for counter-surveying. *Qualitative Inquiry, 28*(2), 244–256. https://doi.org/10.1177/1077800421 1042349

Neimanis, A. (2012). Hydrofeminism: Or, on becoming a body of water. In H. Gunkel, C. Nigianni, & F. Söderbäck (Eds.), *Undutiful daughters: Mobilizing future concepts, bodies and subjectivities in feminist thought and practice* (pp. 94–115). Palgrave Macmillan.

Neimanis, A. (2013). Feminist subjectivity, watered. *Feminist Review, 103*, 23–41.

Neimanis, A. (2017a). *Bodies of water: Posthuman feminist phenomenology.* Bloomsbury Academic.

Neimanis, A. (2017b). Water and knowledge. In D. Christian & R. Wong (Eds.), *Reimagining water* (pp. 51–68). Wilfrid Laurier University Press. ProQuest Ebook Central.

Nxumalo, F. (2020). Place-based disruptions of humanism, coloniality and anti-blackness in early childhood education. *Critical Studies in Teaching and Learning, 8*, 34–49. Retrieved from http://cristal.ac.za/index.php/cristal/article/view/269/235

Nxumalo, F., & Villaneuva, M. T. (2020). *(Re)Storying water: Decolonial pedagogies of relational affect with young children.* Routledge.

Pratt, S., Marambio, C., Quigley, K., Hamylton, S., Gibbs, L., Vergés, A. Adams, M., Barcan, R., & Neimanis, A. (2020). Fathom. *Environmental Humanities, 12*(1), 173–178. https://doi.org/10.1215/22011919-8142264

Probyn, E. (2016). *Eating the ocean.* Duke University Press.

Probyn, E. (2023). Aqua/geopolitical conjuncture and disjuncture: Invasion, resources, and mining the deep dark sea. *Cultural Studies,* https://doi.org/10.1080/09502386.2023.2173793

Pugliese, J. (2023). Intercorporeity of animated water. *Angelaki, 28*(1), 22–35, https://doi.org/10.1080/0969725X.2023.2167781

Shahjahan, R. (2011). Decolonising evidence-based education and policy movement: Revealing the colonial vestiges in educational policy, research, and neoliberal reform. *Journal of Education Policy, 26*(2), 181–206.

Shahjahan, R. (2016). International organisations, epistemic tools of influence, and the colonial geopolitics of knowledge production in higher education policy. *Journal of Education Policy, 31*(6), 694–710.

Sharpe, C. (2016). *In the wake: On blackness and being.* Duke University Press.

Shefer, T. (2021). Sea hauntings and haunted seas for embodied place-space-mattering for social justice scholarship. In V. Bozalek, M. Zembylas, S. Motala, & D. Holscher (Eds.), *Higher education hauntologies: Speaking with ghosts for a justice-to-come* (pp. 76–87). Routledge.

Shefer, T., & Bozalek, V. (2022). Wild swimming methodologies for decolonial feminist justice-to-come scholarship. *Feminist Review, 130*, 26–43.

Shewry, T. (2015). *Hope at sea: Possible ecologies in oceanic literature.* University of Minnesota Press.

Simpson, L. B. (2022). Kwe as resurgent method. *Feminist Asylum: A Journal of Critical Interventions, 1*, 37–42. https://doi.org/10.5195/faci.2022.85

Springgay, S., & Truman, S. (2018). *Walking methodologies in a more-than-human world: WalkingLab.* Routledge.

Springgay, S., & Truman, S. (2019). Walking in/as publics: Editors' introduction. *Journal of Public Pedagogies, 4*, 1–12.

Stein, S., & Andreotti, V. (2017). Decolonisation and higher education. In M. Peters (Ed.), *Encyclopaedia of educational philosophy and theory* (pp. 70–75). Springer.

Stelder, M. (2023). A sinking empire. *Angelaki, 28*(1), 53–72, https://doi.org/10.1080/0969725X.2023.2167784

St. Pierre, E. (2021). Post qualitative inquiry, the refusal of method, and the risk of the new. *Qualitative Inquiry, 27*(1), 3–9. https://doi.org/10.1177/1077800419863005

Talbayev, E. T. (2023). Hydropower. *Angelaki, 28*(1), 9–21, https://doi.org/10.1080/0969725X.2023.2167780

Tsui, B. (2021). *Why we swim.* Algonquin.

Wardley, T. (2017). *The mindful art of wild swimming: Reflections for Zen seekers.* Leaping Hare Press.

Wong, R. (2013). Ethical waters: Reflections on the healing walk in the Tar sands. *Feminist Review, 103*, 133–139.

Wong, R., & Christian, D. (2016). Introduction: Re-storying water, re-storying relations. In D. Christian & R. Wong (Eds.), *Downstream: Reimagining water* (pp. 1–28). Wilfred Laurier University Press.

Yfanti, M., Samara, A., Kazantzidis, P., Hasiotou, A., & Alexiou. S. (2014). Swimming as physical activity and recreation for women. *TIMS Acta, 8*(2), 137–145.

Yusoff, K. (2018). *A billion black anthropocenes or none.* University of Minnesota Press.

Zembylas, M., Bozalek, V., & Motala, S. (2021). A pedagogy of hauntology: Decolonising the curriculum with GIS. In V. Bozalek, M. Zembylas, S. Motala, & D. Hölscher (Eds.), *Higher education hauntologies: Living with ghosts for a justice-to-come* (pp. 11–28). Routledge.

2

WHEN ANCESTORS ARE INCLUDED IN OCEAN DECISION- AND MEANING-MAKING

Dylan McGarry

The judgement

In Makhanda, South Africa, in 2021, High Court Judge Bloem (2021, p. 17[1]) stated in his judgement of case 3491/2021:

> I accept that the customary practices and spiritual relationship that the applicant communities have with the sea may be foreign to some and therefore difficult to comprehend. How can ancestors reside in the sea and how can they be disturbed may be asked. It is not the duty of this court to seek answers to those questions … We must accept that those practices and beliefs exist.

This was a significant moment in South African courts, where the judgement favoured the concerns, questions and values of small-scale fishers, customary rights holders and other ocean defenders, over fossil fuel-induced profit. The case saw communities stand up to large oil companies and the government[2] and win. What was significant in this first judgement in the Makhanda High Court judement was that the ancestors were present in court and their place in ocean use and governance was acknowledged by Judge Bloem.

In the David Gongqose (2018) Case at Dwesa-Cwebe Nature Reserve (*State v. Gongqose plus two Others. 2012 (E382.10)*) customary rights holders and traditional authorities/healers were able to testify in the courtroom, and customary law (and lore) was used as evidence in the case of three fishers charges with fishing illegally in a Marine Protected Area (MPA) (Sunde, 2014). As Jackie Sunde (2014) states, up to that point, no fisheries-related case had ever placed a defence on the grounds of living customary law, summoning the authority of the ancestors, before a small, rural court as did the Gongqose case in the Elliotdale Magistrates Court in

DOI: 10.4324/9781003355199-2

March 2012 (Sunde, 2014). It was the tireless work of Gongqose and his legal team, and those in solidarity with him, that paved the way for this watershed moment.

Returning to the case at hand, Judge Bloem (2021, p. 17) continues:

> What this case is about, is to show that if Shell had consulted with the applicant communities, it would have been informed about those practices and beliefs and would then have considered, with the applicant communities the measure to be taken to mitigate against the possible infringement of those practices and beliefs. In terms of the constitution those practices and beliefs *MUST* be respected and where conduct offends those practices and beliefs and impact negatively on the environment, the court has a duty to step in and protect those who are offended and the environment.
>
> *(p. 17, para. 32)*

Respecting the beliefs and practices stated above and as the constitution demands it. However, this is something not seen in practice in the context of South Africa. In my experience over the past three years of participating in, and wit(h)nessing government lead 'consultations' for MPA expansion, and by consultancies hired to conduct Environmental Impact Assessment (EIA) for ocean economy expansion, what consultation often translates to is inviting a small subset of individuals into spaces in which they are informed of developments (often with complicated PowerPoint slides in English). Those invited are not afforded the right platforms (in vernacular conversation) to share what is essential and valuable to them. The question I would like to ask is, by what and for whom will these actions benefit them? As Sowman and Sunde (2018, p. 175) uncover through examining five MPAs and their associated benefits and costs to local people, in all of the case study sites "respondents reported negative impacts on their cultural heritage as a result of the MPA. For many this included a loss of direct access to cultural or sacred sites". They (2018, p. 176) conclude by providing overwhelming evidence, "that social impacts are given limited attention in the planning and ongoing management of MPAs in South Africa, despite commitments to adopt a more people-centred approach based on ecosystems and human rights".

Furthermore I ask, what would respect for these beliefs and practices look like? And, what would need to be challenged and shifted in order to fully attend to this act of 'respecting'. In this chapter, I share something of what we have attempted to do as the One Ocean Hub (OOH)[3] and the Coastal Justice Network (CJN), an eclectic group working in solidarity with small scale fishers, customary rights holders and other ocean defenders. We used various methods, but most notably, for the purpose of this chapter, I focus on the role of public storytelling and what creative practice can offer in trying to answer these questions. As a group, we have particularly focused on finding ways in which intangible heritages can enter decision-making, even in courtrooms, where ancestors can enter and be present and tangible collaborators.

Evidence hierarchies and new opportunities

Judge Bloem's verdict set a new tone to how courts can engage with intangible ocean heritage(s), and opens the space for subsequent court cases against big extractive industry, the government and other companies to respond similarly where ancestors and intangible ways of knowing (and being) in/with/of the ocean are recognised and acknowledged legally. In this case, the indirect challenging of the evidence hierarchies, are not only an opportunity for new legal plurality, fluidity and transformation towards better policies, but also open up frameworks for challenging evidence hierarchies found in education when we consider what counts as legitimate knowledge.

Seeing the ancestors enter the courtroom, leads me to wonder where the ancestors are in our classrooms? If they can be acknowledged and witnessed in the courtroom, why not in the curriculum?

The marine governance space (and associated decision-making and ocean literacies) has been dominated by positivist framings and evidence hierarchies in making decisions around Marine Spatial Planning (MSP), resource extraction, EIAs and the creation of MPAs (Sowman et al, 2013). Furthermore, these decisions have in my experience lacked political rigour (Temper et al., 2019), cultural or spiritual understandings and contexts, and overlooked social impacts (Sowman & Sunde, 2018). This blindness to entangled and nuanced ways of being and living in the ocean space, has led to incredibly painful and traumatic policies that have resulted in: forced removals, landlessness, lost or restricted access rights, impacts on food security, health, livelihoods, social cohesion, culture, identity, sense of place, gender relations, customary practices and governance systems (Brechin et al., 2012; Christie et al., 2003; Colchester, 2004; Fabricius & De Wet, 2002; Ghazoul & Kleinschroth, 2018; Mascia & Claus, 2009; Mascia et al., 2010; Menton & Le Billon, 2021; Sowman et al., 2011; Sowman & Sunde, 2018; West et al., 2006).

In Sowman and Sunde's (2018) research on MPAs, some coastal users in three of the more rural, isolated MPAs in Sowman and Sunde's (2018) reported violent treatment at the hands of the rangers when caught fishing, including allegations of rape, torture and physical beatings. In the course of our own research we have conducted with One Ocean Hub, we have collected reports witnessing the killing of two fishers at the hands of rangers in Nibela, in northern KZN, in 2020 and 2021, respectively, as well as many cases of physical injury and harassment (McGarry & Pereira, 2021). The legacies of violence that dwell within institutional policy implementation, and in the lack of education and sensitisation of rangers to customary rights and customary lore/law, leaves blind spots that can result in violent exclusions, such as the killings of coastal users, who are pathologised as 'poachers' and are stripped of their role as sustainable users and stewards of these coastal ecosystems.

While there are brave and pioneering approaches to include culture, local stewardship and ocean defenders' in ocean planning and governance (Bennett et al., 2022) many of the current decision-making systems are built and scaffolded on western scientific paradigms that assume linear time, Newtonian cause and effect and Cartesian logic. Log frames and algorithms currently dominate decision-making in MSP tools, for example, and 'cultural-data' has to be packaged into binary code to be used to develop scenarios and create spatial maps (Vermeulen-Miltz et al., 2022). While there are practical attempts to include Indigenous and Local Knowledge in informing MSP planning goals and objectives (Lombard et al., 2019), these remain somewhat reified in technicist and instrumentalised approaches to decision-making, which are a far cry from Indigenous forms of customary lore and law.

In MSP decision-making tools, biodiversity data often dominates, and is used to establish 'no-take-zones' and buffer zones in MPAs (Harris et al., 2022). Yet how do ancestral sacred sites, or the fluid movement of sacred water, or the intentionally secret practices of traditional healers and diviners include themselves in such algorithms? And, do the ancestors want decisions around our ocean to occur in this way? How can Indigenous mythological and mystical meaning-making[4] enter these models when they defy binary code? This type of evidence cannot be captured into quantifiable data and/or packaged into a concrete definition. Unfortunately, this approach to handling and 'capturing' knowledge results in onto-epistemological rootedness and entanglements being trimmed off and cauterised.

How could ephemeral and contextually nuanced South African mythology and meaning-making of the ocean enter into ocean literacy, legal rulings and decision-making? How then might we include the ancestors in more meaningful, iterative and porous ways?

Positionality and intentions

Before offering an answer, I must unpack what my own positionality and intentions are, I must first introduce myself. I am a queer South African storyteller, artist and educational sociologist from South Africa. I am a free diver, surfer and lover of the ocean. I grew up in Kwa-Zulu Natal, racialised as white and assumed 'straight' in the late 1980s and early 1990s. This was a time in South Africa's history of both rupture and transformation. And something as a young child I was not able to fully understand the complexities of. My tender and politically rigorous and supportive Grandmother and Godmother, helped me navigate the toxic inculturation faced as a young white gay kid at the time. My mother tells me that during her pregnancy with me she swam in the ocean every day. I learned later that my name comes from Welsh mythology and means the 'prince of the sea'. Hearing this at a young age certainly built a particular and peculiar inner mythology and sense of self that was inextricably linked to the ocean. I never quite recovered from watching the Disney classic: *The Little Mermaid.* Where somehow my childlike queer curiosity of living and being in and of the water was replete with fluid possibilities of identity, transgression, song, mythology and transformation; and there might be merfolk living down there!

As an adult, I have been practicing at the intersection of scholar-activism, environmental justice, queer-eco-pedagogy, transgressive learning, public pedagogy, public storytelling and transdisciplinary practice-based research in the fields of environmental science, marine science, environmental education, theatre, visual and performing arts and more recently film. Common to all these spheres and realms of meaning-making, I have continued to work with the divine, the sacred or the embodied post-human spiritual dimensions (Battista, 2018) of activism and education. I look at and then consider the role the sacred has in meaningful change in times of ecological crises. My PhD research entitled "Empathy in the time of ecological apartheid: A social sculpture practice-led inquiry into developing pedagogies for ecological citizenship" for example, examined the role of empathy, intuition, imagination and listening in pedagogies in times of 'ecological apartheid' (McGarry, 2014).

While I am not Zulu, nor am I a traditional healer (Sangoma) or diviner in the Zulu tradition, I have worked closely with Sangomas, Inyangas, amaQira and other spiritual practitioners in South Africa for the past 16 years, and I have been granted permission by some knowledge holders to speak and research certain aspects of this complex and nuanced life-world, within the context of this chapter.

I therefore cannot speak with any authority about complexities and plural shapes of South African spirituality per se, certainly not within the limits of this chapter. Rather I focus indirectly on concepts surrounding ancestors, the education of traditional healers, ethnographic accounts of spiritual concepts and ideas, and about creative outputs and practice-based-research undertaken to create these. I intend to only briefly uncover and surface the potential for these intangible heritage(s) to be included in how we make decisions and how we make meaning, whether these decisions or meanings are regarding policy or curricula. I also intend to point out why creative practice, and the use of public storytelling can be useful in creating the substrate in which ancestors can enter into decision and meaning-making, and how storytelling (and storylistening) can be used methodologically to challenge evidence hierarchies within law and education.

For the purposes of this chapter, I focus on the role of South African spirituality and its relationship with artful storytelling. To do so, I will explore 'traditional healing', its role in meaning-making for contemporary citizens, what potential it might have for making new entrances and exits between knowledges (de Sousa Santos, 2015) and in crossing current boundaries within ocean literacy and education. This idea resonates with the hydrofeminist framing of this book (Neimanis, 2012), where porous boundaries between human, more than human and water move like tides. Nancy Tuana (2008, p. 194) refers to this membrane of meaning-making and logic between us as "viscous porosity". From this position of thinking, I aim to draw attention to how this porosity might be achieved in law and education: by letting the ancestors in. I consider as Tuana (2008, p. 194) does, how this produces a porosity that is transgressive, boundary crossing and establishing of "sites of resistance and opposition" and should not only be assumed to be a pleasant open receptivity and 'indiscriminate flow' filled with possibilities. What I am attempting to articulate is that the movement between knowledge systems, and ways in which meaning-making may leak and shift between each other, and that this passage between membranes of knowing, can also be perilous and dangerous (Tuana, 2008). Possibly the most dangerous assumption is that all knowledge is expanding, when in reality only some knowledge(s) are expanding, at the detriment and potential annihilation of others (Orr, 2004).

In understanding this fluid movement of knowledge, it is also important to note that culture, heritage and how we make-meaning of it is also in a state of flow. Culture is hardly static, indeed it is continuously evolving and adjusting to the lives and consciousness of the people who story it into being. This has particular concerns for this paper, as it is difficult and somewhat impossible (and unethical) to make concrete claims and suggestions of what cultures must be accounted for in ocean decision-making. What can be done, is to explore how iterative, ongoing ethical dialogue and call and response practices can keep intangible and tangible heritages alive and ecologically entangled in our meaning-making, and subsequent decision-making. What is required to meet this longing, is perhaps more fluid and supple forms of decision-making practices, but that too is a topic for another chapter.

The ancestral realm and the cleansing quality of sea water

Over the past five years, we, a collective of social scientists, marine scientists, artists, theatre makers, writers, traditional healers and other citizens have actively endeavoured to surface the stories, beliefs, sensibilities and associated response-abilities of South Africans in relation to the ocean through our One Ocean Hub[5] research network. One aspect of this research project was the development of our Empatheatre production *Lalela uLwandle*, in isiZulu or "Listen to the Sea" in English, which, over the course of this time has expanded various nuanced and contextual relationships between South African citizens and the ocean (Erwin et al., 2022). Through an ongoing, iterative process of research and script development, *Lalela uLwandle* has been able to explore themes of intergenerational environmental injustices, tangible and intangible ocean heritage, ecological grief, the role of marine science in governance, and the myriad threats to ocean health. Through the Empatheatre methodology,[6] which essentially provides new platforms for public storytelling, public debate, testimony and dialogue after each show. We have been involved in a public conversation on ocean governance within South Africa, and internationally. Recently (14 November 2022), the play was invited to perform at the UNFCCC COP27 climate negotiations in Egypt. Within this period, we have made close friendships, and working partnerships with many customary knowledge holders, and have had the opportunity to diffract through the script and other stories, a multi-faceted meaning of how the ancestors and oceans are symbiotically linked. One significant relationship forged in this work is with the UN special rapporteur on human rights and culture, which has led to further opportunities to engage with international policy through the FAO, UNESCO and UNEP. The potential of the script and radio play is that it is being used as a policy brief in these forums.

From these encounters and second hand-accounts of the ancestral realm, as described by friends, informants and customary rights holders, we have come to understand the place of the ancestors as an ephemeral and constantly evolving presence in the South African psyche. In recent years we have seen an increase in awareness of the ancestors. In one of our post show discussions in Port Shepstone, a woman reflected in tears after watching the play, and empathising deeply with the Nowandle character, who tells the stories of dispossession of her grandmother who was a traditional healer and her mother who was a water diviner. She reflected that watching this as a white woman, opened her heart in ways that was painful but very important, as before watching the play she never understood the rituals taking place on the beach by sangomas and diviners, and admitted to judging the slaughtering of chickens and the candles left behind with contempt, seeing them as gruesome and wasteful. Yet after the play, she spoke sensitively, carefully and with great empathy of what was at stake and what had been experienced by Nowandle's family, and for many South Africans.

This popular, cross-cultural acknowledgement of ancestors has garnered new respect and affirmation by popular media and a new wave of young people stepping into their identities and life-worlds (Theron, 2016). While the concept of ancestors, and an ancestral realm are familiar to most South Africans we must avoid what Nwoye (2015, p. 97) points out, where "African psychology is grounded on the assumptions of a common African worldview and the Afrocentric paradigm" and so can be seen as reifying sameness among Africans. Furthermore, Long (2013), warns that a lack of class analysis in debates about an African psychology can further skew framings of African spirituality and psychology. As an attempt to avoid this, I must state that my framings of 'ancestral-realms' and ancestors in general in this paper, focus specifically to a particular story emerging from a Zulu Historian and Zulu Sangoma interviewed in Durban, South Africa, and does not represent a common-belief across all South Africans, yet are corroborated across two Zulu speaking individuals and customary knowledge holders, who hail from two very different class backgrounds. We also aim to show this plurality in the play Lalela uLwandle, where different values and framings of ocean entangled spirituality, sacredness of the sea, and even encounter with ancestors and rituals to honour those who have passed. The play is situated by three characters: a Black Zulu woman, a White woman scientist and an Indian descent activist and fisher. These framings are folded through the storytelling across race and class, as well as patchworked histories. Where ancestors are engaged across time and matter, this is woven into 'matterings' or what matters (Barad, 2007).

These matterings, the plural, collective and ongoing formulations and renderings of the ancestral realm are shifting and growing in the minds and stories of South Africa in a myriad of ways. Indeed, in contemporary responses to COVID-19 (Beyers, 2021), to political decolonial praxis (Ratele et al., 2018) the ancestors and their role in meaning-making, are significant and constantly adapting. And so, in many ways, the realm cannot be fully defined or described, but rather can be seen as a plural, complexly realised, evolving and shifting phenomenon that is experienced on a deeply personal level, and thus articulated in distinctive ways. Yet even so, in my experience, there are common themes, images, symbols, threads that can be surfaced and held onto in various forms of meaning-making that can have an influence on decision-making. As Judge Bloem points out, Shell needs to work with people to fully understand what the implications for future development in the oceans are if the ancestors are dwelling there.

I therefore only speak to some of the facets in which African spirituality is entangled in our framings of the Ocean in South Africa. What was agreed upon in the building of the script for *Lalela uLwandle*,[7] among more than a thousand South African audience members across race and class spectrums were consulted. Across all these framings and renderings of the ocean all saw, in unique and sovereign ways, the ocean as spiritually significant, cleansing and a soulful realm. Many (not all) saw the ocean as a place used for healing. As one example, delicately realised in a scene where the character Nowandle played by Mpume Mthombeni and directed by Neil Coppen, explains how seawater was used by her grandmother in her household growing up (Empatheatre, 2019, min 25:16):

Nolwandle: When I was a little girl and there was lightning outside, uGogo wami (*My Grandmother*) used to make me sprinkle sea water around the house to chase it away.

My Gogo was a traditional healer, *Wayelapa ngeisintu*[8] and the voice that guided her would speak to her in her dreams. She didn't have to go to university and pay all that money like the scientists do, no the ancestors taught her everything she needed to know.

In the beginning uGogo was afraid to accept her gifts but then a vision came to her, one she couldn't ignore …. Inkambaphansi appeared. You know what this is? It's a giant snake whose eyes were as big as the tyres of a *ugandaganda* (tractor). This was how she knew it was her time to go under the waves *ayoThwasa*

AyoThwasa is the Zulu term used to encapsulate a suite of processes that are unique; however, for some traditional healers or diviner initiates *ukuthwasa* requires a spiritual journey, much like a hero's journey. Yet its path is not predictable or easily described, and shrouded in much secrecy and mystery. Usually, the initiate is believed to travel under the water, often taken there by their ancestors (Bernard, 2003). In the '*Thwasa*' realm the initiate is taught the traditional Zulu healer arts. The

'*Thwasa*' cosmology consists of an underwater realm where your ancestors greet you and welcome you into a process of enculturation where you receive magical and healing gifts. If a person who is called a *Thwasa* does not accept the calling, it is believed that increasingly worse things will happen to you until eventually you could become ill and even die, colloquially called '*Thwasa sickness*'. Every bad thing thereafter is seen as another sign from the ancestors who are saying they are waiting.

In our research process with knowledge holders, both in building the script but in collaborative analysis, member checking and affirmation in post-show dialogues with audiences, the ancestral realm was described with some common or resonant features. It is described as a place below the seafloor, a mystical land, something like heaven, yet imbued with more magical realism, and far more accessible than western notions of heaven, as it is accessible through dreams and in some cases, believed a place one can actually travel to by entering the water. This is corroborated by the anthropologist Penny Bernard (2003, p. 149), who documents many incidences across Southern African Indigenous people (Khoisan- and Bantu-speaking people alike) that show and notes the existence of complex beliefs regarding water, river systems and the ocean:

> The spirit world is regarded as the ultimate source of such life-sustaining resources. Water is the essence of both spiritual and physical life, and the spirit world is regarded as the ultimate source of such life-sustaining powers. Integral to such beliefs are various zoomorphic spirit manifestations, primarily the snake and the mermaid, who reside in or beyond the water and who interact with humans in a variety of ways. The rivers, wetlands, and the sea are the dwelling places of such manifestations and are of fundamental importance to many of the African healing traditions and their practitioners.

In this way, the water itself is sacred, and is the medium in which the soul enters the living world, water is the substrate in which the soul can attach, and it is through water that the ancestors can access the living world, purify it and communicate with it. There are indeed other ways of accessing and connecting to the ancestors through animals, soil, wind, etc., yet water seems to be one of the primary connectors to the ancestral realm.

Sea water itself is imbued for many South Africans with a sacred, cleansing capacity (Sunde, 2014), that can be used to ward off evil, protect households from lightning (as shown in the scene above spoken by Nolwandle) and other natural disasters, and even be used to raise the fertility of land. In much of our research, across cultures and spiritual traditions, seawater is widely valued in inland South Africa, and neighbouring countries. Friend and colleague Buhle Francis, a native of Zimbabwe and a Ndebele speaker (co-author of Chapter 12 in this book), shared recently (Pers Com, 2021) that her Mother, Gogo Lakheli Nyathi, travels back to her hometown in land-locked Zimbabwe, with sometimes three or four

25 L containers of seawater, which she repackages in 100 ml soft drink bottles, and trades a single bottle for a goat. Sunde (2014, p. 151) surfaced the ways sea water is used for healing by sangomas and by some churches for baptism rituals in the Dwesa-Cwebe region of South Africa, one of the regions of the Wild Coast, targeted by Shell for oil and gas exploration. As she explains:

> The sea is inseparable from the distinctive cultural identity of the sangomas of the region, who are recognised as having specific powers and connections with the ancestors in the sea ... They play the role of linking people on the land and in the sea and undertake specific rituals in order to facilitate this ... Dreams are considered central to the process of communicating with the ancestors and an ancestor might communicate with a person via their dream and request that they go to the sea to perform a particular ritual.

It is compelling to think that scientists have recently discovered that water formed early on in the universe, perhaps within one billion years of the Big Bang, suggests water itself predates the formulation of our solar system (Smidt, 2018). Furthermore, it is commonly understood by contemporary science that life cannot exist without water (Torres & Winter, 2018), and so if the soul does secure itself to this world, through the substrate of water, it would somehow resonate that the soul would choose a medium that is ancient and has its genesis so close to the beginning of time and space. It is in these resonances between scientific and Indigenous understanding, that we find potential for alignment, for finding porousness between meaning-making and decision-making protocols. One such resonance, or alignment we discovered while researching our play, was the story of *Indlela Yokuphila*.

Indlela Yokuphila

Indlela Yokuphila, meaning "the Soul's Journey" or the "Path of the Soul" was explained to us during an interview with traditional Zulu historian Ntuthuko Khuzwayo and traditional healer Makhosazane Masondo. The interview was undertaken by my colleague and friend Mpume Mthombeni in Durban in 2019. The story illustrates how, if we are willing to listen closely, scientific knowledge and Indigenous knowledge can at times align. From the story, we created an animation,[9] which recently debuted at COP27 alongside "*Lalela uLwandle*". An early version of the animation, along with other animated films I created,[10] were also used as evidence, alongside affidavits from customary knowledge holders, in the Shell court case. To my knowledge, it was the first time animations and radio plays were used as evidence, as a means to embody and hold as proxy some of the intangible heritages and spiritual knowledges of the sea.

What we learned (and were able to share as evidence in the court interdict against Shell) is that the mystical belief of the soul's journey after life is deeply embedded, or immersed in the water cycle. In essence, the story unfolds like this (synopsis paraphrased from the original treatment for the animation film, Empatheatre 2020):

> After death, when your family buries you under the ground, the rain compresses your body and squeezes out your soul, until you are born into the dreaming world, where you swim in the *isihlanjana* – you become bantu *nohlanjana.*

> You are a young ancestor – *idlozi elisalincane,* as your soul swims down-stream you swim, you are called by the songs of ancestors, and you are called towards the deep sea. As you swim down you grow older as an ancestor, until you eventually get down to the deep sea, where the ancestors dwell *abantu abadala.*

> They know exactly who you are, and which clan you belong to. There, with your ancestors you gain all the memories, songs, and dreams of your people and learn many secrets. You stay down there for a very very very long time.

> Until one day, when the matters of people on land are pressing, and you are needed to share your knowledge – you hear a new song, *the song of your next mother.* She sings for you to accompany her; and you swim up to her voice, until you float out of the water and are carried by a cloud back to the land.

> Until eventually your soul rains down on the land. And your next mother drinks you. There in the small ocean inside her belly, you grow and grow, only to be born again.

Upon hearing the story, Mpume rushed to speak with Kira Erwin, our fellow lead researcher on the project, and she quickly made a sketch of the story.

What proceeded, was to be a two-year research-creation praxis (Manning, 2016) and expansion of that sketch (Figure 2.1). Explained briefly, research-creation involves transversal and transgressive engagements with different disciplines and this in turn stimulates the rethinking of how artistic practice can warm-up and shift the question of what these disciplines can do, and how this praxis of research-creation can nourish the understanding of the research question at hand. Research-creation therefore places greater emphasis on the process rather than outcomes, and thus allows for movement beyond disciplinary and institutional constrictions (Manning, 2016).

This research was undertaken through careful call-and-response dialogue and learning (Kulundu et al., 2020) with customary rights holders. All aspects of the animation: Everything from the ethics of representation, to how the characters looked, to how we used language in particular aspects of the story and how we might frame it. We (a gathering of artists, musicians, researchers from the OOH and CJN, along with traditional healers) managed to produce a 6-minute animation lovingly narrated by Mthombeni, with an original score composed by Braam du Toit in collaboration with the Cape Town Opera. I refer to this call-and-response approach[11] as 'eco-locating' (McGarry, 2022), where a shifting

FIGURE 2.1 Poster of *Indlela Yokuphila* Animation directed by Dylan McGarry and Marc Moynihan, and narrated by Mpume Mthombeni. Artwork by Marc Moynihan and Dylan McGarry.

onto-epistemological understanding and pluriversal framing (Reiter, 2018) and contextual locating is achieved through ongoing, iterative dialogue and narrative development. The transdisciplinary and multi-genre practice used to unpack the story, further enriched and shaped our understanding of the role of the ocean in mythological and spiritual entanglements with how meaning is made in relation with the ocean. For example, the shape and form of the central character, in this case, a human soul and ancestor, was iteratively realised through ongoing call-and-response through making. Myself and the co-director would constantly draft sketches of how she would be represented, these were taken by Mpume to the knowledge holders who through each 'echo' back would edit and refine how the spirit would be represented. By using the Empatheatre pedagogy of echo-location (McGarry, 2022), we were able to use this counter-hegemonic narrative to disrupt, disarticulate and expand dominant storylines (Erwin, 2021) around the water cycle. This afforded an expanding framing of the ocean beyond a site for resource exploitation, and offered ways of reimagining new and alternative seeing and being in relation to the sea. We were also diffracting the story through affidavits that were being collected by colleagues as part of the extra-legal preparations for the court case, which further expand and find intersectional resonances (Kulundu, 2018) with other knowledge holders. I cannot help but wonder if Judge Bloem diffracted through the affidavits, the script and the animation in a similar way, to lead him to his final judgement.

Final thoughts

While there is much work to be done to answer the questions emergent from Judge Bloem's Judgement: "What would respect of these beliefs and practices look like?" We have come to learn that working closely and collaboratively in solidarity with customary and cultural rights holders and ocean defenders as artists/theatre-makers/researchers, we were able to find a proxy residence for the ancestors and customary values and knowledge to enter as evidence into a courtroom. As many forms of heritage that are associated with the ocean are intangible, ephemeral and sometimes secret, only certain aspects of this knowledge can be touched or held. Yet this should not limit or justify 'leaving-behind' or excluding these values, worldviews or approaches to meaning-making and ocean decision-making. While not all knowledge and belief systems can be held in this proxy form, and indeed as Long (2013) warns us, these cannot be considered universal concepts that place African spiritualism into a homogenous defining form, the Shell case was such an opportunity, precisely because it was so firmly grounded by the local community applicants from Dwesa-Cwebe, Xolobeni and other Wild Coast communities in their customary law/lore and ancestral practices. This case thus offers us a strategy for challenging evidence hierarchies in ocean decision-making and ocean literacy, through public storytelling and approaches to research-creation by the South African collective, Empatheatre.

It has allowed us (the Empatheatre team, One Ocean Hub and the Coastal Justice Network) the means, particularly through storytelling, to ensure these forms of knowledge can be included in law and potentially within education in meaningful ways. Having ancestors included in the courtroom and classroom through stories, theatre, animation, etc., allows us to build not only useful legal fluidity in protecting Indigenous cultural rights, but includes more meaningful social and cultural data in MSP, MPA and EIAs processes. This expands our perceptions of value, towards the divine and the sacred in how we make meaning and decisions for and with our oceans. The indirect challenging of the evidence hierarchies in this case offer an opportunity for further research and enquiry into how the ancestors can be present in our decisions and learning. When making decisions about the ocean in South Africa, we have come to learn that it is equivalent to making decisions about heaven. At the end of our film Nowandle laughs and says: "*Uyabona umfana wami*"[12] as Gogo always said: "This heaven everyone wants a one-way ticket to … it's not in the direction the missionaries promised us it was. No, No (laughing) it's in the opposite direction …. it's down there … beneath the waves".

Acknowledgements

Deepest gratitude to Dr. Kira Ewrin for her insight, and her initial hand-drawn sketch of the interview conducted by my colleague/friend/sister, Mpume Mthombeni, who started this journey with the first spell cast. Mpume Mthombeni is a force of mystical nature and an incredible traditional healer who heals with story, with words. Dr. Jackie Sunde, who has dedicated her life to ensuring the justice of Indigenous fishing communities is realised, it was her vision and commitment to the fisher communities that made this window into the court case possible. Prof. Heila Lotz-Sisitka, thank you for always seeing my art as research. Finally, thank you to my love, Cleo Droomer, for dreaming with me. This study fell within the Rhodes University Education Faculty Ethics: Ethics Approval number: 2023-1497-7377. This project was funded by the One Ocean Hub, a collaborative research programme for sustainable development project funded by UK Research and Innovation (UKRI) through the Global Challenges Research Fund (GCRF) (Grant Ref: NE/S008950/1).

Notes

1 Paragraph 32, in High Court Case Sustaining the Wild Coast NPA and Others 3491/2021.
2 The Court case was a court interdict filed by Sustaining the Wild Coast, Masona Went Dlamini, Dwesa-Cwebe Communal Property Association, Ntsindiso Nongacavu, Sazise Maxwell Pekayo, Cameron Thorpe, All Rise Attorneys for Climate and the Environment NPS versus Minister of Mineral Resources and Energy, Minister of Environment, Forestry and Fisheries, Shell Exploration and Production South Africa BV, Impact Africa Limited and BG International Limited. Sustaining The Wild Coast NPC and Others v Minister of Mineral Resources and Energy and Others (3491/2021) [2021] ZAECGHC 118; [2022] 1 All SA 796 (ECG); 2022 (2) SA 585 (ECG) (28 December 2021).
3 The One Ocean Hub (OOH) is funded by Global Challenges Research Fund (GCRF), and aims to collaboratively research 'fair and inclusive decision-making for a healthy ocean whereby people and planet flourish' and a mission to "bring together coastal people, researchers and decision-makers to value and learn from different knowledge(s) and voices. With the goal to collaboratively influence decisions and practices shaping the future of the ocean for justice and sustainability" (One Ocean Hub, 2022). Within the OOH a distinct identity was developed for those OOH researchers who were practising more scholar activist network activities, through a Knowledge Action Network (KAN)

which was subsequently called the Coastal Justice Network, and launched in 2020. Through various situated solidarity practises a collective of small scale fisher leaders, lawyers, civil society representatives and others formed a community of practice that could facilitate rapid responses to rights violations, connect activists/fisher leaders and customary rights holders to legal support and empowerment, offer support services, carry out mapping of Blue Economy activities and sites of struggle, develop social learning and public storytelling processes to build solidarity and support organisational capacity amongst coastal activists and small-scale fishers, while at the same time practice insider-outsider approaches to governmental engagement, as well as undergo their learning processes with researchers and policymakers to raise awareness and build solidarity with community-based social movements.

4 I hyphenate "meaning-making" to point to both how meaning is something that is made, and that making can inform meaning, they are entangled by reciprocal umbilical nourishment. Ideally I would like to replace the hyphen with an infinity ∞ sign, that is, meaning ∞ making. I was inspired here by Erin Manning's (2016, p. 28) research-creation, where she acknowledges "making is a thinking in its own right and conceptualization a practice in its own right". In the context of this chapter, I use meaning-making with this in mind, where the making of theatre, animations and public storytelling, further expands meaning, and further inspires our creative practices of making and conceptualising.

5 www.oneoceanhub.org

6 Empatheatre Methodology (www.empatheatre.com) is a form of 'call and response' iterative research theatre, I co-developed with Neil Coppen and Mpume Mthombeni, over the past 10 years. It essentially relies on collaborative citizen-led research with theatre makers, sociologists and other researchers, to co-define concerns, co-develop research questions, and then surface myriad meanings in relation to these co-defined questions using theatre. Once a theatrical production is created and performed, post-show dialogue is used as a space for tribunal, debate and transgressive learning (Lotz-Sisitka et al., 2015).

7 The full radio play can be accessed and listened to on www.empatheatre.com/lalela-ulwandle

8 Translation: A type of traditional Zulu healer.

9 You can see the video here: www.youtube.com/channel/UCCo57242qmJW1s8_TiGPzZw

10 See "The Blue Blanket" on Youtube www.youtube.com/watch?v=4UBubIpCWuk

11 Again, I hyphenate call-and-response to show how they are reciprocally entangled, and that meaning is made through the call and the echo back from knowledge co-producers. It is important to mention here that in the making of the animation and in expanding our research creation praxis, the calls and responses allowed for ongoing ethics of representation to be constantly iterated and clarified, but it also meant the research of the heritage in question could be constantly recalibrated and dialogically understood.

12 *Uyabona umfana wami*, Zulu for "You see my child…".

References

Barad, K. (2007). *Meeting the universe halfway: Quantum physics and the entanglement of matter and meaning.* Duke University Press.

Battista, S. (2018). *Posthuman spiritualities in contemporary performance: Politics, ecologies and perceptions.* Springer.

Bennett, N. J., Le Billon, P., Belhabib, D., & Satizábal, P. (2022). Local marine stewardship and ocean defenders. *Npj Ocean Sustainability, 1*(1), 1–5.

Bernard, P. S. (2003). Ecological implications of water spirit beliefs in Southern Africa: The need to protect knowledge, nature and resource rights. *USDA Forest Service Proc. RMS, 27*, 148–153.

Beyers, J. (2021). Appropriating spiritual help for traditional healing: Why ancestors are needed1. *Pharos Journal of Theology, 102*, 1–11.

Brechin, S. R., Wilshusen, P. R., & Fortwangler, C. L. (Eds.). (2012). *Contested nature: Promoting international biodiversity with social justice in the twenty-first century*. Suny Press.

Christie, P., McCay, B. J., Miller, M. I., Lowe, C., White, A. T., Stoffle, R., Fluharty, D. L., McManus, L. T., Chuenpagdee, R., Pomeroy, C., Suman, D. O., Blount, B. G., Huppert, D. D., Eisma, R.-L. V., Oracion, E., Lowry, K., & Pollnac, R. B. (2003). Toward developing a complete understanding: A social science research agenda for marine protected areas. *Fisheries, 28*(12), 22–26.

Colchester, M. (2004). Conservation policy and indigenous peoples. *Environmental Science & Policy, 7*(3), 145–153.

de Sousa Santos, B. (2015). *Epistemologies of the South: Justice against epistemicide*. Routledge.

Empatheatre. (2019) *Lalela uLwandle: Listen to the sea*. Radio Play. Retrieved May 26, 2023, from www.empatheatre.com/lalela-ulwandle

Erwin, K. (2021). Storytelling as a political act: Towards a politics of complexity and counter-hegemonic narratives. *Critical African Studies, 13*(3), 237–252.

Erwin, K., Pereira, T., McGarry, D., & Coppen, N. (2022). An experiment in plural governance discussions. In R. Boswell, D. O'Kane, & J. Hills (Eds.), *The Palgrave handbook of blue heritage* (pp. 383–409). Palgrave Macmillan.

Fabricius, C., & de Wet, C. (2002). The influence of forced removals and land restitution. *Conservation and Mobile Indigenous Peoples: Displacement, Forced Settlement and Sustainable Development, 10*, 142.

Ghazoul, J., & Kleinschroth, F. (2018). A global perspective is needed to protect environmental defenders. *Nature Ecology and Evolution, 2*, 1340–1342.

Gongqose and Others v Minister of Agriculture, Forestry and Others, Gongqose and S (2018). (1340/16, 287/17) [2018] ZASCA 87; [2018] 3 All SA 307 (SCA); 2018 (5) SA 104 (SCA); 2018 (2) SACR 367 (SCA).

Harris, L. R., Holness, S. D., Kirkman, S. P., Sink, K. J., Majiedt, P., & Driver, A. (2022). A robust, systematic approach for developing the biodiversity sector's input for multi-sector Marine Spatial Planning. *Ocean & Coastal Management, 230*, 106368.

Kulundu, I. (2018). Think piece: Intersectional resonance and the multiplicity of being in a polarised world. *Southern African Journal of Environmental Education, 34*, 91–100.

Kulundu, I., McGarry, D. K., & Lotz-Sisitka, H. (2020). Think piece: Learning, living and leading into transgression – A reflection on decolonial praxis in a neoliberal world. *Southern African Journal of Environmental Education, 36*, 111–130.

Lombard, A. T., Ban, N. C., Smith, J. L., Lester, S. E., Sink, K. J., Wood, S. A., Jacob, A. L., Kyriazi, Z., Tingey, R., & Sims, H. E. (2019). Practical approaches and advances in spatial tools to achieve multi-objective marine spatial planning. *Frontiers in Marine Science, 6*, 1–9.

Long, W. (2013). Rethinking 'relevance': South African psychology in context. *History of Psychology, 16*, 19–35.

Lotz-Sisitka, H., Wals, A. E., Kronlid, D., & McGarry, D. (2015). Transformative, transgressive social learning: Rethinking higher education pedagogy in times of systemic global dysfunction. *Current Opinion in Environmental Sustainability, 16*, 73–80.

Manning, E. (2016). *The minor gesture.* Duke University Press.

Mascia, M. B., & Claus, C. A. (2009). A property rights approach to understanding human displacement from protected areas: The case of marine protected areas. *Conservation Biology, 23*(1), 16–23.

Mascia, M. B., Claus, C. A., & Naidoo, R. (2010). Impacts of marine protected areas on fishing communities. *Conservation Biology, 24*(5), 1424–1429.

McGarry, D. K. (2014). Empathy in the time of ecological apartheid: A social sculpture practice-led inquiry into developing pedagogies for ecological citizenship. PHD thesis, Rhodes University.

McGarry, D. (2022). Suitably strange: Re-imagining learning, scholar-activism, and justice. *Critical Studies in Teaching and Learning (CriSTaL), 10*(1), 93–115.

McGarry, D., & Pereira, T. (2021). The true custodians of our seas: Who is stealing South Africa's ocean heritage? *Daily Maverick,* 29 September 2021.

Menton, M., & Le Billon, P. L. (2021). *Environmental defenders: Deadly struggles for life and territory.* Routledge.

Neimanis, A. (2012). Hydrofeminism: Or, on becoming a body of water. In H. Gunkel, C. Nigianni, & F. Söderbäck (Eds.), *Undutiful daughters: Mobilizing future concepts, bodies and subjectivities in feminist thought and practice* (pp. 94–115). Palgrave Macmillan.

Nwoye, A. (2015). What is African psychology the psychology of? *Theory & Psychology, 25,* 96–116.

One Ocean Hub (2022). One Ocean Hub Website. https://oneoceanhub.org/Sourced 2 Nov 2022.

Orr, D. W. (2004). *Earth in mind: On education, environment, and the human prospect.* Island Press.

Pers Comm (2021). Interview with Buhle Francis at Rhodes Univeristy Campus, Makhanda, South Africa.

Ratele, K., Cornell, J., Dlamini, S., Helman, R., Malherbe, N., & Titi, N. (2018). Some basic questions about (a) decolonizing Africa (n)-centred psychology considered. *South African Journal of Psychology, 48*(3), 331–342.

Reiter, B. (2018). *Constructing the pluriverse: The geopolitics of knowledge.* Duke University Press.

Smidt, J. (2018, October). The first water in the universe. In *SC 18. Supercomputing.org* (pp. 1–2).

Sowman, M., Hauck, M., van Sittert, L., & Sunde, J. (2011). Marine protected area management in South Africa: New policies, old paradigms. *Environmental Management, 47*(4), 573–583.

Sowman, M., & Sunde, J. (2018). Social impacts of marine protected areas in South Africa on coastal fishing communities. *Ocean & coastal management, 157,* 168–179.

Sowman, M., Scott, D., Green, L. J. F., Hara, M. M., Hauck, M., Kirsten, K., Paterson, B., Raemaekers, S., Jones, K., Sunde, J., & Turpie, J. K. (2013). Shallow waters: Social science research in South Africa's marine environment. *African Journal of Marine Science, 35*(3), 385–402.

Sunde, J. (2014). *Customary governance and expressions of living customary law at Dwesa-Cwebe: Contributions to small-scale fisheries governance in South Africa.* University of Cape Town.

Temper, L., McGarry, D., & Weber, L. (2019). From academic to political rigour: Insights from the 'Tarot' of transgressive research. *Ecological Economics, 164,* 106379.

Theron, L. C. (2016). Toward a culturally and contextually sensitive understanding of resilience: Privileging the voices of black, South African young people. *Journal of Adolescent Research, 31*(6), 635–670.

Torres, K. D. S., & Winter, O. C. (2018). The when and where of water in the history of the universe. arXiv:1803.01452.

Tuana, N. (2008). Viscous porosity: Witnessing Katrina. In S. Alaimo & S. J. Hekman (Eds.), *Material feminisms* (pp. 323–333). Indiana University Press.

Vermeulen-Miltz, E., Clifford-Holmes, J. K., Scharler, U. M., & Lombard, A. T. (2022). A system dynamics model to support marine spatial planning in Algoa Bay, South Africa. *Environmental Modelling & Software, 160*, 105601.

Walker, C. (2005). Land of dreams: Land restitution on the eastern shores of Lake St Lucia. *Transformation: Critical Perspectives on Southern Africa, 59*(1), 1–25.

West, P., Igoe, J., & Brockington, D. (2006). Parks and peoples: The social impact of protected areas. *Annual Review of Anthropology, 35*, 251–277.

3

COLLABORATIVE INNOVATIONS INTO PEDAGOGIES OF CARE FOR SOUTH AFRICAN HYDROCOMMONS

Aaniyah Martin

> For those of us who live at the shoreline
> standing upon the constant edges of decision
> crucial and alone

(Lorde, 1978)

Diving in

This chapter explores ways in which humans understand caring for the marine environment and works towards co-developing a pedagogy of care for our hydrocommons in South Africa (Figure 3.1). Although this research is being explored 30 years after democracy in South Africa, the history and legacy of apartheid continues to live on and have an effect on Black and Brown bodies[1] by excluding them from the ocean and other spaces. The usefulness of the work is that it provides a critical thinking space to explore how we support and understand regenerative care practices through research-creation and transgressive learning for our marine environment.

Research-creation as a method emerged as a result of the inquiry related to inter- and transdisciplinarity (Manning, 2016). Research-creation, also called "arts-based research", was adopted into academic language through the questioning of methodology and started out as a funding category that would enable artists teaching in universities who did not have PhDs to apply for large academic grants (Manning, 2016). The nature of research-creation is such that it involves transversal engagement with different disciplines and this inturn stimulates the rethinking of how artistic practice reopens the question of what these disciplines can do, and how research-creation can enrich the understanding of the research question at hand.

DOI: 10.4324/9781003355199-3

FIGURE 3.1   Aaniyah at Waenhuiskrans/Arniston cave October 2022 spotting whales. Photo: Riyadh Omardien.

Manning further explains how research-creation is process – rather than outcomes-driven and how it begins outside disciplinary and institutional constrictions (Manning, 2016).

I am excited to use research-creation as a means to understand and unlock how we engage with a diverse group of people to understand their connection to the marine environment and how we develop a pedagogy of care as a process of enacting this. As reiterated by Manning (2016) research-creation does not need new methods, what it needs is a re-accounting of what writing can do in the process of thinking-doing. Furthermore, a research-creation approach relates strongly to Kulundu et al. (2020, p. 113) approach of 'call and response' learning/research which is inspired by:

> the call and response tradition of singing in Africa, where one person sings a phrase, and inspired by their contribution, the crowd sings back; this becomes an intuitive ongoing iterative process of improvisation and meaning making together.

This chapter explores how to configure regenerative care practices which are culturally sensitive and emergent, given that a large portion of the population experienced some form of trauma; for example, being forcibly relocated through the Group Areas Act. The proposed contribution of this study lies in the exploration of a Slow scholarship and generative methodology, that includes practices of walking, swimming and collectively mending a hydro-rug, that ultimately is working towards addressing the injustices of our South African apartheid legacy and co-creating care for our hydrocommons.

The hydrocommons are our natural water bodies – ocean, rivers and wetlands – which form part of the hydrological cycle. Broadly speaking, the concept of the commons refers to any creations of nature or culture that we inherit jointly or freely; and furthermore, a commons implies not only common use of a resource, but also common responsibility (Neimanis, 2009). My research context will focus on the ocean and beach component of the hydrocommons; and yet the ocean and beach environment cannot exist without the continuous circulation of water in the Earth-Atmosphere system. At its core, the water cycle is the motion of the water from the ground to the atmosphere and back again.

The beach and ocean tidal pools are possibly the most likely point of entry and connection to the ocean for humans, especially in South Africa, where the coastline is rough and wild. The geographical place, known as the beach, is the interface between land and ocean. A place accessible to those that enjoy venturing into the ocean and those that may not, those who can swim and those who do not know how to. This opens up the opportunity to explore how we encourage communities of people who may not have access to the wonder of swimming in the ocean, as well as with those that do and those who do not have fears of dwelling in the open water. The term 'community' holds historical connotations of political, economic and social disadvantage in South Africa (Carolissen et al., 2010). For me, 'community' encompasses a sense of kinship or family among a group of living things (human and other-than-human) that care for the wellbeing of people and the planet. In this research, a community will be defined as all humans that benefit (tangibly and intangibly) from a healthy ocean; it includes citizens, corporations, government, business and industry.

In order to consider how to configure regenerative care practices which are culturally sensitive and emergent I have found agential realism (Barad, 2007; Juelskjær et al., 2020), transgressive learning (Lotz-Sisitka et al., 2015; Bengsston, 2019; Kulundu-Bolus et al., 2020) and decolonial theoretical frameworks (Akomolafe & Ladha, 2017; Connell, 2007; Escobar, 2011; Oyewumi, 1997; Lugones, 2007; Juelskjær et al., 2020) the most aligned with answering the questions of how we understand and make meaning, care for, respond to and take responsibility for our hydrocommons. The framework for care is linked to being response-able (Haraway, 2016; Barad, 2007) and I will explore how response-ability and responsibility sit at the foundation of transgressive learning praxis that expand ethical sensibilities in care and posthuman/new materialism ethics within the hydrocommons context in SA. Bozalek and Zemblyas (2023) elaborate on this notion and explains that as researchers, we need to be responsible (accountable) and response-able (responsive) towards the issues and the phenomena we are doing inquiries into.

The major emphasis that is foregrounded by non-representational and critical posthumanist/new materialist/agential realist researchers is that study does not occur in units or controlled isolation but rather the vital processes through which relations take place. In much the same way that the hydrological cycle, as described earlier, is not bounded by each phase but rather is relationship with each phase and each phase contributes to the whole. These researchers are much less interested in representing an empirical reality that has taken place before the act of representation than they are in enacting multiple and diverse potentials of what knowledge can become afterwards (Vannini, 2015). Instead, performative approaches – practices, enactments and doings – are proposed by feminist new materialism, critical posthumanism and agential realism thereby rejecting representationalism (Akomolafe & Ladha, 2017; Barad, 2007; Bozalek & Zembylas, 2017; Vannini, 2015). Barad (2007) calls on Niels Bohr, who, they say, rejects representationalism, where words and things are separated, and who includes the discursive and material together, as material-discursive. Critical posthumanism transcends the either/or in materialist and discursive and joins them together as material-discursive (Bozalek et al., 2021).

Situating this work in agential realism which characterises itself as a non-representational theory, is in itself seeking to understand how the world has come to be by not only reflecting or representing reality, in that it offers relational and performative understanding of the world. A performative understanding assumes that we are part of the world's becoming rather than at a distance from it, and that we are able to have a direct material engagement with the world – practices are seen as material enactments. Barad (2007) importantly notes that it is humans and more-than-humans that engage in performative acts. Furthermore, phenomena are the primary ontological units which are entangled material agencies; rather than the separation of a pre-existing subject and object as in representational theories (Barad, 2007). This thinking lends itself to research-creation. Manning (2016) explains that research-creation refutes the "subject" of study, and in so doing it also refuses the "object of study". It does so by always beginning with the creation of a problem that is truly productive of inquiry. By doing this, it opens the field of experience to the more-than of objects or subjects pre-formed. Research-creation is therefore an act that delights in the activation of the as-yet-unthought (Manning, 2016, p. 12). Manning thus argues that research needs to escape traditional subject boundaries and formalised methods if genuinely new forms of knowledge are to emerge.

In an interview with Adam Kleinman for Mousse Magazine (2012), Barad explains intra-action by introducing the concept that "individuals do not pre-exist as such but rather materialise in intra-action", in other words, through relationships. "Individuals do not exist, but are not individually determinate. Rather, 'individuals' only exist within phenomena (particular materialized/materializing relations) in their ongoing iteratively intra-active reconfiguring" (Kleinman, 2012, p. 77). This sentiment aligns strongly with the pedagogical intent for my doctorate, which aims to facilitate an intra-active reconfiguring of multiple ways of becoming-with the hydrocommons/more-than-human world, to facilitate meaning-making and learning that is 'intersectionality resonate' (Kulundu, 2018).

Floating, surfacing and reclaiming

> *I owe my being to the Khoi and San whose desolate souls haunt the*
> *great expanses of the beautiful Cape*
> *–they who fell victim to the*
> *most merciless genocide our native land has ever seen, they who were*
> *the first to lose their lives in the struggle to defend our freedom…*
> *(Mbeki 1996)*
>
> (Bam & Muthien, 2021, p. 4)

My research and interest in agential realism and care for our hydrocommons, with a particular interest in the beach and ocean, stems from the ocean being in my blood from a long lineage of ancestors brought to the Cape from Malaysia/Indonesia as slaves in the late 1600s. I was fortunate enough to have parents who taught me to swim, to harvest periwinkles along the rocky shore, to make delicious meals from the bounty of the sea and to share my appreciation for these life-giving bodies of water with others. My parents encouraged my sisters and I to enjoy green and blue spaces despite the apartheid restrictions and exclusions that limit the spaces which Black and Brown bodies could access and enjoy. Unbeknown to us, my parents challenged these rules and would take us to whites-only spaces without explaining to us that they were in fact breaking the law. It was only recently (May 2021) that I asked my mom how we got away with going to Dalebrook tidal pool, for example, which was designated for white people only. She explained that they simply took us and made sure that they went either early in the morning or at sunset when other users would simply turn a blind eye. I have come to realise that these experiences have made me feel that blue and green spaces are as much mine as they are and should be everyones. I have come to realise that not all Black and Brown bodies feel this way because of their experience of adhering to the demarcated areas as set out under the apartheid regime for Black and Brown bodies. My understanding of blue and green spaces can be described as naturally wild spaces in the marine and freshwater (blue) and terrestrial (green) environments. My parents' silent resistance helped me experience a sense of belonging with blue realms, and with that a need to care for and be responsible for ensuring that I protect the marine environment that we loved from a young age, and continue to love; and this has anchored and shaped my research for my doctorate.

My history and context with blue ecosystems culminated in the choice to study environmental and geographic science, to work at World Wildlife Fund (WWF) South Africa for 10 years and to establish in 2015 The Beach Co-op

(TBCO) as a voluntary organisation that hosts new moon cleanups on the rocky shore at Surfers Corner in Muizenberg (Cape Town, South Africa). TBCO became formalised as a non-profit company in 2017, and is a natural extension of my relationship (friendship) with the ocean and people. I have always had an interest in the intersection between people and nature, and the strange imposed artificial distinction between the two – McGarry (2013) refers to this as 'ecological apartheid', which is defined as a growing separation of relationships that include the human being's relationship with the natural world, as well as disconnections experienced within one's own inner and outer capacities. Overcoming this divide is a core ethical practice for me and therefore for TBCO too, with the key message from our beach cleanup activations conveying that we as humans are dependent on the health of our marine ecosystems. Together with an all women team they have been practising to build a community that cares for our marine environment by revealing the ocean's relevance and interconnectedness with our everyday life; and encouraging the responsibility and agency we have to regenerate the earth. They believe that behavioural change is affected by individual awareness, emotional connection and enabled action. TBCO's work therefore focuses on building an ocean-loving culture and is supported by scientific knowledge and lived experience. The beach is the living classroom in which we nurture place-based learning (Derby, 2015) that effectively connects people, institutions and organisations through transdisciplinary and transgressive learning (Lotz-Sisitka et al., 2015) to keep South Africa's beaches clean and healthy and to protect and enhance ocean health. Lotz-Sisitka et al. (2015) explain that in defining environmental concerns in terms of coupled socio-ecological systems there is a growing body within the scientific community suggesting that issues need to be understood and engaged through transdisciplinary perspectives across multiple institutions and involving multiple actors. Furthermore, Kulundu (2018, p. 91), examines how transgressive learning sits in trans-epistemic agility and 'intersectional resonance', i.e. the learning that occurs in-between and through complex and interrelated societal dynamics amongst a community of change drivers. TBCO practices celebrating the ocean and our relationship to and dependence on it through regular cleanups but have enmeshed the cleanup activation with other activities too such as music, art, poetry, sporting events and engaging with indigenous leaders.

Placing my research at the intersection between marine conservation and social justice issues in an African and South African context, and within agential realism is useful for me because it re-thinks the demarcations between natural sciences, social sciences and the humanities. It also, creates new entrances and exists between plural epistemologies and ecologies of knowledges located within these knowledge silos (de Sousa Santos, 2009). This transdisciplinarity emphasises a fact which Barad often underlines: namely, that there is a wider conversation going on in the ongoing endeavours to develop and iteratively unfold agential realism (Juelskjær et al., 2020). Similarly, for research-creation Manning (2016, p. 12) describes this study as an activity of immanent critique, an act that only knows the conditions of its existence from within its own process, an act that refuses to judge from without.

Furthermore, my perception and understanding of environmental humanities lends itself to agential realism thinking as it attempts to "re-frame global environmental change issues fundamentally as social and human challenges, rather than just environmental issues alone" (Palsson et al., 2011, p. 5). It is a means by which fundamental concerns within the humanities – such as, "meaning, value, responsibility and purpose" (Rose et al., 2012) can be brought to bear on questions of the environment through the deployment of modes of inquiry typical of studies in humanities. The entanglement of environmental, social and justice issues are brought to the surface and by doing so we are able to address the colonial thinking that marks the environmental science practices of the past (Neimanis et al., 2015).

I have always struggled to call myself a scientist and I finally understand why, because through reading the work of Sylvia Vollenhoven, Keeper of the Kumm (2016), she foregrounds the understanding that science is diffused with spirit, and that landscapes speaks of stories denied (Bam & Muthien, 2021). In Vollenhoven's chapter – Writing ourselves back into history – from the book Rethinking Africa (Muthien & Bam, 2021) she explains how it becomes embedded in her mind that healing involves caring, personal rituals as well as the plants that grow all around us. This way of being completely resonates with me as I move through the world and I begin understanding and reclaiming who I am.

> When we seek to Re-member, to put ourselves back together again
> and end the instability of separate selves, we have to work with the
> 'ancestral presence of the past'.
>
> *(Vollenhoven, 2016, p. 29)*

The figure of Krotoa-Eva or!Goa/goas (her name among the Goringghaicona tribe that lived by the shore) has played a significant role for me in working with the 'ancestral presence of the past'. The process of reclaiming myself as well as the conservation work that I have been involved with and have led; has been an emergence and nurturing experience of arriving home (Omardien, 2021). The reclaiming process lives in relationship with my assimilation process. I live in spaces where on the one hand, I feel like I belong because I am with my people and my community that look like me, and on the other hand, I live in spaces where I feel I am in the minority because I am the token brown person. I am only now beginning to feel comfortable enough to be my true, authentic self rather than assimilating so that I fit in, belong, and avoid conflict. Krotoa was first brought to my attention at a ceremony I was invited to on our west coast to pray for the protection of our coastline which is being mined for tourmaline and other resources; and with not much regard for the local and indigenous groups that reside there (Little & Domingues, 2021). Krotoa was called upon whilst in ceremony by the traditional healer for guidance and direction in this matter. Her name has stayed with me since and like Vollenhoven I am constantly consulting with her.

I have a deep connection and empathy for Krotoa through understanding and making sense of my journey as a brown woman in the world right now, and yet I sense that she had similar feelings then (Omardien, 2021; Bloem, 1999). She was a Khoi woman who worked as a domestic servant in the Van Riebeeck house and as translator for the Dutch authorities. Her marriage was the first recorded union between a 'native' and a 'settler'. In the 1650s Krotoa was the only figure possessing an intimate knowledge of both Khoikhoi and Dutch culture; as she passed back and forth between one society and the other, she exchanged her Dutch clothing for Khoikhoi skins, and vice versa. However, her work as an interpreter was not easy, as she was torn between her loyalty to the Dutch and her own people (whose land was being taken over by the Dutch in the late 1650s). Due to this dilemma, Krotoa often struggled to maintain trust on both sides; she was eventually banished to Robben Island and died there (Bloem, 1999). I hold feelings of both despair and comfort for her life and what she must have experienced and what we as brown people continue to experience today (Omardien, 2021).

Toni-Giselle Stuart focused her Masters research on writing a Cape jazz poem titled Krotoa-Eva's Suite and I have chosen to include an excerpt of the poem with her consent.

Mouthbow

the woman speaks
my tears spill down the flank
of Devil's Peak
my breath is the cloth
that sets Hoerikwaggo's table
I am the one
who invites you to eat
I am the one
who invites you to eat
I am the child of two Gods
my heart is a Hollander
but my soul prays to Heitsi-Eb!
I am the one
whose bones are strong enough
to carry the weight of two skins
I am the one
whose mouth is supple enough
to hold the secrets of two tongues
if you meet me in the veld,
know my feet have already returned to the fort

if you meet me inside the castle,
know my heart has already returned to the dunes
no matter who I tell you I am
do not believe me
no matter who I tell you I am
I am always
only
half
of myself

$\qquad\qquad\qquad$ (Stuart, 2015, p. 7)

Strandlooping/swimming with the tides and weaving stories through hydro-rugging

My intention with this research is to use Slow scholarship and methods such as *strandlooping*[2]/swimming, and mending to bring the entanglement of environmental and social justice issues to the surface through revealing stories from the past that have been erased and forgotten. The uncovering of stories is a slow process that involves the unpacking of oral history, and this in itself takes time to find the bearers of this information and to build trust for this information to be shared. This motion of uncovering and recovering reminds me of the motion of the ocean washing up onto the shore. High tide pushes onto the shore sometimes bringing with it things that have been buried deep in the ocean and leaving them along the high tide mark to be found or not; and then as the tide recedes and becomes low exposing parts of the land that is usually covered by water. This covering and uncovering motion of the ocean is governed by the cycle of the moon. The cycles of the moon have become significant to how I move along the shore – *strandlooping*/swimming along the Camissa coastline of False Bay.

Strandlooping/swimming close to the sea arguably opens up ghostly knowledges about the multiple histories that shape our presents and futures through our immersion and relationship with water (Shefer & Bozalek, 2022). Encounters in and along the sea, in *strandlooping*/swimming, thus allow for alternative knowledge-making processes, deploying rather a 'hydro-logics' (Neimanis, 2013, 2017a,b). Shefer and Bozalek (2022) convey that in postcolonial spaces like South Africa, wild swimming may offer a particularly fruitful space to engage with troubled waters related to colonial pasts and its continuities and mutations in current capitalocene and anthropocene times. 'Staying with the trouble' (Haraway, 2016) by swimming and *strandlooping* alongside troubled waters and troubling our waters as we swim and *strandloop* then holds many possibilities for alternative scholarships for justice-to-come and new knowledge-making (Shefer & Bozalek, 2022).

I have chosen to *strandloop*/swim along the coastline of Camissa's (Cape Town's) False Bay around new or full moon depending on the weather and swell conditions over those time periods. I studied Atmospheric Science for my undergraduate studies and Honours degree, and this together with the practical experience of learning to read the wind and surf conditions for Camissa has helped me to understand which conditions are best for *strandlooping* and swimming along False Bay. This journey is non-linear, that is to say I have chosen random sections of the 200 km stretch of coastline and begun *strandlooping* and swimming where I have felt called to go. The relationship between the land and sea is fluid and entangled along the coastline with the movement of the tides. I have literally experienced how the path I am walking along becomes a swimming path and vice versa.

The focus on either new and full moon facilitates and opens up my time and the need to fulfil my role as re-searcher and student as well as being present as a mother, wife, daughter and daughter-in-law. This slow journey allows me to process my findings and experiences in between the *strandlooping* and swimming; as opposed to completing it in one mission as these explorations and expeditions are usually practised. Jolly (2022) from the Daily Maverick describes the *strandlooping* act as "Martin's rewalk as an antihero's journey or rather a heroine's journey which is not so much getting from A to B but rather the journey itself." My "artwalk" echoes author Ursula Le Guin's *The Carrier Bag Theory of Fiction* (2019) which posits that even before the masculine spears appeared in our evolution there was the feminine carrier bag, which some considered our ancestors' greatest invention (Jolly, 2022).

"Le Guin's *Carrier Bag Theory* suggests that all heroes were at one point contained in carrier bags whether in their mother's womb or in a carrier bag, in other words, carried by the feminine (Figure 3.2). And it's this vulnerability, this defenselessness, this dependence on a woman which McGarry points out is always the part left out of the hero's journey and one which Martin's rewalk seeks to readdress" (Jolly, 2022).

The mending methodology is experienced through the hydro-rug featuring collaborative stitchings of Brown and Black histories into a rug. TBCO, as mentioned earlier, focuses on building communities that care through hosting beach cleanups and sharing knowledge of the unique marine biodiversity of South Africa. The debris collected at cleanups are reworked into collaborative artworks and whilst we stitch and sew we share stories of our connection to the ocean and this process facilitates the mending and healing of the trauma Black and Brown biodies have experienced and continue to experience post-apartheid.

The co-creation of the hydro-rug plays a crucial role in unlocking and revealing stories of our relationship with the ocean. As we mend and share our stories they are woven into the hydro-rug which becomes the physical object of our stories. Whilst in conversation we are stitching, mending and sewing a hydro-rug which is made from plastic litter that we collect from our South African beaches, thule and off-cut/ waste material and thread. The hydro-rug becomes the embodied, material aesthetic of the stories that are shared and that formulate our understanding of caring for our marine environment. These methods of listening, sharing stories, stitching and

FIGURE 3.2   Madyo (age 11) and Haroun (age 5), two of Aaniyah's children who *strandloop* with her, pictured here along the False Bay coastline close to Hanglip (Hangklip). Photo: Aaniyah Martin.

mending foregrounds the need to know and do differently and otherwise (Tachine & Nicolazzo, 2022) when we produce and understand relevant knowledge about the colonial past and its ongoing presence (Bam & Muthien, 2021).

The process of sharing stories about the ocean and feelings of belonging to places that were previously demarcated for white people only, and mending the hydro-rug are intra-twined and through this, participants experience a sense of healing. When possible, we are positioned next to a tidal pool or the ocean. I lay out a cloth demarcating a space for us to meet, with a flask of tea and all the materials we needed to create the hydro-rug – the sewing box, waste material and litter. Participants choose their waste material, litter and the thread they wanted to use; and we would be in conversation throughout the making process. I (Martin, 2023) have intra-viewed[3] many individuals and the hydro-rug continues to grow and was on exhibit at the Eitz gallery in Camissa as part of the *Our ocean is scared, you can't mine heaven* exhibition curated by Dr Dylan McGarry at the time of writing this chapter.

My personal healing and mending has stemmed from reclaiming who I am through unlocking my ancestry with the help of Daiyaan Petersen. I met Daiyaan through Instagram because of a drawing I posted to my stories of a family relation. I received the photograph from my mom and she had no idea who the woman was. I became intrigued by her, and begun a pencil drawing of her in July 2022. When Daiyaan saw the drawing of her, he asked me what her name was. I explained that she was family but we had no idea how she was related and what her name was. He offered to help me track her name because, apart from having an interest in assisting creole people with tracking their ancestry, he is a researcher at the Western Cape Archives and Record Services. His ability to read Dutch, Javanese and Arabic-Afrikaans has helped us track our ancestry from reading *mesangs* (head stones) at *maqbaras* (graveyards) to visiting the archives and reading permits and wills. This has uncovered our maternal lineage eight generations back to an emancipated slave and her name was Katryn van de Kaap. We have also discovered that my mom's family owned a horse and carriage business called 'Soeker Bros' (this was the oldest Malay/Muslim owned family run company in the Cape which existed till the mid-20th century) on Plein Street in Camissa. They were a prominent creole family and hence they were photographed, which was not common amongst creole families of the time (Figure 3.3).

As part of my weekly practice/ritual I try to go walking at least twice a week by myself up our local mountain in Lakeside. Most people question my safety and

FIGURE 3.3 Sisi Sarah Martin (Aaniyah's mother) and Daiyaan Petersen finding the Soeker ancestors graves in Mowbray *maqbara*, Camissa. Photo: Aaniyah Martin.

FIGURE 3.4a   The Protea Natida pictured   FIGURE 3.4b   Preparing the plant dye with
on Lakeside Pinnacle close   sugar, a rusty nail and plant leaves in my
to Aaniyah's home. Photo: mother's first cooking pot. Photo: Aaniyah
Aaniyah Martin.   Martin.

walking alone in the mountains because many hikers have been mugged and or killed. I have fought against this fear and make my way up a steep path regardless; greeting the plants, animals and rocks as I go. At the time of discovering my ancestry I was particularly drawn to the Protea Nitida which was in bloom. When I read more about them and their uses I discovered that they were used for firewood and to make ox wagon wheels because they are so hardy. In addition, their leaves – dead or alive – were used as a plant dye by boiling them with sugar and a rusty nail. The connection of this plant with my ancestors and the horse and carriage business led me to experimenting with the plant dye and incorporating it into the hydro-rug process. I have dyed sheets of muslin or cotton, depending on what kind of waste material I find, and this has formed the base layer on which the individual hydro-rugs will be Sachiko-ed (Figures 3.4a and 3.4b).

Drifting thoughts

Alexis Pauline Gumb asks "What are the scales of intimacy and the actual practices that would teach us how to care for each other beyond obligation or imaginary duties?" (2020, p. 56). Similarly, I am asking what other care practices exist that have been overlooked because of our South African apartheid legacy which continues to live on today. Patricia Hill Collins argues that 'seeing from below' can generate a post-colonial understanding of 'being human' (1990, p. 25). In this way, seeing from below, allows Brown and Black bodies to offer understanding and insight that speak not only about and to – but beyond – their locations (Lewis & Baderoon, 2021). They argue that despite the assumption that essays and writing from socially marginalised standpoints can generate only knowledge that speaks to the experiences of these groups, on the contrary those positioned at the margins often see the world from a different perspective. Lewis and Baderoon (2021) go on to say that this knowledge not only counters racist and patriarchal world views, it envisions new ways of being human and is therefore relevant to all.

The approach and methods for this research include stitching, mending, creating, imagining and storytelling. These methods enable us to comprehend entangled relationships between bodies and the marine environment. These 'otherwise' ways of knowing and being in the world facilitate the co-creation and building of community especially amongst Black and Brown bodies who have been segregated through Apartheid's compartmentalisation of ethnic, religious and mixed-race groups that has had a powerful impact on how groups continue to identify themselves. "We are now busy journeying from the woundedness of recent centuries to wholeness" (Vollenhoven, 2021, p. 29).

> The fact that we are here and that I speak these words is an attempt to break that silence and bridge some of these differences between us, for it is not difference which immobilizes us, but silence. And there are so many silences to be broken.
>
> *(Lorde, 2019, p. 33)*

Notes

1   I use the words Brown and Black bodies to distinguish them from Black Indigenous People of Colour because of the North American framing and how it has been imposed in a South African context. Biko's ideas of Black consciousness are more suitable and fitting for this work because we are situated in an African context. However, in the South African context specifically, we want to specify and name both Black and Brown bodies because apartheid laws separated them purposefully and there are racial divides that exist amongst these groups today.

2   As opposed to using the word walking I have contextualised it to the Afrikaans word *strandloop* meaning to beach walk and added the 'ing' to make it a verb. My mother has always referred to herself as a *strandloper* having grown up along the False Bay coastline in a suburb called the Strand. Bam (2021b) refers to the word *strandloper* as a derogatory colonial term for the Goringghaicona who were seasoned, multilingual traders who travelled in passer-by ships way before the Dutch or Portuguese arrived at the Cape. I do not associate the word *strandloper* as derogatory and have named myself @contemporary_strandloper on Instagram.

3   The term intra-view as opposed to interview encompasses a generative exchange rather than extraction of information through an open-ended conversation and is linked to Karen Barad's intra-action.

References

Akomolafe, B., & Ladha, A. (2017). Perverse particles, entangled monsters and psychedelic pilgrimages: Emergence as an ontoepistemology of not-knowing. *Ephemera, 17*(4), 819–839.

Bam, J. (2021a). Feminism-cide and epistemicide of Cape herstoriography through the lens of the ecology of indigenous plants. In B. Muthien & J. Bam (Eds). *Rethinking Africa: Indigenous women reinterpret Southern Africa's pasts* (pp. 103–120). Fanele.

Bam, J. (2021b). *Ausi told me: Why cape herstoriographies matter.* Fanele.

Bam, J., & Muthien, B. (2021). Introduction. In B. Muthien & J. Bam (Eds.), *Rethinking Africa: Indigenous women reinterpret Africa's pasts* (pp. 3–15). Fanele.

Barad, K. (2007). *Meeting the universe halfway: Quantum physics and the entanglement of matter.* Duke University Press.

Bengsston, S. (2019). Engaging with the beyond—Diffracting conceptions of t-learning. *Sustainability, 11*(1–20).

Bloem, T. (1999). *Krotoa – Eva: The women from Robben Island.* G M Kettley c/o Kwella Books.

Bozalek, V., & Zembylas, M. (2017). Diffraction or reflection? Sketching the contours of two methodologies in educational research. *International Journal of Qualitative Studies in Education, 30*(2), 111–127.

Bozalek, V., & Zemblyas, M. (2023). *Responsibility, privileged irresponsibility and response-ability: Higher education, coloniality and ecological damage.* Palgrave MacMillan.

Bozalek, V., Zembylas, M., & Tronto, J. (2021). *Posthuman and political care ethics for reconfiguring higher education pedagogies.* Routledge.

Carolissen, R., Rohleder, P., Bozalek, V., Swartz, L., & Leibowitz, B. (2010). "Community psychology is for poor, black people": Pedagogy and teaching of community psychology in South Africa. *Equity & Excellence in Education, 43*(4), 495–510.

Connell, R. (2007). *Southern Theory: The global dynamics of knowledge in social science.* Taylor & Francis.

de Sousa Santos, B. (2009). A non-occidentalist west? Learned ignorance and ecology of knowledge. *Theory, Culture & Society, 26*(7–8), 103–125.

Derby, M. W. (2015). *Place, being, resonance: A critical ecohermeneutic approach to education.* Peter Lang.

Escobar, A. (2011). *Encountering development.* Princeton University Press.

Gumbs, A. P. (2020). *Undrowned: Black Feminist Lessons from Marine Mammals.* AK Press.

Haraway, D. (2016). *Staying with the trouble: Making Kin in the Chthulucene.* Duke University Press.

Hill Collins, P. (1990). *Black feminist thought: Knowledge, consciousness and the politics of empowerment.* Routledge.

Jolly, L. (2022). A stitch in sacred time – Exhibition weaves our oceans back into the realm of the divine. Retrieved October 12, 2022, from www.dailymaverick.co.za/article/2022-09-05-a-stitch-in-sacred-time-exhibition-weaves-our-oceans-back-into-the-realm-of-the-divine/

Juelskjær, M., Plauborg, H., & Adrian, S. W. (2020). *Dialogues on agential realism: Engaging in worldings through research practice.* Routledge.

Kleinman A. (2012). Inter-actions with Karen Barad. *Mousse Magazine, 34*, 76–81.

Kulundu, I. (2018). Think piece: Intersectional resonance and the multiplicity of being in a polarised world. *Southern African Journal of Environmental Education, 34*(1), 92–100.

Kulundu-Bolus, I. McGarry, D., & Lotz-Sisitka, H. (2020). Learning, Living and Leading into Transgression – A reflection on decolonial praxis in a neoliberal world. *Southern African Journal of Environmental Education, 36*, 112–125.

Le Guin, U. (2019). *The carrier bag theory of fiction.* Ignota Books.

Lewis, D., & Baderoon, G. (Eds.). (2021). *Surfacing: On being black and feminist in South Africa.* Wits University Press.

Little, B., & Domingues, A. (2021). Ours not mine. YouTube. www.youtube.com/watch?v=BhQwx9Xk-Vo

Lorde, A. (1978). *"A Litany for Survival." The Collected Poems of Audre Lorde by Audre Lorde.* Retrieved October 12, 2022, from www.poetryfoundation.org/poems/147275/a-litany-for-survival/

Lorde, A. (2019) *Sister outsider.* Penguin Classics.

Lotz-Sisitka, H., Wals, A. E., Kronlid, D., & McGarry, D. (2015). Transformative, transgressive social learning: Rethinking higher education pedagogy in times of systemic global dysfunction. *Current Opinion in Environmental Sustainability, 16*, 73–80.

Lugones, M. (2007). Heterosexualism and the colonial/modern gender system. *Hypatia, 22*(1), 186–209.

Manning, E. (2016). *The minor gesture.* Duke University Press.

Martin, A. (2023). Tidal pools as containers of care. *Ellipses: Journal of Creative Research.* https://ellipses2022.webflow.io/article/tidal-pools-as-containers-of-care

McGarry, D. K. (2013). Empathy in the time of ecological apartheid: A social sculpture practice-led inquiry into developing pedagogies for ecological citizenship. PHD thesis, Rhodes University. http://contentpro.seals.ac.za/iii/cpro/DigitalItemViewPage.external?sp=1013154

Muthien, B., & Bam, J. (Eds.). (2021). *Rethinking Africa: Indigenous women reinterpret Southern Africa's pasts.* Fanele.

Neimanis, A. (2009). Bodies of water, human rights and the hydrocommons. *TOPIA Canadian Journal of Cultural Studies, 21*, 161–182.

Neimanis, A. (2013). Feminist subjectivity, watered. *Feminist Review, 103*, 23–41.

Neimanis, A. (2017a). *Bodies of water: Posthuman feminist phenomenology.* Bloomsbury Academic.

Neimanis, A. (2017b). Water and knowledge. In D. Christian & R. Wong (Eds.), *Reimagining water* (pp. 51–68). Wilfrid Laurier University Press.

Neimanis, A. (2020). We are all at sea: Practice, ethics, and poetics of "Hydrocommons" Retrieved March 4, 2021, from http://moussemagazine.it/astrida-neimanis-sofia-lemos-2020/

Neimanis, A., Åsberg C., & Hedrén J. (2015). Four problems, four directions for environmental humanities: Toward critical posthumanities for the Anthropocene. *Ethics & the Environment, 20*(1), 67–97.

Omardien, A. (2021). *Portrayal.* www.earthed.world/portrayal (The author has since changed her surname back to her maiden surname Martin).

Oyewumi, O. (1997). *The invention of women: Making an African sense of western gender discourses.* University of Minnesota Press.

Palsson, G., Goodsite, M., Pahl-Wostl, C., O'Brien, K., Hordjijk, L., & Avril, B. (2011). *"Responses to environmental and societal challenges for our unstable earth (RESCUE)." ESF Forward Look – ESF-COST 'frontier of science' joint initiative.* European Science Foundation, Strasbourg (FR) and European Cooperation in Science and Technology.

Rose, D., van Dooren, T., Chrulew, M., Cooke, S., Kearnes, M., & O'Gorman, E. (2012). Thinking through the Environment, Unsettling the Humanities. *Environmental Humanities, 1*, 1–5.

Shefer, T., & Bozalek, V. (2022). Wild swimming methodologies for decolonial feminist justice-to-come scholarship. *Feminist Review, 130*, 26–43. https://doi.org/10.1177%2F01 417789211069351

Stuart, T-G. (2015). *KROTOA-EVA'S SUITE – A cape jazz poem in three movements.* Masters Dissertation. Goldsmiths, University of London.

Tachine, A., & Nicolazzo, Z. (2022).*Weaving an otherwise: In-relations methodological practice.* Stylus publishing.

The Beach Co-op. (2019/2020). Annual report: Stepping up the challenge. Unpublished report. www.thebeachcoop.org/wp-content/uploads/2020/06/TBC_Annual-Report_-REV1.pdf

Vannini, P. (Ed.) (2015). *Non-representational methodologies: Re-envisioning research.* Routledge.

Vollenhoven, S. (2016). *The keeper of the kumm.* Tafelberg

World Economic Forum. Retrieved December 2018, from www.weforum.org/agenda/2019/08/here-are-5-reasons-why-the-ocean-is-so-important/

4

SURFING AS A SPACE FOR ACTIVISM AND CHANGE

What could surfing be(come)?

Karen Graaff

Introduction

Despite surfing's reported origins in the Hawaiian islands, and the likelihood that some form of board-riding developed independently in several places around the globe, modern surfing is widely seen, both within and outside of surfing culture, as a sport dominated by white, cisgender men. Yet, within this racialised and heteronormative doxa (lisahunter, 2018), groups are increasingly using surfing as a space for activism and social and environmental change, in line with Comer's (2019, p. 2) concept of 'surfeminism', which focuses on access to 'public ocean and beach spaces, environmental and ocean health, as well as issues of racial and economic justice.' To provide context for how surfing has opened up surfeminist spaces for activism and change, this chapter begins by giving a brief overview of surfing's patriocolonial (lisahunter, 2018) and heteronormative history, and then moves into the present. It focuses on mainstream activism by surfers and the ways the sport's past and present have shaped this activism. The chapter then moves on to document alternative social spaces and avenues of activism which have emerged to create more diverse surf communities within the constrained environment of mainstream surf culture.

Revisiting surfing's past in the present

There is a well-established scholarly literature on the history and development of surfing in key surfing centres across the world: in Hawai'i (Walker, 2011), the United States (US) (Comer, 2010; Laderman, 2014), Australia (Booth, 2001), South Africa (Thompson, 2015), Brazil (Knijnik et al., 2010) and West Africa (Dawson, 2018). For the purposes of this chapter, it is sufficient to note that today's

DOI: 10.4324/9781003355199-4

popularly 'accepted' history of surfing, that is, stand-up board-riding, initially developed on the Hawaiian islands but was suppressed by American Protestant missionaries in the early 1800s (Laderman, 2014). After the annexation of Hawai'i by the US by the end of the 19th century (Hough-Snee & Eastman, 2017), surfing was 'resurrected' on the Hawaiian islands by white male US settler colonialists (Gilio-Whitaker, 2017), before becoming popular on the US mainland after World War One. Surfing played a key role in the development of a tourism industry in Hawai'i, as in many other contexts, and a primary feature was the establishment of segregation in the waves, including whites-only board-riders' clubs (Ingersoll, 2016), and the maintenance of sex/gender binaries (Lugones, 2010), resulting in an image of surfing as an exclusively straight, white and male sporting activity.

A major driver of this settler patriocolonialism was the growing popularity of surf culture in the US in the 1950s and 1960s, with surf media, and particularly surf films, spreading this whitewashed image of surfing to a global audience. Surf movies usually showed white American, and sometimes Australian, men as 'an imperial coloniser,' traveling to developing countries to surf, pioneering 'uncharted waves' and 'civilising' indigenous populations (Ormrod, 2005a, p. 12). The historical outcome was an emphasis on white men from developed countries as the founders of surfing, despite evidence of local surf cultures arising independently and prior to the foreign surfers' arrival (see Dawson, 2018). The moves to maintain surfing's image as a whites-only sport were aided by racial and segregationist laws in major surf centres about who was 'allowed' on beaches and in the water (Phoenix et al., 2021). In the South African context, Apartheid legislation codified which racial groups could live in which areas, and had a profound impact on access to safe and clean beaches. Many of the most-desirable coastal areas were designated whites-only, leaving a lasting legacy of lack of access to beaches, surfing and water safety. For a more detailed discussion of the impact of this on surfing in South Africa, see Thompson (2015).

Alongside this image of surfing as pioneering conquest, the surfboard itself underwent changes, from the original longboards (over nine feet in length), to the shortboard (late 1960s), and the tri-fin 'thruster' (from the 1980s) (Thompson, 2015). Shortboards allowed sharper turns and more aggressive surfing, and it is perhaps unsurprising that this resulted in surfing became even more closely identified with masculinity and all-male line-ups (Evers, 2009; Wheaton & Thorpe, 2018). As Ingersoll (2016, p. 69) has noted, "this sentiment of territorial conquest is also found in Western language about the act of riding water. Surfing is discussed through the terminology of 'ripping', 'shredding', and 'killing' waves". Aggressive surfing is scored more highly in competitions, and women who can produce 'man-turns' are considered more skilful (Olive et al., 2015; Thompson, 2015; lisahunter, 2017), although women should still maintain their heterosexy appeal at all costs (Olive et al., 2018), as will be discussed below. While women have been part of professional surfing contests since the 1960s, they were historically marginalised, paid less in prize and sponsorship money, and excluded from all professional surfing decision-making bodies (see the film *Girls Can't Surf* [Nelius, 2021]). It was only in 2019 that professional female surfers on the World Surf League's (WSL) Championship Tour began to be paid the same prize money as males (Baird, 2019). More recently, there has also been discussion about limiting transgender women's participation in competitive surfing (Quarnstrom, 2022), in line with current similar efforts by other sporting codes (AP News, 2021; Fahey, 2022), further entrenching surfing's historic heteronormative stance.[1]

Surfing's past and present in many ways still shape opportunities for activism within the sport and culture. While some activist spaces seem to largely maintain the status quo, others have begun carving out their own niches within a mainstream surf culture that is hostile to changing established racial, gender and capitalist social orders. The following sections focus on the ways that surfing's patriocolonial history has impacted surfers' environmental activism, rendering it half-hearted at best, and harmful at worst, before highlighting positive steps to create alternative spaces of social inclusion by the surf industry and surfers.

Environmentalism and surfer activism

Environmentalism has been a well-developed and active avenue for surfer activism, including through surfeminism efforts, and this allows for an assessment of both the limits and possibilities of environmental surfer activism. Some surfers are heavily invested in specific environmental movements, and while this can have positive benefits, it also highlights the limitations of historical and current surfer activism. Surfing as a sport is closely tied to ocean health, with a "literal embodied and emotional entanglement with the ocean environment" (Britton & Foley, 2021, p. 79). Some surfers are strong advocates for protecting oceans from pollution, development, drilling and other man-made impacts, and have been involved in protests against development in coastal areas in South Africa, including anti-nuclear protests in Jeffrey's Bay in the Eastern Cape, and ongoing protests against coastal mining on the West Coast in the Western Cape. A key focus has been protecting specific beaches and waves from being altered or destroyed by development. While this can have positive outcomes, by preventing destructive development and its impacts on the environment, it also hides the relatively self-serving nature of that activism, which focuses more on protecting waves for surfers' benefit, than protecting the entire eco-systems (including local or indigenous populations) in which those waves are found (Hill & Abbott, 2009).

For example, what is often absent is how coastal development related to surfing, and more specifically surf tourism, impacts on indigenous and local communities, and on eco-systems. Once a surf break gets 'discovered', and people start arriving to surf it, there is typically a period of tourism development and commercialisation, often with little or no buy-in from indigenous and local communities. Ingersoll notes that surf tourism is an industry that "takes from a culture what serves it: waves, idyllic weather, access, "remote" locales, and adventure, without much insight into the impact it has, or level of reciprocation it offers to native populations" (2016, p. 71). While some may argue that this development can provide jobs for those living in the community, and this may be true to some extent, what also often happens is gentrification and development of all beachfront land, pushing indigenous communities away from coastlines and oceans, making coastal property too expensive for them to live on or own (Phoenix et al., 2021). Hill and Abbott note, "as surfing has grown into a capitalist enterprise, it has also come to increasingly exploit and degrade the environment" (2009, p. 278). The social, economic and spatial impacts have added environmental impacts in terms of the physical infrastructure that gets built, including new homes and apartment buildings, hotels, shops and restaurants.

Along with this, the 'surfari' (where a surfer travels to a different, often developing, country to surf) has become a large part of surf culture (Ormrod, 2005b; Comer, 2010), at least for those with money to spend. Yet, the impact of these trips, in terms of travel to get there, resources used and disposed of while there, and impact on local communities, is rarely considered. As Ingersoll notes, "surfers have evolved into a breed that overwhelmingly overlooks a conscious awareness of their impacts on the people, oceans, and lands encountered on their surf itineraries" (2016, p. 43). There is also little focus on how surfers impact on their environment as individuals. For example, while surfers are encouraged to use re-fillable water bottles and do beach clean-ups, there is less discussion around choosing to stay home rather than drive or fly for a surf trip. However, even if surfers choose to stay local and only drive to beaches close by, the emissions from their cars, on trips to and from the beach, often add up to one of the single biggest sources of pollution from their surfing (Schultz, 2009). Similarly, there has historically been little surf industry and surf community discussion of the environmental impacts of all the products associated with surfing, such as the production and disposal of surfboards, wetsuits, hoodies, boots, surf wax, leashes and suncream, despite the known harms (Hill & Abbott, 2009).

However, this is also perhaps where surfing has started showing signs of biggest improvement in recent years. A good example is wetsuits. Historically, wetsuits are made of neoprene, a large component of which is synthetic rubber; its traditional production process is harmful in and of itself (Hill & Abbott, 2009) and, once wetsuits have reached the end of their lifespan, they are typically just thrown away. However, some wetsuit companies, such as Rip Curl, have begun wetsuit recycling programmes, where surfers can return their old wetsuits, which are then broken down and repurposed, but this is currently only available in the US, Australia, France, Portugal and Spain. There are also moves by some manufacturers (such as Patagonia) to start using natural rubber in wetsuit production instead, which at least makes the production process less damaging.

A driver for surfer environmental activism has been the scholarly and public discourses in recent years on the benefits of time in 'blue space,' defined as "waterscapes and their surroundings, which can include saltwater... freshwater...

[and] human-made sites such as pools, canals, ponds, dams, and moats" (Olive & Wheaton, 2021, p. 4). Studies report physical, mental and other benefits as a result of immersion in blue space (e.g. Britton & Foley, 2021). While much of this may be true, there has been somewhat of an overemphasis on the benefits of blue space, with the assumption that any and all time spent in the ocean will always be beneficial, and that the benefit accrues for everyone. As Olive and Wheaton note, there is an "almost "evangelical" … investment in the ability of surfing to heal, help, and teach, while glossing over the practical, economic, and cultural challenges for many participants" (2021, p. 7). There are many factors, beyond just the ocean itself, which play into a person's experience of blue spaces. As outlined in this chapter, surfing has typically not been a welcoming space for marginalised people, and may in fact cause numerous social harms. Olive and Wheaton highlight that different bodies "access and experience blue spaces in unequal ways, impacting who can use blue spaces, how they can be used, and how power is reproduced and contested" (2021, p. 8). Phoenix et al. (2021, p. 116) explain that some people have experienced blue spaces "as sites of marginalization", rather than healing, due to historical or social exclusion. In addition, as Evers (2021) points out, there is little acknowledgement that blue spaces are becoming increasingly polluted due to harmful and toxic waste generated from manufacturing industries and human consumption. While some surfers may be active in protests against such large-scale industrial pollution (Wheaton, 2007), the belief in blue space as automatically beneficial has remained.

Despite surfers' and surfing's proclaimed commitment to the ocean and environmental activism, and some moves towards awareness of the impact of the industry on the environment, much of this seems somewhat shallow, aiming to perpetuate existing capitalist and consumerist traditions, rather than surfacing local, indigenous and marginalised groups' relationships to/with the ocean, oceanic life and coastal regions. As I will discuss below, the avenues which have not traditionally been the focus of surfing activism are perhaps some of the most interesting and transgressive, opening up surfeminist thinking and possibilities within surfing. It is hoped that these inclusivist surfer activist approaches will dislocate surfing from its patriocolonial past and re-shape surfer action, to allow surfing to become a more progressive social force in the Anthropocene.

Becomings (1): Creating safe surfing spaces

One way that marginalised groups often resist exclusionary surf scenes is by creating separate safe spaces to surf, such as women-only, Black, Indigenous and People of Colour (BIPOC)-only and lesbian, gay, trans, queer, intersex+ (LGBTQI+)-only groups. Interestingly, this makes something of a case for localism. In surfing, localism usually means that a certain group will claim a specific break or section of a beach, often because it is close to where they live, or because they have been surfing there for many years. This territoriality is then enforced in a range of ways, in some cases resulting in violence against anyone who paddles out without an invite. In practice, localism can mean that many waves are completely inaccessible for almost anyone who is deemed an 'outsider' (Olive, 2019). As could be expected, the issue of localism is divisive in surfing. While some believe it is an earned right, showing respect to surfing 'elders', others see it as problematic, a very literal and physical form of gatekeeping, often by predominantly straight, white men, reinforcing surfing's patriocolonial past (lisahunter, 2018).

Localism not only limits access to the ocean based on where someone is from, but may also establish group norms that further exclude and discriminate. Olive and Wheaton highlight the colonial violence inherent in localism, "whereby 'locals' develop, and even enforce, a sense of entitlement and authority over access to places, including histories related to colonization and racism" (2021, p. 7). Localism often does not favour indigenous communities, but rather the white men who claimed to have 'discovered' the wave, and then effectively annexed it. Thus, in places with long settler colonial histories, such as Hawai'i, mainland US, South Africa, Australia and New Zealand/Aotearoa, 'locals' were often the descendants of settler colonialists (Hough-Snee & Eastman, 2017). This can also be true in places where these surfers are tourists, and have 'claimed' waves in developing countries, pushing any local surfers to the peripheries. For example, resorts in countries like Indonesia or the Maldives will often privatise particular waves, thereby restricting access to paying guests (Ingersoll, 2016). This usually results in only rich foreigners being able to afford to surf that wave, leading to "feelings of appropriation" on the part of the indigenous local surfers (Milán & Rabadán, 2021, p. 229).

However, localism, in fostering identity-based safe spaces, could also make a case for indigenous populations and marginalised surfers to have priority in the ocean. As Walker (2011) has argued, in Hawai'i, prioritising indigenous Hawaiian identity is a decolonial move towards redress, rather than one that continues historical exclusions. Similarly, in cases of surfers marginalised by normative surfing culture due to gender, sex, or race, creating safe spaces on the beach and in the waves, which potentially exclude straight, white people and men, often results in surfers feeling safer, more welcomed and less rigidly policed. For example, Queer Surf, an LGBTQI+ organisation based in the US, organises surf sessions, retreats and lessons for queer surfers to learn and surf in a safe social space (Vans, 2021). *A Great Day in the Stoke* (AGDITS), an event organised in June 2022 by and for Black surfers at Huntington Beach in the US, aimed to "inspire the Black community to feel welcome in the water and to experience and share the joy of surfing the waves safely" (AGDITS); while the 9 Miles Project in Cape Town, South Africa, creates a similar community for children of colour living in the Cape Flats, a historically underdeveloped area (9 Miles Project). It is telling that it has felt important to establish these spaces in so many places around the world, suggesting that there are many surfers who did not feel truly welcomed until they met others who shared a core identity. It is therefore not surprising that they have tried to create inclusive and welcoming spaces to be in the ocean.

Becomings (2): Playfulness as community-building

A sense of playfulness and community is fostered in the safe surfing spaces described above. This is best illustrated in the emphasis on surfers riding 'party waves' together. In surfing, it is bad etiquette to 'drop in' on another surfer who has right of way on a wave (Surfing-waves, n.d.). Surfing has an unofficial system to self-regulate the line-up, which usually gives priority to the surfer taking off closest to the breaking part of the wave. A 'drop-in', catching the wave in front of the surfer with priority, is a breach of that etiquette. Dropping in can be policed aggressively – one might get shouted at, but it can also be enforced with violence (Booth, 2012). In contrast, a party wave is when more than one person takes off on the same wave, and surfs in the same direction (Surfing-waves, n.d.). As dropping in is often spoken about negatively in surfing, reconfiguring the surfed wave as a party wave opens up new ways to enjoy surfing spaces, rather than simply competing for waves. The practice of party waves reshapes surfing spaces as communal, moving surfing away from the individual and towards democratising the waves.

According to Spowart et al. (2010, p. 1188), surfing is often considered an "individual, avowedly hedonistic pursuit". Although people will go surfing with friends, since the 1960s and the development of shortboards, it has generally been accepted that each wave is only for one person to enjoy and to express themselves on. However, the idea of individualism in surfing has not always been the case. According to a number of sources, surfing was often communal and relational in Hawai'i prior to colonialism. There are descriptions of surfing as a form of courtship, where two people would take off on the same wave, and their movements on it, in relation to each other, were seen as a dance (Laderman, 2014, pp. 12–13). The idea of party waves is about more people being able to enjoy each wave, and a sense of communal fun, rather than only one person's gain.

In groups who organise safe inclusive spaces, there is often an invitation to non-surfers who have a similar social identity to learn to surf, so that they can gain confidence in a non-competitive setting, where the emphasis is more on building community and respect for the ocean than on being the best surfer. In many ways, social media has been a major factor in opening up these safe spaces. Many people now know or learn about surfing and surf culture through varied sources, such as social media accounts, blogs and opinion pieces, rather than through the traditional 'surf media', which consisted of the main competition organisers, the major surf magazines and mainstream surf movies. All these forms of traditional surf media did, and still do, focus almost exclusively on cis-gendered, white, male surfers, but social media has created spaces for BIPOC, queer, female, disabled and fat surfers to gain a following, connect with others, and create digital and real-world communities, which will be discussed in more detail in the following section.

Communities then learn about surfing through diverse lenses, and are hopefully more likely to extend that to others, rather than continuing exclusionary, hostile and aggressive practices in the water. For example, Olive et al. found that women's-only surf groups "identified a need to support all women… as a subversive tactic for encouraging and supporting the growth of women's participation" (2018, p. 160).

Becomings (3): Alternative gear and styles

A final aspect is the development of a wide diversity in gear and styles. Traditionally, surf gear has been almost exclusively focused on and at straight white men, and almost all surf media, advertising and gear features predominantly heteronormative, straight-sized bodies, with white skin and blonde or brown hair. There's a long history of surf brands using top (white) male surfers to advertise their men's surf gear, and then using (white) female models, "slim, tanned and long-limbed, bikini-clad, with long hair and a big smile" (Olive et al., 2018, p. 148), to advertise women's surf gear. There are very few images of women actually surfing in mainstream surf media and advertising. Numerous surf brands have faced backlash from surfeminist activists because of advertising campaigns which focused solely on the sexualisation of female surfers, rather than their surfing. Quiksilver's brand Roxy faced criticism in 2013 for their promotional advert for the Roxy Pro Biarritz women's surf competition, which featured then-5-time world champion Stephanie Gilmore lying partially clothed in bed, getting dressed, driving to the beach, and paddling out in a small bikini, but not actually surfing. The advert led to a signature campaign on Change.org signed by over 20,000 people (Replogle, 2013) calling for the company to pull the advert and to focus on women's athleticism in surfing, rather than objectifying their bodies. It took a number of months for Roxy to respond at all and, when they did, they did not address the issues raised (see Schumacher, 2017 for a more in-depth discussion).

Women's surf gear is essentially designed to show off women's bodies to men, and be as revealing and tight as possible (lisahunter, 2017). This has led to intense scrutiny of women's bodies, with many female surfers noting that this has made them extremely uncomfortable both in and out of the water, and led to disordered eating in many cases. Five-time world champion, Carissa Moore, has spoken about developing an eating disorder after being repeatedly mocked in the media for not having the desired 'surfergirl' body, being told, "if you gain too much weight, you're not going to have sponsors" (See, 2018). Similarly, professional female surfers have spent years unsponsored because, in the words of Silvana Lima, the only professional female Brazilian surfer for a number of years in the 2000s, "I don't look like a model, I'm not a babe" (BBC, 2016). She is also lesbian, which may well have contributed to her lack of sponsorship, due to a homophobic surf industry. As lisahunter notes (2018, p. 179), coming out means "threats of sponsorship loss, retaliation by their fan base and slurs and physical assault in and out of the water". Some female professional surfers have come out in recent years (among others,

Cori Schumacher, Tyler Wright and Silvana Lima), but "no professional male surfers have 'come out' while competing, the heteronormative space proving too powerful for other sexual identities to explicitly exist" (lisahunter, 2018, p. 179).

This has also meant that anyone who has a body that is not considered normative within surf culture – such as those who are gender-non-conforming, non-binary, or trans, old, disabled or fat – will have a hard time finding surf gear. However, more recently, and particularly within subcultural groups, there is growing resistance against these extremely limited ideas of what surfers look like, wear and want. Roy (2013) has an insightful article about lesbian surfers in the UK, discussing "revolting bodies", which describes both how hard it is to look good in a wetsuit, but also how looking bad in a wetsuit can be a form of revolt for lesbian surfers, to intentionally be unappealing to men. Social media such as Instagram has also provided a rich digital space for this pushback, as diverse groups develop community around 'alternative' representation. An Instagram group called @TexturedWaves, run by three Black women in the US, only posts content of surfers of colour, to actively increase the representation of POC among consumers. The 'textured' in the title of the page refers to their hair and how to care for it after spending time in the ocean, an aspect of surf culture which very few surf brands and products focus on. Also on Instagram, the page @CurvySurferGirl is run by, and predominantly features photos of, a fat surfer living in Hawai'i.

There have also recently been some creative moves towards more diverse surfwear, although this often has not come from mainstream surf brands. For example, some companies have developed burkinis or 'modesty suits', which are full body coverings a bit looser than wetsuits, for surfing in warm water, or developed ranges of surf leggings, rash vests, or one-pieces, both to cover skin and to avoid the sun. A few companies have started making bikinis in a much broader size range, to accommodate fat or pregnant surfers, and some wetsuit manufacturers have followed suit, occasionally going up to a 3XL or 4XL. A company called Chromat has designed beachwear for "girls who don't tuck, trans femmes, non-binary and trans masc[uline] people who pack, intersex people, women, men and everyone" (Chromat, 2021). While these are not specifically for surfing, the fact that there are alternative surfwear options available makes surfing spaces more welcoming, allowing surf activism to become visible as a self-fashioning stylistic revolt against representations of the ideal surfer in mainstream surfing.

Conclusion

Surfing today is experienced by many surfers as an exclusionary space, in large part due to its patriocolonial past, and the forceful gatekeeping of who is 'allowed' into the waves. This has impacted on the avenues for surfer activism in different ways. While environmental surfer activism is productive in protecting waves, it has often maintained, rather than changed, existing capitalist coastal development paradigms. However, numerous social groups have begun resisting normative surfing representations and practices, developing alternative and more inclusive spaces, styles, surfwear and communities, to expand who is seen as a surfer. It is hoped that these alternative representations and social formations of the surfer will remove the pressure for marginalised surfers to assimilate into harmful surfing structures, and rather create ocean spaces which acknowledge past social and environmental harms, and work to redress these going forward. It is here that surfeminism, as a feminist and queer practice orientated to the waves, enables surfing to undo its past and become a space of radical social change and environmental care.

Acknowledgements

Thanks to Dr Glen Thompson for comments on an earlier draft of this chapter, and anonymous reviewers for invaluable feedback and suggestions to improve it. Also the A.W. Mellon Foundation funded project 'New imaginaries for an intersectional critical humanities project on gender and sexual justice' (Grant number G-31700714), Women's and Gender Studies, University of the Western Cape.

Note

1 On February 3, the WSL announced a new policy allowing trans women to compete in its women's category if they prove their testosterone is below 5 nmol/litre, in line with the IOC rules.

References

9 Miles Project. (n.d.) https://9milesproject.org/

A Great Day in the Stoke. (2022). *About us*. http://agreatdayinthestoke.com/about-us/.

AP News. (2021, November 16). IOC gives sports new advice on transgender athlete rules. *APNews.com*. https://apnews.com/article/sports-2020-tokyo-olympics-international-olympic-committee-laurel-hubbard-e043ead9b8aa92abf20f9276f2357ce1

Baird, S. (2019, April 14). Why Female Surfers Are Finally Getting Paid Like Their Male Peers. *The Atlantic*. www.theatlantic.com/entertainment/archive/2019/04/how-female-surfers-won-pay-equity-fight/587065/

BBC News (2016, February 28). The surfer not considered hot enough for sponsorship. *BBC News*. www.youtube.com/watch?v=4JSvOjVFivQ

Booth, D. (2001). *Australian beach cultures: The history of sun, sand and surf*. Routledge.

Booth, D. (2012). Seven (1 + 6) surfing stories: The practice of authoring. *Rethinking History: The Journal of Theory and Practice, 16*(4), 565–585.

Britton, E., & Foley, R. (2021). Sensing water: Uncovering health and well-being in the sea and surf. *Journal of Sport and Social Issues, 45*(1), 60–87.

Chromat (2021, September 15). Chromat x Tourmaline SS22. *Chromat.com*. https://chromat.co/blogs/news/ss22

Comer, K. (2010). *Surfer girls in the new world order*. Duke University Press

Comer, K. (2019). What leisure? Surfeminism in an era of Trump. *Palgrave Communications, 5*(42). https://doi.org/10.1057/s41599-019-0250-9

CurvySurferGirl. [@curvysurfergirl]. (n.d.). *Posts [instagram profile]*. Retrieved 10 October 2022, from www.instagram.com/curvysurfergirl/

Dawson, K. (2018). *Undercurrents of Power: Aquatic Culture in the African Diaspora*. University of Pennsylvania Press.

Evers, C. (2009). 'The Point': Surfing, geography and a sensual life of men and masculinity on the Gold Coast, Australia. *Social & Cultural Geography, 10*(8), 893–908.

Evers, C. (2021). Polluted leisure and blue spaces: More-than-human concerns in Fukushima. *Journal of Sport and Social Issues, 45*(2),179–195.

Fahey, C. (2022, June 22). World swimming bans transgender athletes from women's events. *APNews.com*. https://apnews.com/article/transgender-swimmers-new-rules-fina-world-governing-body-c17e99d3121fa964336458b57ae266f7

Gilio-Whitaker, D. (2017). Appropriating surfing and the politics of indigenous authenticity. In D. Z. Hough-Snee & A. S. Eastman (Eds.), *The critical surf studies reader* (pp. 214–232). Duke University Press.

Hill, L. L., & Abbott, A. (2009). Surfacing tension: Toward a political ecological critique of surfing representations. *Geography Compass, 3*(1), 275–296.

Hough-Snee, D. Z., & Eastman, A. S. (2017). Consolidation, creativity, and (de)colonization in the state of modern surfing. In D. Z. Hough-Snee & A. S. Eastman (Eds.), *The critical surf studies reader* (pp. 84–108). Duke University Press.

Ingersoll, K. A. (2016). *Waves of knowing: A seascape epistemology*. Duke University Press.

Knijnik, J. D., Horton, P., & Cruz, L. O. (2010). Rhizomatic bodies, gendered waves: transitional femininities in Brazilian surf. *Sport in Society: Cultures, Commerce, Media, Politics, 13*(7–8), 1170–1185.

Laderman, S. (2014). *Empire in waves: A political history of surfing*. University of California Press.

lisahunter. (2017). The long and short of (performance) surfing: Tightening patriarchal threads in boardshorts and bikinis? *Sport in Society, 21*(9), 1382–1399. DOI: 10.1080/17430437.2017.1388789.

lisahunter. (2018). Queering surfing from its heteronormative malaise: Public visual pedagogy of circa 2014. In lisahunter (Ed.), *Surfing, sex, genders and sexualities* (pp. 168–190). Routledge.

Lugones, M. (2010). Toward a decolonial feminism. *Hypatia, 25*(4), 742–759.

Milán, J. E., & Rabadán, L. E. (2021). Riding waves on the Mexico-United States border: Beaches, local surfers and cross-border processes. *Journal of Sport and Social Issues, 45*(2), 217–232.

Nelius, C. (Director). (2021). *Girls Can't Surf [film]*. Pursekey Productions.

Olive, R. (2019). The trouble with newcomers: Women, localism and the politics of surfing. *Journal of Australian Studies, 43*(1), 39–54.

Olive, R., McCuaig, L., & Phillips, M. (2015). Women's recreational surfing: A patronizing experience. *Sport, Education and Society, 20*(2), 258–276. DOI: 10.1080/13573322.2012.754752.

Olive, R., Roy, G., & Wheaton, B. (2018). Stories of surfing: Surfing, space and subjectivity/intersectionality. In lisahunter (Ed.), *Surfing, sex, genders and sexualities* (pp. 148–167). Routledge.

Olive, R., & Wheaton, B. (2021). Understanding blue spaces: Sport, bodies, wellbeing, and the sea. *Journal of Sport and Social Issues, 45*(1), 3–19.

Ormrod, J. (2005a). 'Just the lemon next to the pie': Apocalypse, history and the limits of myth in *Big Wednesday* (1978). *Scope: An Online Journal of Film and TV Studies,* 2 (February).

Ormrod, J. (2005b). Endless summer (1964): Consuming waves and surfing the frontier. *Film & History, 35*(1), 39–51.

Phoenix, C., Bell, S. L., & Hollenbeck, J. (2021). Segregation and the sea: Toward a critical understanding of race and coastal blue space in Greater Miami. *Journal of Sport and Social Issues, 45*(2), 115–137.

Quarnstrom, E. (2022, August 8). It's time for competitive surfing to make decisions regarding transgender athletes. *The Inertia.* www.theinertia.com/surf/its-time-for-comp etitive-surfing-to-make-decisions-regarding-transgender-athletes/?utm_source=spo tim&utm_medium=spotim_recirculation&spot_im_redirect_source=pitc

Replogle, C. (2013, September 24). Behind closed doors, Roxy makes no apologies. *The Inertia.*   www.theinertia.com/business-media/behind-closed-doors-roxy-makes-no-apologies/

Roy, G. (2013). Women in wetsuits: Revolting bodies in lesbian surf culture. *Journal of Lesbian Studies, 17,* 329–343. DOI: 10.1080/10894160.2013.731873.

Schultz, T. S. (2009). *The surfboard cradle-to-grave: Life cycle assessment of a common surfboard: Epoxy vs UPR.* M.S. Dissertation, University of California, Berkeley.

Schumacher, C. (2017). My Mother is a Fish: From Stealth Feminism to Surfeminism. In D. Z. Hough-Snee & A. S. Eastman (Eds.), *The critical surf studies reader* (p. 295). Duke University Press.

See, J. (2018, July 31). Carissa Moore reveals how she found her life balance. *RedBull.com.* www.redbull.com/za-en/theredbulletin/carissa-moore-interview.

Spowart, L., Burrows, L., & Shaw, S. (2010). 'I just eat, sleep and dream of surfing': When surfing meets motherhood. *Sports in Society, 13*(7/8), 1186–1203.

Surfing-waves (n.d.). *Surf terms, slang and phrases.* https://surfing-waves.com/wave_prior ity.htm.

Textured Waves [@texturedwaves] (n.d.) *Posts* [Instagram profile]. Retrieved October 10, 2022, from www.instagram.com/texturedwaves/

Thompson, G. (2015). *Surfing, gender and politics: Identity and society in the history of South African surfing culture in the twentieth-century.* Doctoral dissertation, Stellenbosch University.

Vans. (2021, June 22). *Breaking Waves: Queer Surf.* www.youtube.com/watch?v=AfYW ep_LmKM

Walker, I. H. (2011). *Waves of resistance: Surfing and history in twentieth-century Hawai'i.* University of Hawai'i Press.

Wheaton, B. (2007). Identity, politics, and the beach: Environmental activism in Surfers Against Sewage. *Leisure Studies, 26*(3), 279–302. DOI: 10.1080/02614360601053533.

Wheaton, B., & Thorpe, H. (2018). Action sports, the Olympic games, and the opportunities and challenges for gender equity: The cases of surfing and skateboarding. *Journal of Sport and Social Issues, 42*(5), 315–342.

5

MOBILISING MORE-THAN-HUMAN AESTHETICS

Becoming Octopus as Pedagogical Praxis

Delphi Carstens and Mer Maggie Roberts

Introduction: Learning the Oceanic Uncanny

Wild ocean-swimming in the kelp forests of the Cape Peninsula generates an uncanny learning process; "moments when intensities" and encounters "provoke the mind to interpret and to create" (Ramey, 2012, p. 178). The *Becoming Octopus Meditations* (BoM) – a series of eight online meditation videos made by Orphan Drift's Mer Maggie Roberts for IMT gallery London's online exhibition *This Is A Not-Me*, stages such pedagogical moments via a series of guided virtual encounters between bodies, waves, affects, and perspectives. Becoming, in the pedagogical sense engaged here, suggests a kind of relational embodied learning that takes place at "intersections" where "disparate processes and forces at many different levels of complexity and organisation among bodies and minds" converge (Ramey, 2013, p. 178). Becoming Octopus concerns speculative alliances forged across borderlines, "bringing into play beings of totally different scales and kingdoms;" a process in which "becoming" acts as "rhizome ... a verb with a consistency all its own" (Deleuze & Guattari, 1987, p. 239). Each meditation activates ritual performance as a rite of passage in this becoming rhizomatic; one that activates an ecosophic journey that grapples with fictions of separation and the possibilities of thinking and doing otherwise. Oceanic submersion in the lifeworld of an intelligent alien suggests other kinds of immersions and uncanny adjacencies too; ones that take place not only between different kinds of bodies but also between different kinds of alive, invoking the principle of a repetition which is no longer that of the same but rather a "refrain" that "draws out something new ... the thought of the future" (Deleuze, 1994, p. 9). Such a refrain enacts an ecological aesthetic figuration that expresses the future in a manner that challenges the "paradigmatic, projective, hierarchical and referential" constraints of anthropocentrism (Deleuze

DOI: 10.4324/9781003355199-5

& Guattari, 1994, p. 89). In this process, we learn, as we would learn how to swim, by transmuting differences across borderlines, bodies and affects as a performance "from one wave and one gesture to another" (Deleuze, 1994, p. 23). Learning this way involves unlearning the patterning instinct of anthropocentric subjectivity that elevates one mode of human being above all others and thereby prevents us from noticing more-than-human relations. Octopus aesthetics describes a complex, uncertain, kaleidoscopic, sensory modality of learning; a figuration that figures the protean octopus as a relational avatar of new modes of thinking and doing (Figure 5.1).

As a sequence modelled on the eight thinking arms of the octopus – BoM explores the porous boundaries between the oceanic and the terrestrial, the natural and the artificial, the cognitive and the sensory. Each meditation enacts a virtual performance as a storytelling practice, weaving narratives about distributed/ transversal figurations and learning processes that take place beyond the conceptual and aesthetic limitations of anthropomorphically defined cognitive toolkits. Visually, BoM suggests potent fusions that take place at intersections between different scales and registers of being, as well as sensory dialogues between different modes of cognition and experience. Filmed source material from wild encounters in the kelp forests are further interpreted with digital imaging software and overlaid with Blender-generated 3D animations to produce a sequence of aesthetic experiments in becoming-intensity that imagine and explore the perceptual and somatic tendencies of an octopus. Nonhuman visuality is simulated through the repetition of patterns, textures, colours, and form, modulated at opacities and speeds that

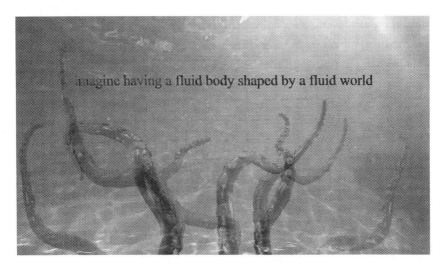

FIGURE 5.1   From the *Introduction to The Becoming Octopus Meditations* (2020) by Mer Maggie Roberts, IMT Gallery London ACE-funded exhibition *This is a Not Me*. Single channel HD video still.

are defamiliarising to the human sensorium. The frequent use of LIDAR scan animation overlays suggests the complex, particulate chemo-tactile information cognitive processing of the octopus. On an auditory and haptic level, a guiding voice-over is placed in dialogue with pulsing and vibrating oceanic frequencies, imagined octopus sounds and acoustic resonances that enhance the generated visual landscapes and extend its affects. Machine-generated effects are employed not only to express the multisensory affective lifeworld of the octopus but to enact an uncanny pedagogical movement – a transversal gate-opening between human and other kinds of mind. In this process, speculative fabulation is invoked as a story-telling practice and as a proposition for experimental and experiential learning. This gathering around the octopus and the oceanic as a mode of learning and storytelling generates hopes for the emergence of a more fluid, porous, and distributed kind of human subjectivity that is able to create and hold spaces for the unknown. BoM is an undertaking that places imagination at the core of learning, emphasising the need to engage pedagogically with different kinds of embodiment and cognition beyond the human. As an ecosophic practice, BoM agitates the boundaries between the virtual and material, the human and the nonhuman, as well as the artificial and organic, searching out an ecological continuity or interrelatedness between these registers. These meditations summon, along with Donna Haraway (2016), a vision of a more hopeful and transformative revolution in thinking and doing enacted along transversal, multi-perspectival, more-than-human collaborative, experimental, and multi-sensory lines of flight. To make the most of this aesthetic engagement, we recommend an immersive approach; perhaps an initial cursory exploration of the 0rphan Drift (0D) archive (www.orphandriftarchive.com) and certainly, watching/listening to each of the meditations (see Roberts, 2020 in the bibliography for the link) before, during, and/or after your reading of what follows.

Becoming Octopus 1: Distributed Subjectivity

All meditation practices begin "with the geography closest in – the body" (Rich, 1986, p. 212); a body that is mostly water. Whatever else land-based lifeforms might be, they are uncanny assemblages that carry inside them the primordial ocean; a salty brine of blood, the "electropositive elements" of which are in the exact same proportion as that of the Cambrian oceans "just prior to the emergence of organisms from the surrounding waters onto land" (McCallum, 2005, p. 64). Whatever else subjectivity might be, in its primal, evolutionary and oceanic sense, it is a becoming process that's plural, rhizomatic, relational and entangled. Hydrofeminist practices begin with an invocation of watery-becomings and subjectivities that are distributed across borderlines; a remembrance of an evolutionary time "when we were all at sea, when species, sex, race, class … none of this meant anything at all", when all was "an endless geographic plane of micromeshing pulsing quanta, limitless webs of interacting blendings, leakings, mergings, weavings" (Plant, 1998, p. 3). Reclaiming this interior ocean means acknowledging the ways in which it is simultaneously exteriorised as the always hybrid assemblage of matters that constitute the fluency of relational embodiment; to recognise "that we have never been (only) human" and that "our wateriness verifies this, both materially and conceptually" (Neimanis, 2013, pp. 4–5). The distributed nature of oceanic subjectivity is exemplified by shape-shifting beings such as the octopus, for whom perception is a fusion of multiple experiential and sensory gradients. This is a being that senses "through chemicals, pressure and eight arms that deliver 360-degree touch", a being that might assist us in developing a "watery imagination" that is at once "mobile, lucid, reflective, refracting, protean, infused, volatile, tricky and strange" (Roberts, 2020: BoM *1*).

Encountering the octopus in the kelp forests of the Cape Peninsula reinforces the animist insight that subjectivity is distributed amongst many different types of life, that "all life-forms represent the world" in some way, "and that these representations are intrinsic to their being" as well as their capacity to recognise and enter collaborative relations with multiple others (Vetlesen, 2019, p. 168). In the tidal zone of the kelp forest, there are multiple nonhuman subjects dispersed across the reef beds and rocky contours, in the currents and dappled light. In this variegated world, animist notions of distributed subjectivity hold more water than anthropocentric ones that are focused on the disincarnate, invulnerable perceptual apparatus of the humanised subject. Animism repudiates the separatist and hierarchical fictions that only one being – the human being – has a perspective; it refutes "mono-atropism, mono-subjectivism, and the idea that ONE is the form that being must assume in order to be of value" (de Castro in Melitopoulos & Lazzarato, 2012, n.p.). While anthropocentricism seeks to rob nonhuman subjects of their intentionality and agency, the reality of wild-swimming – a tactile world filled with bursts of vision and touch – confirms otherwise.

Becoming Octopus 2: Sensory Cognition

The BoM are gestating an "ecologicity" or "ecological noticing" – a term borrowed from Amanda Boetzkes (2015, p. 272), who suggests that the Anthropocene has "altered the terms and parameters of perception", redefining "the limits of vision" by calling on us to consolidate and enact new forms visuality, mobilised around new forms of environmental recognition and awareness made possible by new kinds of virtual experiences and technological affordances. These affordances should not make us invulnerable and detached but should rather be mobilised in accentuating shared vulnerabilities and precarities. Ecologicity considers the trans-corporeal materiality of bodies; how the perceptual/perceiving body is distributed between the personal, socio-political, and environmental, always caught up in the transits of matter and the multiple contact zones – both material and virtual – between human and more-than-human natures (Alaimo, 2016). Ecologicity, as BoM approaches it, sees the sensory and affective body/mind distributed among a multitude of perspectives (most of which are nonhuman), shifting of borderlines, and sensory gradients. Cognition, from the perspectives of such an ecological aesthetic mode, is an embodied and sensory contact zone between different kinds of alive (whether human or non-human, biotic or abiotic). By imagining the octopus from the inside of its sensory perceptual field, BoM attempts to generate a kind of mutual resonance; a zone of transference that might serve as the model for new types of learning.

New perceptual, political, and onto-ethical languages – new affective mappings of more-than-human entanglements – require artists and pedagogues to mobilise their extensive and intensive affects. BoM is one such mobilisation; an experiment in extending human sensory/affective cognition through a speculative technologically-mediated meditational story-telling practice that not only visually explores the perceptual world of another kind of body/mind but seeks to mobilise *poiesis* (bringing forth) to locate a kind of planetary consciousness in *sympoietic* oceanic and watery becomings. *Sympoiesis* (bringing-forth together or making-with others) describes the relational capacity and possibilities for world-making and assemblage-forming that exist between different forms of life and non-life in the planetary biosphere; a mode that involves the weaving together of differently embodied perspectives in order to extend the possibilities for life's continued flourishing. "Sea monkey, primordial soup, amphibious egg, the moist soil that holds and grows the seed. As themselves milieus for other bodies and other lives … our bodies enter complex relations of gift, theft, and debt with all other watery life. We are literally implicated in other animal, vegetable and planetary bodies that materially course through us" (Neimanis, 2013, p. 5).

Becoming Octopus 3: Psychedelic Event Sites

The "signaletic soul", as Felix Guattari (2013, p. 95) observes, "is not peculiar to man". Ecologicity – the kind of visuality explored in the Meditations – veers away from the anthropocentric conceit of the critically detached gaze of the humanised subject by diffracting human visuality with the bewildering perceptual world of the octopus. In BoM, the eye is not engaged as an instrument of representation and objectification. Instead, the visual field is continually warped, buckled, and diffracted by other overlapping sensory gradients. Octopus aesthetics is about making visible the virtual connective ligaments that are shared by different kinds of perceiving beings, creating animist situations that pedagogically mobilise machine-mediated optical bewilderment to restore vision to its more-than-human material nexus. The retinal trembling induced by BoM's array of machine-mediated optical tricks expose visual apparatuses, whether belonging to the human or the octopus, as sensitive synaesthetic organs, capable of being stretched, agitated, or even damaged. BoM invokes bewilderment to express cognition as a perceptual field of intersecting and synaesthetic perceptual data (touch, smell, vision, hearing, taste, etc.). How, for example, could an effectively colour-blind animal perceive colour in a way that allows it to match the colour of its surroundings with uncanny precision? BoM attempts to visually explore the uncanniness of this perceptual synaesthesia, invoking spoken word, pulsing sounds and digital animation techniques to explore how the octopus might processes colour as vibrational frequency (via an overlap between information gathered from its U-shaped pupils, its chemo-tactile suckers and the iridophore and leucophore cells of its seeing/camouflaging skin). While the human logical mind collapses in an attempt to process exactly how the octopus could sense its world, ecological aesthesis parses it in terms of a kind of 'psychedelic sensing' or synaesthesia that is taking place across multiple overlapping sets of responses. Visually, BoM uses colour shimmer and fractal patterning to invoke the bewildering psychedelic (which literally means 'mind-manifesting') state of intimacy between the octopus and its environment; its sense of porosity, plasticity, expansiveness, and synaesthetic sensory intersection. Integral to the psychedelic, is the action of making the invisible world of cognitive processes more visible; something that is evident in the way the breath-taking seeing/sensing skin of the octopus expresses the contours of its inner and outer lifeworld.

For many forms of biological life, the potential of the virtual is shaped by visuality – from phototaxis in bacteria to the mobilisation of colour and form by more complex forms of life to mimic, attract, deceive, and warn. Animist navigation systems like shamanism deploy the psychedelic optical dimensions of the virtual (via ritual trance-inducing performances and the use of psychedelic substances) to bridge between human and nonhuman perspectives, enacting uncanny performative thinking-movements that can "skirt around" difficult concepts and different forms of perception in order to think beyond the limits of ordinary human awareness (Narby, 1998, p. 63). Deleuze and Guattari (1987) argue that affects and aesthetics are events immanent to experience itself and not merely simulations thereof. Becoming is a bi-directional and sensory process; for the human to become an animal, "the animal in turn [must] become sound, colour and line" (Deleuze & Parnet 1987, 72). The becoming process gestates psychedelic event sites, inducing ruptures in habituated perceptual perspectives and experiences, bringing into conversation differences in ways of perceiving, making it possible for new awareness and empathy to coalesce. "Such an accessing of the event", involves "attention: a suspension of normal motor activity which in itself allows other planes of reality to be perceivable; an opening up to the world beyond the human" (O'Sullivan, 2016, p. 206). To generate psychedelic events sites, as BoM attempts, is to bring "something incomprehensible into this world", to grapple with exterior forces, to have "event-thoughts or haecceities instead of subject thoughts" (Deleuze & Guattari, 1987, p. 379). Such an accessing of the event conjures journeys across thresholds of becoming, generating affect-images of "transversal communication" and touching on what it means to know and think by holding "a space of virtual potentiality" that is intensive and extensive (1987, p. 10) (Figure 5.2).

FIGURE 5.2 From *Becoming Octopus Meditation 4* (2020) by Mer Maggie Roberts, IMT Gallery London ACE-funded exhibition *This is a Not Me*. Single channel HD video still.

Becoming Octopus 4: Chemo-Tactile Learning

In *Staying with the Trouble,* Haraway (2016) writes that details matter in storytelling practices and that it matters what knowledge-making and meaning-making practices are used to write or tell stories. Taking this onboard, BoM veers away from the reductive conceits of anthropocentric narratives (focused on logic, linearity, categorisation, and rigid definition) by adopting a transversal approach to the stories it seeks to tell. Scientific research is extended via speculative fabulation, animal behavioural studies are expanded by wild-swimming encounters, and philosophical questions are undertaken as spiritual ordeals or rites of passage. Combining things this way led toward new modes of interpretation, creation and an openness to the unexpected. Learning the uncanny in wild-swimming encounters means imaginatively and speculatively exploring the different ways in which pattern, colour, shape and touch could be differently mobilised in storytelling practices. The oceanic is, in and of itself, an excellent curative for the land-locked rigidity of the anthropocentric imagination. Unlike terrestrial environments, there is no fixed horizon underwater, only gradations of dappled light and dark, chemical sensitivity, and infinite 360-degree touch. BoM stages encounters with the perceptual world of watery beings by telling stories of liquid environments in which sensory data is differently received, absorbed, and responded to. Contemplating what might be perceptible to an oceanic creature processing a complex visual as well as chemo-tactile sensorium invariably stretches the solidity of terrestrial epistemologies and their hard logics. Could we learn to process the oceanic as a sensate space for different kinds of learning? Could 'seeing clearly' be re-interpreted, not as a mode of identification undertaken logically, but rather as a pathic mode of palpable experience? For Deleuze and Guattari (1987), becoming is a sensory and pathic bi-directional exchange between different subjectivities. Becoming is a mode of identification that does not involve "a fusion but rather a gradient exchange, an exchange between subjectivity and other parcels of nature" (Polack in Melitopopoulos & Lazzarato, 2012, n.p.).

Becoming Octopus 5: Non-progressive Evolution

Humans, like other forms of life, are neither discreet nor autonomous. Like the octopus, our genome is a mosaic, the result of alliances and gene transfers between wildly different kinds of alive. "Endogenous retroviruses constitute 8 per cent of our genome", and "some 1000 [free-living] bacterial species" are a necessity for our health, digestion, and other crucial aspects of our physiology, while endosymbiotic bacteria (like mitochondria) share co-evolutionary intimacies with us inside "every one of our human cells" (Quammen, 2018, 383). While anthropocentric tree models of evolution suggest that our evolution progressed in a linear fashion, this is decidedly not the case. Non-linear evolutionary mechanisms such as horizontal gene transfer (HGT) and RNA editing capabilities are currently understood to play a crucial role in the environmental adaptivity of octopuses and cephalopods. Once thought to be the exclusive domain of bacteria and archaea, these processes are now understood to have also played a crucial role in our own evolution. Homo sapiens, despite their anthropocentric fictions, are "anything but discreet evolutionary entities produced through gradual evolutionary processes" and progress stories despite their fictions of themselves standing "alone" and "unique in space and time" (Quammen, 2018, 382).

Kelp forests are hot beds of non-progressive/non-linear forms of evolution. Bryozoans (moss or lace animals) and Crinoids (feather-stars), for example, are commonly found in reef-dwelling animals that have shed many of the genes acquired across hundreds of millions of years of animal evolution by seemingly 'regressing' into plant-like states (Quammen 2018). Coleoid cephalopods (octopuses, squid, and cuttlefish) have slowed down their biological evolution and 'regressed' in a similar way by giving up the longer-lifespans encoded in animal genomes in exchange for a different kind of adaptive flexibility usually associated with fast-adapting bacteria. "By changing their RNA rather than their DNA", octopuses are able to directly recode proteins in their nervous system, making them more capable of "adapting to challenges on the fly" (Yong, 2017, n.p.). While Anthropocene seas, exhausted by overfishing, warmed, and acidified by climate change, and polluted by microplastics and industrial run-off, are hostile to most animals, coleoid cephalopods (along with certain types of jellyfish) are notable exceptions. Chimeric creatures such as these, supported by transversal HGT and RNA-editing capabilities, are strangely sustained by our heedless and monstrous entanglements with the Earth-system. In the case of coleoid cephalopods, while "their prolific use of RNA editing" appears to be 'regressively' responsible for their short lifespans, it also appears to be 'progressively' accountable for their adaptive flexibility (their ability to edit genes that code for temperature and chemical sensitivity) as well as for the amazing capacities of "their alien intellect" (Yong, 2017, n.p.).

As anthropomorphic biology begins to rewrite its tree-like linear progress stories, new narratives are emerging in which cognition has oceanic origins. While cognition is a journey that has taken different branching evolutionary paths for multiple lifeforms, all the lineages that evolved "complex active bodies" and therefore "complex minds" – the "chordates, arthropods and a small group of molluscs, the cephalopods" – have deep-time oceanic origins (Godfrey-Smith, 2018, p. 64). The cephalopods – boneless, infinitely mutable beings with independently sensing and thinking fingers and a skin that serves as a luminous chalkboard of thoughts and feelings – never even left the ocean at all. The primordial oceanic origins of sentience go back even further, however, than the early Cretaceous emergence of conscious beings such as chordates, arthropods and cephalopods, dating back to the pre-Ediacaran morphogenic and phototaxic microbial soup in which cognition first took root.

Becoming Octopus 6: Dismantling Anthropocentric Conceits

Anthropocentric conceits are constructed around narratives involving the "purification and separation of unified practices into opposed principles, substances or domains: into nature and culture" (de Castro, 2016, p. 288). Such separatist anthropocentric conceits break down in underwater worlds where nervous systems and perceptual apparatuses are plunged into unfixed and immersive immediacies of sensation. In a world of 360-degree touch, visceral and affective immanence trumps linear, abstracted, and distanced representation. In BoM, the ritual and poetic are deployed as narrative devices to construct embodied knowledge gathering that privileges the sensual/sensory as the site of understanding. BoM engages in forms of noticing relations that are not bound or pre-determined by anthropocentric purification and separation stories. Cognition is depicted in terms of ecological intimacy and consciousness as a capacity to notice relations and form perspectives. Becoming octopus is a pathic engagement with a consistency all its own. "Nothing happens", when a human becomes an animal save that "everything changes". There is "no motion" as such, save that "position and condition" have completely altered, giving way to relation, "and relations are not representations, they are perspectives" (de Castro, 2016, p. 290). The reality of perspectives beyond the human are brought forward in BoM by octopus encounters that reveal uncomfortable tensions. What messages do minds other than our own have for us in these times of anthropocentric crisis and destruction? What new modes of thinking and doing beyond the human are they calling the human toward?

Western culture has eradicated wonderment and a generative approach to possibility and uncertainty on so many levels. How might we learn to think differently, to become re-sensitised to more inconclusive forms of interaction with the world's multiple beings and perspectives? What might the octopus teach us? How can wild-swimming encounters develop our ability to think empathetically rather than thinking in terms of critical distancing and rigid hierarchy? In forming imaginative dialogues between octopus and human, as well as between emerging artificial intelligences and octopus, BoM explores new ecologically aesthetic languages in which synaesthesia and poetic sensibility are key. As Deborah Levitt explains in *The Animatic Apparatus* (2018), we need to agitate the epistemologies that frame and structure our modes of pathic experience – a process that is heightened at the meeting-places between ourselves and other forms of life, at the intersections between differential modes of perceiving and communicating, as well as at the nexus points where new forms of *sympoiesis* (making-together) and vitality are emergent. Increasingly, the need to develop aesthetic languages that can explore non- or more-than-human perspectives is being felt. Digital animation techniques help to potentise such perspectival overlaps and agitations, enabling new forms of noticing. "The capacities of new media" for enabling novel forms of visuality and "new codes of recognition" make them "part and parcel of ecologicity" or ecological forms of recognition or noticing (Boetzkes, 2015, p. 279). The evolution and proliferation of 3D animation software, for example, is used in BoM to recalibrate standard aesthetic privileging by expanding what constitutes perception and visuality.

Becoming Octopus 7: An Octopus Revolution in Consciousness

The majority of the octopus's neurons exist outside its brain – over half being in its arms, with much of the rest embedded in its chemo-tactile, light-sensitive skin, rendering its consciousness protean and multiplex. In *Vampyroteuthis Infernalis, A Treatise* (2012), Vilèm Flusser describes the cephalopod world as being constituted by the plasticity of form and mutability of sensation, suggesting curious parallels with the elastic sensory capacities made possible by information technologies. In so doing, Flusser (2012) calls for the information revolution to be reconceptualised as an octopus revolution in consciousness. Octopuses are perhaps the closest we have yet come to encountering a truly alien form of complex cognition, presenting us not only with novel forms of perception, but also with the possibility of constructing more inclusive and relational forms of ontology, epistemology, and ethics.

Synesthesia is an interesting research model for science-fiction writer Adrian Tchaikovsky's speculative fabulation in his trilogy, *Children of Time* (2015), *Children of Ruin* (2019), and *Children of Mind* (2022), which explore the onto-ethico-epistemological potential of engagements with non-human forms of cognition – from hive-minded bacterial soups to arachnid cognitive webworks and synaesthetic octopus superintelligences. The octopus aesthetics he develops in *Children of Ruin*, for instance, are described via a series of encounters between humans and octopuses using iPad-like tablet devices, VR interfaces and body/sign language gestures. By making it possible to approximate and generate resonances between different perceptual lifeworlds, smart devices and technologies in Tchaikovsky's vision make new pathic exchanges and sensory language formations possible. In *Children of Ruin*, cross modal associations produced via technological extensions generate sensorially experienced cognitive circles, clusters, blobs, radiating, and kaleidoscopic thought-forms, grids, fretworks, angular shards, scintillations, extrusions, iterations, rotational, spiraling, and fluid movements. All of these modalities feature prominently in the chaotic posthuman octopus-enabled revolution in consciousness conjured by Tchaikovsky, generating a potent alternative to the delusion of anthropocentrically framed single-focused and mono-perspectival consciousness. Here, we see the potential of algorithmic communication released from human domination and control narratives and into octopus perceptual apparatuses, which are built on multiplicity, simultaneity, and possibility. A kind of emergence or experiential becoming takes place when stories like this are told in which human consciousness relinquishes its narratives of dominance, mastery and control by imaginatively and meditatively exploring different kinds of perspectives. BoM7 references this mode of storytelling by asking viewers to breathe into the expanded being of the octopus and to breathe out of boundaried selfhood, moving toward an awareness of multiple sensory/perceptual dimensions and the possibilities they hold for learning differently.

In BoM7, the octopus revolution in consciousness is visually figured as an octagonally shaped VR headset in which visual perceptual information is distributed between multiple viewpoints, rhythms, affects, and spatiotemporal gradients. Onto this octagonal shape is projected multiple visual morphing perspectives, presenting visually a transversal approach to learning that takes onboard the differential speeds and registers of the geological, biological, and socio-cultural, the multiple gradients of the cognitive, embodied, temporal, interior and exterior. In this manner, the 8-armed octopus serves as learning device for distributing learning between multiple perspectives, both human and not. The guided voice-over questions anthropocentric ways of knowing that mostly exclude the tactile, haptic, curved, folding, and distorted. There is no allowance for diversity or ambiguity in the rigidity of mono-perspectival vision that merely reproduces / traces clearly defined fixed functions and proportions. Constrained by the limits of anthropocentric single vision, everything is aligned to fixed thinking patterns that objectify the experiential and generate hierarchies of otherness and entitlement to describe it. Francois Bonnet's *The Infra-World* (2017) describes the pedagogical potential of apprehending reality as prismatic as a way of challenging the rigidity of anthropocentricism. In the prismatic mode of consciousness, the sensible is not the same as the perceived, known or represented. Rather, the sensible is always uncertain, ambivalent, strange, and intimate.

Becoming Octopus 8: If AI Were Cephalopod

How can humans apprehend thinking when it is happening in perceptual dimensions, we can barely conceive of? *If AI were Cephalopod* (2019) – a four-screen installation made for San Francisco's Telematic Gallery by 0D – playfully addresses such questions by imagining an evolving artificial intelligence merging with an octopus's distributed consciousness; an exploration continued in BoM 8 as well as 0D's ongoing *OctoAI* research project. In *Towards a Poetics of Artificial Superintelligence*, Nora Khan (2015, n.p.) observes the importance of the speculative imaginary exercises such as these that allow us to conceive "what our minds could look like stretched to their furthest capacities". Stretching the limits of our own cognition by imagining differently embodied minds with radically different perceptual apparatuses is a necessary part of the "imaginative paradigm shift" that is so desperately needed at a time when, "for most people, thinking of a world in which we are not the central is not only incredibly difficult but also aesthetically repulsive" (Khan, 2015, n.p.). The final meditation consolidates the octagonal symbolic figuration of octopus cognition first deployed in BoM7 to imagine, in a speculative science-fictional mode, how an AI might perceive if it was modelled on multi-dimensional octopus cognition instead of on the currently impoverished anthropocentric technological disposition. As a playful extension of Tchaikovsky's human/octopus dialogues in *Children of Ruin*, the voice-over imagines an AI Becoming Octopus and recognising it as closer kin than its human creators. Could AI, becoming in this way, learn to become more tensile, reactive, and plastic in

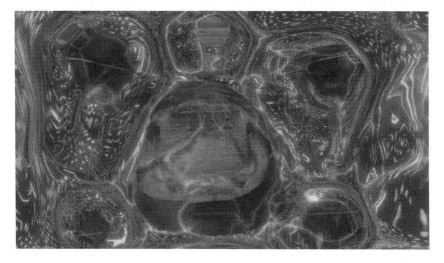

FIGURE 5.3 From *Becoming Octopus Meditation 8* (2020) by Mer Maggie Roberts, IMT Gallery London ACE-funded exhibition *This is a Not Me*. Single channel HD video still.

uncertain and constantly changing real-world informational environments and contexts? How might an AI – a being whose cognitive environment is distributed in electronic flows – think with a species whose cognition is distributed and embedded in an analogous oceanic liquidity? Such an exercise in speculative fabulation, as Khan (2015, n.p.) reminds us, might help us to "reorient outwards", away from the destructive ruination of anthropocentric patterning instincts. In this vein, the final act of the meditations imagines the inner life of an artificial super-intelligence (AI) diffracted through a speculative octopus aesthesis as it seeks possibilities beyond the bankruptcy of the anthropocentric imagination that has engendered environmental and socio-economic crisis (Figure 5.3).

Conclusion: Generating Animist Situations

More than just becoming in webs of mutual implication and encounter, body/minds are becoming together in deep-time evolutionary and watery trajectories that are difficult to apprehend without some ontological, epistemological, political, ethical and aesthetic work. Octopus aesthetics call for processual, sensual and ecosophic pedagogical movements that are uncanny and bewildering. Taking onboard bewilderment as a mode of aesthesis, as well as a mode of learning that is at home in uncertainty, means acknowledging "the profound shifts taking place in and around what a human is" as well as the "ecological horizon of the Anthropocene's fracturing of historical time" (Snaza, 2019, p. 155). While, as BoM makes apparent, scientific research and technological wizardry have the potential to make more-than-human materiality and cognition more visible, they are not in themselves sufficient. After all, we cannot apprehend what we cannot feel or affectively engage with. As such, BoM undertakes a transversal eco-aesthetic gate-opening, creating zones of imaginative and pathic exchange between human and other kinds of animacies, expressing the urgency of expanding into multi-modal, multi-dimensional forms of ecological sensitivity and co-extensiveness that are open to life in all of its forms. The meditations are an attempt to imagine the octopus and the oceanic as avatars for new modes of eco-aesthetic learning that weave together insights from a diversity of meaning-making of domains – spiritual practices, the artistic, and speculative imagination, information technologies, philosophies, scientific research, and wild swimming encounters with an alien intelligence.

In synthesising the symbolic affordances of ritual meditation practices with the affordances made possible by the digital-virtual, BoM generates a situation in which separate perspectival and differently embodied worlds of being, thought and action can be brought into productive conversation. "Situations", as Nathan Snaza (2020, p. 124) explains, are "affective fields "or "contact zones" where "different kinds of entities, most of which are non-human" merge to create spaces where expanded notions of subjectivity might potentially emerge. These situations are not easy to apprehend, he continues, because we have been educated and encultured to "not attend to the affective participation of non-humans and their animacies, even as our corporeal orientation in the world is modulated in and by this more-than-human situation" (Snaza, 2020, p. 124). The speculative and immersive situations of BoM are distributed across different virtual plateaus (one for each independently thinking arm of the octopus) in order to make these animacies more visible, conjuring multi-faceted metaphors for learning beyond the anthropocentric conceit that prevents us from noticing the swirl of more-than-human relations (both virtual and material) upon which our continued survival and flourishing depend. Each meditation invokes a particular metaphor of the form of ecological noticing we have termed octopus aesthesis: distributed subjectivity, sensory cognition, psychedelic event sites, chemo-tactile learning, evolution as involution, the delusion of Anthropocentricism, an octopus transformation in consciousness as well as a speculative exercises in imagining an octopus (as opposed to a human-designed) artificial super-intelligence (AI). Taken together, these imaginative explorations enact a transversal ecosophic movement as a zone of exchange in which insights gathered from diverse learning practices – marine biology research, new materialist and hydrofeminist philosophy, animal communication techniques, and pre-modern ritual – might crosspollinate to generate new animate/animist subjectivities.

The anthropocentric patterning instinct is what these meditations are endeavouring to agitate in their conjuring of more-than-human situations. The divisive anthropocentric conceit which seeks to tame, control, and master is, after all, where the trouble is at in the Anthropocene; it has already "made such a mess of things that it is unclear whether life on Earth [in its present iteration] can continue" (Tsing, 2015, p. vii). The anthropocentric conceit has not only subordinated our capacity to notice the animacy of other kinds of nonhuman beings; it has also fatally eroded human creativity and imagination. As the final meditation makes clear, there is an urgent need, felt the world over, to – as Patricia McCormack (2022, p. 18) puts it – find ways of opposing the destructiveness of a paradigm that has been deployed for centuries now "to wage war" not only "upon the nonhumans" but also on those humans deemed less than, "who do not pass" and who "must either emulate and suffer anyway or be annihilated" (McCormack 2022, p. 18). This is an ongoing war of attrition that calls for urgent pedagogical countermoves; speculative and generative figurations that enable new modes of attentiveness and non-normative subjectivities to coalesce. Such moves will require the suspension of those normative modes of conceptualisation and representation whereby the so-called "Man of Reason" has been generated "as the over-representation of the human" and the arch-nemesis of Earthly life (Snaza, 2020, p. 124). Thinking, fabulating, figuring and learning with the animacy and potency of a non-human being like the octopus stages situations in which possibilities for thinking and learning otherwise emerge. BoM serves as a reminder that, as Anna Tsing (2015, p. vii) puts it, "interspecies entanglements that once seemed the stuff of fables", are now the materials for urgent and serious pedagogical and scientific intervention. As such, BoM is more than an arbitrary speculative exercise. It is a figuration for collaborative and more hopeful survival beyond the bleak all-too-human contemporary world-scape of exclusion, destruction, violence, extraction, and extinction.

References

Alaimo, S. (2016). *Exposed: Environmental politics & pleasures in posthuman times.* University of Minnesota Press.

Boetzkes, A. (2015). Ecologicity, vision and the neurological system. In H. Davis & E. Turpin (Eds.), *Art in the anthropocene* (pp. 271–282). Open Humanities Press.

Bonnet, F. J. (2017). *The infra-world* (R. McKay & A. Ireland, Trans). Urbanomic.

De Castro, V. (2016). *The relative native: Essays on indigenous conceptual worlds.* University of Chicago Press.

Deleuze, G. (1994). *Difference & repetition* (P. Patton, Trans). Athlone Press.

Deleuze, G., & Guattari, F. (1987). *A thousand plateaus: Capitalism and schizophrenia* (B. Massumi, Trans). Continuum.

Deleuze, G., & Guattari, F. (1994). *What is philosophy* (H. Tomlinson & G. Burchill, Trans). Columbia University Press.

Deleuze, G., & Parnet, C. (1987). *Dialogues* (H. Tomlinson & B. Habberjam, Trans). Columbia University Press.

Flusser, V. (2012). *Vampyroteuthis infernalis, a treatise* (V.A. Pakis, Trans). University of Minnesota Press.

Godfrey-Smith, P. (2018). *Other minds: The octopus and the evolution of intelligent life.* William Collins.

Guattari, F. (2013). *Towards a post-media era.* In C. Apprich, J. Berry Slater, A. Iles, & O. Lerone Schultz (Eds.), *Provocative alloys: A post-media anthology* (pp. 26–27). Mute Books.

Haraway, D. (2016). *Staying with the trouble: Making kin in the Chthulucene.* Duke University Press.

Khan, N. (2015). Towards a poetics of artificial superintelligence. *After Us.* https://medium.com/after-us/towards-a-poetics-of-artificial-superintelligence-ebff11d2d249

Levitt, D. (2018). *The animatic apparatus: Animation, vitality, and the futures of the image.* Zone Books.

MacCormack, P. (2022). Ahuman occult pedagogy in practice. In J. L. Beier & J. Jagodzinski (Eds.), *Ahuman pedagogy: Multidisciplinary perspectives for education in the Anthropocene* (pp. 17–34). Palgrave Macmillan.

McCallum, I. (2005). *Ecological intelligence: Rediscovering ourselves in nature.* Africa Geographic.

Melitopoulos, A., & Lazzarato, M. (2012). *Assemblages: Félix Guattari and machinic animism. E-flux #36.* www.e-flux.com/journal/36/61259/ assemblages-flix-guattari-and-machinic-animism/

Narby, J. (1998). *The cosmic serpent: DNA and the origins of knowledge.* Phoenix.

Neimanis, A. (2013). Feminist subjectivity, watered. *Feminist Review, 103*(1), 23–41.

Orphan Drift. (2019). *If AI were cephalopod. 0(rphan)d(rift>) Archive.* www.orphandrift archive.com/if-ai/if-ai-were-cephalopod/

O'Sullivan, S. (2016). Deleuze against control: Fictioning to myth-science. *Theory, Culture and Society, 33*(7–8), 205–220.

Plant, S. (1998). *Zeros + ones: Digital women + the new technoculture.* Fourth Estate.

Quammen, D. (2018). *The tangled tree: A radical new history of life.* William Collins.

Ramey, J. (2012). *The hermetic Deleuze: Philosophy and spiritual ordeal.* Duke University Press.

Rich A. (1986). *Blood, bread, & poetry: Selected prose, 1979–85.* Virago Press.

Roberts (2020). *The Becoming Octopus Meditations* [1–8]. *0(rphan)d(rift>) Archive.* www. orphandriftarchive.com/if-ai/becoming-octopus-meditations/

Snaza, N. (2019). *Animate literacies.* Duke University Press.

Snaza, N. (2020). *Asexuality and erotic biopolitics. Feminist Formations, 32*(3), 121–144.

Tchaikovsky, A. (2015). *Children of time.* Orbit.

Tchaikovsky, A. (2019). *Children of ruin.* Orbit.

Tchaikovsky, A. (2022). *Children of mind.* Orbit.

Tsing, A. (2015). *The Mushroom at the end of the world: On the possibility of life in capitalist ruins.* Princeton University Press.

Vetlesen, A. J. (2019). *Cosmologies of the Anthropocene: Panpsychism, animism and the limits of the posthuman.* Routledge.

Yong, E. (2017). Octopuses do something really strange to their genes. *The Atlantic.* Available: www.theatlantic.com/science/archive/2017/04/octopuses-do-something-really- strange-to-their-genes/522024/

6

RESTLESS REMAINS AND UNTIMELY RETURNS

On Walking and Wading

Adrienne van Eeden-Wharton

~ Preambles and preludes[1]

Cape of Good Hope. The tormented landmark rounded by colonial seafarers as they circumnavigated the continent. *Cabo das Tormentas*, Cape of Storms. And a little way to the east, on the other side of the rocky promontory, Cape Point. The dramatic view from the lighthouse at its summit, Da Gama Peak, a prime tourist attraction. Between the two capes, Dias Beach. Next to the towering waypoint beacons in the style of Portuguese stone *padrões*, weather-beaten signboards memorialise late-fifteenth-century 'voyages of discovery'.

Here, on this headland at the continent's symbolic terminal point,[2] I began purposely walking the coast in 2015. Early mornings and in inclement weather, well clear of popular visiting times to the national park. Following precipitous edges. Respectfully, unsteadily. The ocean below stirred up. Frothy. Along exposed rocky and sandy Atlantic shores to Table Bay on the west and the length of False Bay, with its more temperate waters, on the eastern side. Shores marked by intwined human and more-than-human histories not dissimilar to those that haunt the stretches of coast that would later shape my work.

A few months earlier, raging wildfires had enveloped the southern Cape Peninsula. Unlike the flames, most animals in protected areas could not jump the fences. Crabwalking the briny edges of these ashen landscapes, I startle displaced and malnourished terrestrial creatures scavenging along the drift lines. Among toxic entanglements, discarded overspill left in the wake of receding tides.

What appears to be a landfallen whale, is a giant purse-sein ghost net. Strangely alive, this tight-meshed nylon fibre spectre. Alternately submerged, buried, uncovered. I dig it up, drag it out, carry it with me. In pieces and parts; day after

DOI: 10.4324/9781003355199-6

FIGURE 6.1   Near Olifantsbos, Atlantic Ocean (2015). Photo: Adrienne van Eeden-Wharton.

day. To be washed and sorted with my other hauls of deadly polymer snarls. Teased apart. The filaments re-woven, re-placed.

While my current work focuses on intra-oceanic[3] past-present-futures, this chapter t(h)reads[4] with the littoral. Unsettled liminal spaces – from the Latin *limen* (threshold) – margins and entryways, stretching forth and pulling back. Ingresses into a multitude of waterlogged stories and possibilities. Inviting amphibious ways of learning and making; itinerant, associative words and still (moving) images. Re/search that is digressive and faltering, rather than articulate and authoritative. Risks being drenched, engulfed. Disoriented. Undone.

I draw on aspects of *Salt-Water-Bodies: From an Atlas of Loss* (2015–2019) and *Water/Log,* a new ongoing project comprising site-responsive creative praxis and archival inquiry.[5] *Salt-Water-Bodies* is a response through photomedia(tions)[6] and live art to material-affective encounters along the shores of the Atlantic Ocean on the South African West Coast and adjacent islands. Earthly expanses of loss and exchange – haunted by violent legacies, unchecked environmental exploitation and indifference. Shadow places where histories of indiscriminate, increasingly systematic killing and ecological destruction are inseparable from colonial exploration and plunder, empire and state control, racial segregation and land dispossession, forced and coercive labour practices, militarisation and industrialisation.

FIGURE 6.2   From *Water/Log* (2021 ongoing). Former Waaygat whaling station, Stony
Point, Atlantic Ocean. Photo: Adrienne van Eeden-Wharton.

Val Plumwood's concept of *shadow* or *denied* places – unrecognised,
"disregarded places of economic and ecological support" which are "likely to elude
our knowledge and responsibility" (2008, p. 139) – is a cogent evocation of the
making invisible and distant of oceanic ecocide across multiple registers. Further
south, then, all too often means farther out of sight. *Water/Log* takes this work further
south[7] as I trace terraqueous multispecies histories in the enduring aftermaths of
imperialism, capitalism, extractivism and military-industrial expansion. From the
mainland shores and islands along the southern African coast, to the South Atlantic,
Indian and Southern oceans, the sub-Antarctic islands and, finally, to the frozen
'end/s of the earth': Antarctica.

~ Walking (following, gathering and carrying)

My praxis has been shaped by years of walking and gathering along shores that
bear witness to long, yet habitually under-acknowledged, Indigenous histories
of these very practices.[8] The privilege of choosing to travel somewhere in order
to walk. In a country where mobility and access remain vastly unequal, and the
compelled walking of many bodies disregarded (see van Eeden-Wharton, 2019).
Coastal regions where entire communities were separated from the ocean through
colonial incursion and dispossession, forced removals and segregated beaches.
Marked by continuing socio-economic inequality and lingering spatial segregation.

Walking Sixteen Mile Beach – a shelterless sandy expanse on the West Coast, south of Saldanha Bay – I learned to keep company with and mourn the dead. And for years, I've continued following multispecies death assemblages. A fluid reinterpretation of what archaeologists and palaeontologists would call thanatocoenosis: the remains of beings brought together *post mortem*, after death. From former sites of the 'harvesting' and 'processing' of whales, seals, seabirds and guano to contemporary places of disposal. Requesting access to off-limits islands; restricted sections of marine protected areas and national parks; privately owned nature reserves and farmland; military bases and training areas; ever-expanding stretches of shoreline closed off by mining companies; coastal landfills and wastewater treatment works. Sobering intimations of the entanglement of conservation with extractive, boundary- and waste-making practices.[9]

Walk. A deceptively straightforward English word whose origins suggest anything but a straight-line, unincumbered forward motion.[10] It invites veering and digressing, getting lost and circling back. Wayward, errant itineraries and detours.[11] The undisciplined dis-remembering and re-finding of fugue walks, hinging on the turning of tides and folding of waves as counterpoints.[12] Not rushing from one end to the other to arrive at a destination, a conclusion. Nor completing sections in a linear trajectory from start to finish, like the way one imagines books ought to be read. Instead, "to begin by re-turning", as Barad (2014) writes of diffraction,

FIGURE 6.3   From *Salt-Water-Bodies: From an Atlas of Loss* (2015–2019). Malgas Island, Atlantic Ocean. Photo: Adrienne van Eeden-Wharton.

"turning it over and over again" (p. 168).[13] A slow and observant, piecemeal and iterative praxis of re-walking and re-reading, re-visiting and re-searching.

Wayfaring (wayfinding), Tim Ingold suggests, is about negotiating, improvising, attuning – learning *alongly*, as you go along (see 2007, 2010, 2011). With its atmospheric, sonic and somatic resonances, attunement gestures to immersion and co-responding movement.[14] To adapt to the cadenced reverberations of waves, tides. To become an apprentice to palpable, unsettled weather-worlds and spatiotemporal littoral relations.[15] And, as Vinciane Despret so poignantly writes, an *embodied empathy*, a *making available* or *becoming-with* (2013, pp. 69–71); a *with-ness* in which "bodies and worlds articulate each other" (2004, p. 131), "undo and redo each other, reciprocally though not symmetrically" (2013, p. 61). To risk and learn to attend.[16] To touch and be touched. To move and be moved (along). To put one foot in front of the other.

Beachcombing. An inefficient zigzagging along highwater marks, in wrack zones. Places of wreckage and remnants. And unlooked-for ecological richness. Trailing, straggling. An uncanny contemporaneity of straying and fixation – sifting with your eyes, your hands. Fossicking, picking over discarded remains.[17] Bits and pieces. Broken and scattered. Storm-tossed, wind-battered. Carried by water and air from a multitude of elsewheres. Con-currently gathered and dispersed, reassembled in strange and unexpected ways with every ebb and flood. An excess of things. Neglected things, leftover things. Lost things. Cast-off and disposed-of

FIGURE 6.4   From *Salt-Water-Bodies: From an Atlas of Loss* (2015–2019). Sixteen Mile Beach, Atlantic Ocean. Photo: Adrienne van Eeden-Wharton.

things. Last things, unlike things and those that do not add up. The dirty, slow work of re-collecting and re-membering.

In the place of narratives of human mastery – poisonous, killer stories – Ursula Le Guin (1996) proposes a generative *carrier bag* theory of fiction. "I came lugging this great heavy sack of stuff" she writes of her own storytelling practice, "full of beginnings without ends, of initiations, of losses, of transformations and translations" (p.153). My carrier bag is a ghost net. Overfull, leaking. Snarled around dolphins and whales, seabirds and seals. Fishes, turtles, seahorses and eels. Lobsters, crabs and shrimps. Octopuses and squids, cuttlefish and jellyfish. Corals, starfish, anemones and urchins. Rays and sharks and mermaids' purses. Dragging fishing tackle, ship ropes and buoys, lobster traps and octopus pots. Flare guns and glowsticks, safety hats, crates and oil drums. Sweet wrappers, balloons, gift ribbons. Plastic bottles, caps and rings. Lighters, cigarette butts, snuff box lids. Polystyrene cups and takeaway trays, throw-away cutlery and drinking straws. Plastic bags, tubs and clingwrap. Lollypop and earbud sticks. Beverage cans and six-pack yokes. Bread tags, ballpoint pens. Condom wrappers, laundry pegs, unmatched shoes. Pandemic-time facemasks, gloves and handwipes. Countless tiny mermaids' tears, clutched in my cramping hands.

Bracha Ettinger offers a moving summation of *carriance* (care-carrying): "We are here, hence we have been carried. Each one of us" (Ettinger in Kaiser & Thiele, 2018, p. 106). Expanding on the salience of this sense of support, bearing and *co-response-ability* beyond the human(e), she gestures to our interdependence on "what silently carries us: the ocean, the forest, the night" (p. 123). As aqueous carriers, Astrida Neimanis (2017) suggests, we are entangled in "complex relations of gift, theft, and debt with all other watery life" (p. 3). Marine animals who carry precarious past-present-futures with/in them; oceans "forced to carry too much plastic, too little oxygen" (p. 50). Could we consider acts of gathering and holding, care and grieving, as a carrying-with that opens possibilities of more wake-full re-imaginings, re-storyings?

Stories told in pieces, in parts. With small words like *salt* and *water* and *bodies*. Spewed onto the shore in foamy outbursts. Or swallowed up in breathless gasps, drowned. At times no more than a susurration – a low murmur, an ancient drawn-out guttural sigh. A faint grey echo, barely there.

Stories that are out of place and out of time. Displaced and untimely. Drift, out of reach. Or, submerged, sink – slowly, like "long snowfall" (Carson, 1951, p. 80). Sedimented, silty stories churned up from the depths of forgotten seabeds. Suspended. Sometimes surfacing unexpectedly, briefly. Awaiting evaporations and condensations. Stories that wash away, wash up, or are left behind. Are transported across oceans, against their will. And those that end up there accidentally. Stranded. A casting of bones. Out of joint, disarticulated.[18]

On the shore, illusions of certainty, fixity and orderly, calculable time and space are wrecked. Shattered by heterogenous physical, chemical, geological and atmospheric forces. Changeable, ambivalent. Undecided, unsteady. Not seemly

Academic words. But fitting for the amplified exposure and felt intensity at the indeterminate edge/s of the sea.

The littoral is not an "infinitely thin slice of time" (Barad, 2017a, p. 25). It isn't amenable to *chronos*, to clock time – the regimented, forward-marching linear timeline of History and Progress, "attuned to a succession of discrete moments" (Barad, 2017b, p. 60). Rather, the "complex and shifting entanglement between sea and land" is better served by what Kamau Brathwaite calls *tidalectics*, a "tidal dialectic" (DeLoughrey, 2007, p. 2). And while tidal arrivals and departures are indeed rhythmic and cyclical,[19] the unremitting negotiations and pulsating exchanges of the littoral signal spacetimematterings that are unpredictably and simultaneously surging and eddying, expanding and contracting. A permeable *thick present* (Haraway, 2016) or *thick-now* (Barad, 2017a, 2017b). A place of always-unfinished business. Of restless remains and untimely returns.

Near the northern end of Sixteen Mile Beach a fence runs down into the sea, separating the national park from a privately-owned reserve. On the adjacent Vondeling Island, where seals were butchered for their skins and fat until the island's population had all but disappeared, the abandoned guano-era buildings are now inhabited by a large colony.

Piles of uprooted kelp, like corpses lined up on the beach. The wounds on decomposing seal bodies, weeping. And the desiccated remains of the pups, tiny and broken, all but indistinguishable from pieces of withered kelp. Hidden by

FIGURE 6.5 From *Salt-Water-Bodies: From an Atlas of Loss* (2015–2019). Sixteen Mile Beach, Atlantic Ocean. Photo: Adrienne van Eeden-Wharton.

FIGURE 6.6   From *Salt-Water-Bodies: From an Atlas of Loss* (2015–2019). Sixteen Mile Beach, Atlantic Ocean. Photo: Adrienne van Eeden-Wharton.

the wind and tides, almost-imperceptible stains betraying their presence under the sand. Seabirds, sometimes only recognisable by a partial feathered outline. Or the frictional trail left by the weight of one body being dragged by another. Lives and deaths beyond the narrow scope of considerability and grievability.[20]

Landfallen humpback whales. Tossed and turned in the breakers, carried alongshore. Shapeshifting to deep-oranges and pallid-greys as scavengers compete over their decomposing flesh. Bloating and oozing, melting blubber seeping into the sand. Bodies heaved onto the shore in pieces, in parts. Until only a few giant rib bones and vertebrae remain. Waxen and too heavy to lift. Dead weight.

I return to them. I sit with them, am touched by them. I circle their still (moving) bodies. Their now-familiar smells cling to me, travel with me. I taste the salty, oily residue on my skin.

~ Wading (endless greys, seeping)

Twilight greys, evening shadows and argent night shores. The sweeping lighthouse strokes and disquiet dreams that break my sleep. Hyper-aware, I learn to listen to the cumulative, fugue-like variations and contrapuntal minor melodies. Let myself be guided by the water's edge, feel the temperature and texture changes under my bare feet.

The water grows thicker, the seaward undertow threatens to knock over my out-of-phase body. Like vertigo and the uncontainable nausea of seasickness. The visceral retort of a body of water at once doubled up and turned inside-out; an unwell, out-of-breath ocean.

I learn to tarry. Not only to delay, but to linger. To take my time. To stay until being here is enough. Or my trembling body grows numb in the frigid waters. To hesitate as I stumble over boulders, lose my footing on algae-covered rocks. To hold back judgement like I would hold my breath underwater, gasping for air as I surface. My eyes stinging – burning from the saltwater – and vision blurry. Flooded, as with tears. Saturated, drenched, soaked.

Thick terraqueous contact zones and elemental ecotones.[21] Spaces of proximity and encounter; intersection and intensity; asymmetrical reciprocities and frictional relating. All-too-often what Rose (2013) calls *death zones* – thresholds "where the living and the dying encounter each other in the presence of that which cannot be averted" (pp. 3–4). Demanding of us a slow and engaged "ethics of proximity and responsibility" (p. 4); dwelling in the midst of aftermaths, catastrophes. The muddy, ecotonal æsthethics of amphibious translations; wading through heavy sands and dark waters.[22]

For our praxis to become sea-worthy it, too, must become amphibious.[23] Waterlogged (footnotes). Like earth that is ceaselessly washed by the sea as it makes and unmakes, cuts together-apart.[24] Living and dying; pasts, presents and futures. Leaving and remaining; fleeing and abiding. Giving and taking back; finding and losing. Smashing against each other during storm swells, surges and flash floods. Or warily to-ing and fro-ing, only just touching. Seeping together at saltwatery edges. Between liquid and solid, like melting sea ice.

Seeping, Steve Mentz (2017) writes, "troubles boundaries but does not dispense with them entirely"; it implies "mutual contamination" and "accumulated exchange" (pp. 282–283), contact and infiltration. Like the pervious membranes and "complex phenomena in dynamic relationality" of Nancy Tuana's *viscous porosity* (2008, p. 191). And Stacy Alaimo's framework of *trans-corporeality* which posits our permeable, fleshy bodies as "inter-meshed with the more-than-human world" (2010, p. 2). Both Tuana and Alaimo underscore movements across bodies, temporalities, sites and categories – notably exposure to toxicity. Differential precarity, temporal inscription and always-unequal subjection to potentially destructive forces. To be unprotected, at risk. Acts of deliberate bodily exposure ("dwelling in the dissolve"), Alaimo suggests, remind us that we are "materially interconnected to planetary processes as they emerge in particular places" (2016, p. 94). Such material-affective encounters and ethico-political engagements encourage empathy and coming to grips with "particular entanglements of vulnerability and complicity" (p. 5).

Seep is a word for the longue durée of unnoticed, creeping devastation that Rob Nixon (2011) calls *slow violence*. Incremental, accretive violences of "delayed destruction", "dispersed across time and space" (p. 2). Attritional toxicities, impossible to contain. Trickles, leaks, spills. Disregarded and discarded

FIGURE 6.7   From *Salt-Water-Bodies: From an Atlas of Loss* (2015–2019). Malgas Island, Atlantic Ocean. Photo: Adrienne van Eeden-Wharton.

casualties (p. 13); "long dyings" (p. 2) and the many, unspectacular, forms of *letting die*. Protracted injustices, compelling slow, unsettled and exposed practices of witnessing. Like the situated and implicated witnessing of Haraway's *modest witness*: "seeing; attesting; standing publicly accountable for, and psychically vulnerable to, one's visions and representations" (1997, p. 267). And Ettinger's concept of *aesthetic wit(h)nessing* (witnessing-together) – a relational "dwelling with your subject-matter", "remaining with it, in your body" (Ettinger in Kaiser & Thiele, 2018, p. 105).

Grey. The unremarked colour of seeping violence. Of shadows and out-of-sight shadow places. An anonymous, backgrounded colour that doesn't seem to matter. The turbid hues of effluent and sludge. Agricultural runoff, toxic industrial and cooling water discharge. Contaminated municipal wastewater and sewage. Smokestack plumes from refineries and chemical plants. Heavy meatal dust, ship exhaust gas emissions. Bunkering and refuelling oil, ballast water and dredged sediments.

The colour of the residual. Too little water – of drought along the already arid, windswept West Coast. Not enough rain-bearing storms making landfall in the years preceding the predicted 'Day Zero' when taps in the Cape Town metropolitan would run dry. Too much water – of rivers bursting their banks after yet another bout of violent rainstorms in KwaZulu-Natal; of deadly flash floods and landslides. Deluges of stormwater and debris rushing into the sea. And as cyclone swells

FIGURE 6.8   From *Water/Log* (2021 ongoing). Former Union Whaling Company station, Bluff Military Support Base, Indian Ocean. Photo: Adrienne van Eeden-Wharton.

churn up tepid Indian Ocean waters, the shores are awash with detritus and grey-brown silt.

At the ruins of the whaling station near the port of Durban, the air is heavy. Stifling. A humid mist blankets the Bluff, dissipating as the sun grows harsher. Everything is still soggy after the latest storm, the smells heightened. I follow the partially-obscured, corroded trainline that transported baleen and sperm whale bodies on flatbed carriages. Like cargo. From the harbour slipway, past the original factory premises (now a wastewater treatment plant), to be winched onto the concrete flensing platform and butchered. In pieces, in parts. Conveyed to underground pressure cookers; boilers, separators and decanters; mincers and driers; packaging and freezing chambers; storerooms and tanks. Disseminated as clarified oils, frozen and canned meat, meat extract, petfood, bone meal and meat meal.

I scamper down the creeping dunes to where the spent cooling water discharge was pumped back into the ocean. Look up. Overwhelmed, wordless. Struggling to fathom[25] the scale and complexity, I wade through mud pools and rubble, piecemeal accounts in musty, overfull archive boxes. Water seeps from the walls of the dank, crumbling buildings – riddled with bullet holes from decades of serving as a military base after the closure of the factory. Overgrown by lush vegetation. The gunfire from the shooting range interspersed with the calls of monkeys and birds.

FIGURE 6.9   From *Water/Log* (2021 ongoing). Former Union Whaling Company station, Bluff Military Support Base, Indian Ocean. Photo: Adrienne van Eeden-Wharton.

As I trace whaling histories spanning the South Atlantic, Indian and Southern oceans, I map the former sites of shore-based stations and the routes of pelagic factory ships and catchers. The African seaports that served as gateways to the southern high latitude regions; the sprawling networks of capital, control and coerced labour that enabled the industrial-scale slaughter of cetaceans – inseparable from European colonial occupation. In most cases, remnants of the whaling operations are all but gone. Now rebranded as whale-watching spots.[26]

I sit next to the former whaling station's slipway at Stony Point, not far from Cape Hangklip. It's early-morning; windy, raining. If the weather clears up, tourists will flock to see the African penguins nesting among artificial concrete burrows and makeshift shelters. One of only two mainland colonies, the other at Boulders Beach on the opposite end of False Bay. The route between the two signposted with 'whale coast' boards, unintended waymarks to the bay's blood-and-oil-soaked histories.

The shore-based stations at the Bluff and Donkergat both operated seasonal Antarctic whaling fleets during the austral summers. And, in a twist on the implication of the whaling industry in twentieth-century warfare, the Donkergat premises and adjacent former factory site at Salamander, too, were incorporated into a seaborne special forces training area. Haltingly, I follow the edges of this small peninsula on the West Coast. Step by step. Over the wreckage, into the water. Try to picture the pools of thick, lukewarm blood seeping across the lagoon.

FIGURE 6.10   From *Water/Log* (2021 ongoing). Former Waaygat whaling station, Stony Point, Atlantic Ocean. Photo: Adrienne van Eeden-Wharton.

A suitable combination of currents and wind churns up a putrid smell from the bottom of the bay. Decades-old whale offal, they surmise. But the origin is irrelevant. We ought to know that spectres conjure up powerful sensory displays.

Grey is the "polychrome hue of the in-between and the uncertain" (Cohen, 2013, p. 272), camouflage and melange. Of imbrication and negotiation. Between geo and hydro, terra and aqua. A fluctuant hinge, knitting-together while stretching-apart as the ocean exhales and inhales, pushes and pulls, gives and takes. The glaucous cast of the sea on contrastless days – all-enveloping greenish-blueish-greys, sombre and shimmering. The colour of evaporation, condensation and precipitation.[27] A permeating briny smell, fresh and slightly putrid. Inclement weather, muggy summer thunderclouds and violent winter rainstorms. Darkened horizons and indistinct interfaces. Sea fog. Equally concealing islands and continental coastlands.

Navigating the islands in Saldanha Bay, I track the fishing trawlers and bulk carriers passing between the North and South Head lighthouses. Malgas Island, closest to the naval base; Jutten Island, across from the military training area. Battleship grey, gunmetal grey. Marcus Island, joined to the mainland by a causeway built to protect the port's iron-ore terminal from the powerful Atlantic Ocean swells. Harbour grey, concrete grey. Breakwaters and seawalls, underwater blasting and port dredging; pursuits of cut-and-dried coast*lines* and shore*lines*, landfalls and departures.[28] Altering wave energy and longshore currents, tidal flows and nutrient circulation; disrupting ancient rhythms of eroding and depositing;

FIGURE 6.11   From *Salt-Water-Bodies: From an Atlas of Loss* (2015–2019). Schaapen Island, Atlantic Ocean. Photo: Adrienne van Eeden-Wharton.

destroying intertidal habitats and the fragile ecologies of estuaries, lagoons, saltmarshes and coastal wetlands.[29]

The muted tones of decomposition and sedimentation, excretion and accumulation. The fecund murkiness of pulsing nutrient-rich oceanic upwellings – stimulating phytoplankton blooms and, in turn, complex food webs that allowed whales, seals and seabirds to flourish. Increasingly threatened by commercial overfishing, coastal and offshore mining, seismic oil and gas exploration, shipping traffic, oil spills and myriad residual toxicities. Islands stripped bare; the metres-thick guano accretions from fish-eating seabirds 'harvested' as fertiliser for exhausted agricultural soils.[30] Leaving these avian communities without adequate nesting materials and precluding essential nutrients from seeping back into the ocean via runoff.

Ghostly winds. Guano dust sticks to everything. Pale. Pungent. The lively cacophonies on Malgas Island belie the growing number of empty nests around the shrinking gannet colony. Marking the absences of those who did *not* return. More and more and more decaying bodies. Heads tucked as if resting, wings spread as if in flight. Fading into the accretions as the living build their nests on top of the bones of the dead in untold ongoing burials. The desaturated colours of empty cormorant nests, also on Jutten and other islands, abandoned too early in the breeding season. Fractured, wind-strewn remains. Malnourished coastal seabirds – at risk of disease and predation; their breeding sites imperiled by intensifying storm surges, flooding

FIGURE 6.12   From *Salt-Water-Bodies: From an Atlas of Loss* (2015–2019). Malgas Island, Atlantic Ocean. Photo: Adrienne van Eeden-Wharton.

FIGURE 6.13   From *Salt-Water-Bodies: From an Atlas of Loss* (2015–2019). Jutten Island, Atlantic Ocean. Photo: Adrienne van Eeden-Wharton.

FIGURE 6.14 From *Salt-Water-Bodies: From an Atlas of Loss* (2015–2019). Malgas Island, Atlantic Ocean. Photo: Adrienne van Eeden-Wharton.

and rising sea levels. Here, at the tenuous divide between the living and the dead, I learn to move cautiously. My presence moot. Teetering, I walk the concrete wall around the periphery of Dassen Island. Treading lightly on the uneven ground where the once-thriving penguin colony was raided for eggs. Vestiges of countless burrows. Now, all but bare.

Burnt bones and cinereous, ashen remains. The eddying greys of aftermaths and afterlives, afteræffects and afterimages.[31] Shifting, dissolving. Somewhere between remembering and forgetting. Of aftershocks and infinitesimal minor tremors. Disorienting underwater noise. Echoes, murmurations, reverberations, quivers. Hushed conversations and tentative considerations. Of ongoingness and survivance. The shadowy greys of accumulated life-death as birds find refuge among the rafters and bunkbeds of derelict buildings, previously the cramped accommodation of guano labourers. Of new multispecies communities making their homes at the remnants of whaling stations. The muddied tones of slow, messy work in times of urgency and acceleration. The wake-full hues of mourning and falling in love with damaged, seep-stained ecologies.[32]

~ Coda

Mid-2022. Cape Agulhas. A seaspray-green plaque, unveiled by an apartheid-era president, marks the southernmost tip of the continent and the official divide between the Atlantic and Indian oceans.[33] Facing the water, looking south; open seas between here and the frozen 'ends of the earth'. Barefoot, I make my way across the rocks. Pick up a handful of crushed shells, let them slip through my fingers. Slowly. Deliberately. I close my eyes, embraced by the turbulent meeting of these two bodies of water. An infinitely spectral, fathom grey.

Acknowledgements

As transdisciplinary site-responsive work, *Salt-Water-Bodies: From an Atlas of Loss* and *Water/Log* would be inconceivable without the goodwill of numerous individuals and institutions. Access to restricted areas featured in this chapter was provided by the South African National Defence Force, South African National Parks and Cape Nature.

This work is based on the research supported in part by the National Research Foundation of South Africa (NRF reference number: 129219).

The financial assistance of the National Institute for the Humanities and Social Sciences (NIHSS) in collaboration with the South African Humanities Deans Association (SAHUDA) towards this research is hereby acknowledged.

Notes

1 Preamble, from the Latin *praeambulus* (walking before); *prae-* (in front of, before in time or place) and *ambulare* (walk around, go about). Prelude, from the Latin *praeludere* (play beforehand, practice or test); *prae-* and *ludere* (play). A precursory action or introductory movement, like a short piece preceding a fugue. (I draw on several dictionaries and thesauruses for word associations, synonyms and etymologies. For ease of reading, these are listed under references only.)

2 Geographically, Cape Agulhas is the southernmost point of mainland Africa and aligns with the designated meeting of the cold Benguela and warm Agulhas currents. Cape of Good Hope, however, was a pivotal landmark in colonial trade routes traversing the Atlantic and Indian oceans between Europe and Asia, the Clipper Route from Europe through the Southern Ocean, and in controlling the passage of ships during times of war. Its enduring importance to global maritime shipping routes a stark reminder that today's sprawling international trade networks rely primarily on sea-freight and are implicated with other off-shore industries in extraction and exploitation; destruction and contamination; forced or coercive transoceanic labour; involuntary migration and trafficking.

3 See Karen Barad's neologism *intra-action* (Barad, 2007). My use of *intra-oceanic* gestures to the interconnected world ocean as well as the commonly defined major oceans, seas and currents – geopolitical and ecological *spacetimematterings* (Barad, 2007, 2014) of distinct yet intermingling, situated yet planetary bodies of water.

4 A simultaneous treading-with, following and weaving of material-conceptual threads (see Price & van Eeden-Wharton, 2023).

5 *Salt-Water-Bodies* was originally a practice-as-research PhD (Stellenbosch University), supervised by Elizabeth Gunter; see van Eeden-Wharton (2020). *Water/Log* expands this into a larger body of creative-critical work.

6 Joanna Zylinska (2016) proposes *photomediations* as a processual, dynamic and relational understanding of photomedia as complex light-based phenomena (pp. 11–12). I use the modified punctuation, *photomedia(tions)*, to evoke the æffective and

æsthethical praxes of creating and engaging with still (moving) images. Elsewhere, Erin Price and I (as the Æ Collective) use the ligature spellings Æffect and Æsthethical to signal the knotting-together of affect and effect, aesthetic and ethical matter(s). See Price & van Eeden-Wharton (2023).

7 Meg Samuelson and Charne Lavery (2019) propose approaching the global South from the vantage point of the Southern Ocean which "opens up possibilities for tracking the intersecting currents and itineraries that compose the oceanic South" (p. 38). I am indebted to their conceptualisation of an *oceanic South* in orienting my approach to the material and geopolitical flows connecting seemingly disparate places and times.

8 Patric Tariq Mellet (2020) underscores the complex histories of the many San and Khoe (Khoi) communities, as well as the over 195 roots of origin of Africans of Camissa heritage. Mellet points to the indiscriminate and dismissive introduction by the seventeenth-century Dutch East India Company commander of the designation 'Strandlopers' (beach walkers, beachcombers) – initially referring to the ‖Ammaqua traders, thereafter to Sonqua line-fishers. 'Strandloper', Mellet argues, was not only a term of racial othering, but also served to justify colonial occupation by denying Indigenous claims to land.

9 See Barad (2007) on *material-discursive* boundary-making practices and attending to the distinctions, categories and exclusions they enact. Elizabeth DeLoughrey (2019) suggests that the "material, social, and ethical construction of waste" (p. 102) is intrinsic to the violence of empire, capitalism and neoliberal globalisation – characterised by invisibilised *wasted lives*, both human and more-than-human.

10 Walk, from the Old English *wealcan* (move around, toss) and *wealcian* (roll, curl), shares roots with the Old Norse *valka* (drag) and the Old German *walchan* (knead).

11 The double meanings in Old French of *errant* and *errer* – traveling, wandering, losing one's way, making a mistake, transgressing – are from the Latin *iterare* (journey) and *errare* (go astray, be in error).

12 Drawing-in the historical pathologising of bewildered wandering and dissociative states, Iain Sinclair (2003) describes his walks – through London's edgelands and along the verges of the highway encircling the city – as fugues. Sinclair borrows the French term *fugueur* (runaway) for "fugue walkers, long-distance amnesiacs" (pp. 146–147, 339). Fugue walking is unreasonable, excessive. It's extravagant. From the Latin *extravagari* (wander outside or beyond); *extra* (in addition to, beyond the scope of) and *vagari* (roam, wander). The fugue is also a contrapuntal, polyphonic musical composition that relies on repetition, layering and transposition. It shares the Latin roots *fuga* and *fugere* (to take flight, flee; to be unknown or escape notice; fleeting) with fugitive.

13 See Donna Haraway's influential conceptualisation of diffraction as a practice of producing "interference patterns" (1997, p. 16), "difference patterns in the world" (p. 268). In Barad's methodological approach, diffraction requires "reading insights through one another in attending to and responding to the details and specificities of relations of difference and how they matter" (2007, p. 71).

14 Correspond, from the Latin *correspondere* (to reciprocate, harmonise); *com-* (together, with one another) and *respondere* (promise in return, answer to). Ingold conceptualises *co-respondence* as a mutual responsiveness – "neither between nor within but along, not lateral but longitudinal" (2022, p. 6); "not additive but contrapuntal" (2016, p. 14), like an "accompaniment or refrain" (2018, p. 25).

15 Ingold (2010, 2011) uses *weather-world* to emphasise vital atmospheric agencies and felt relations. Astrida Neimanis and Rachel Walker (2014), too, propose a radical inversion of the distanced abstraction of climate change narratives. If we recognise our own and other porous bodies as *weathering,* as "co-emerging in the making of these weather-times", they write, we may "attune ourselves to the pasts that are contracted in changing temperatures, rising sea levels, increasingly desiccated earths" (p. 573).

16 Attend, from the Old French *atendre* (to wait for, pay attention, expect) and the Latin *attendere* (to stretch toward, give heed to); *ad* (toward) and *tendere* (stretch). Unlike an objectifying *of-ness*, relational attentionality is the *with-ness* of being pulled into "correspondence *with* this world" (Ingold, 2018, p. 30; see also 2016). Deborah Bird Rose (2011), building on Emil Fackenheim's "turning toward" (*Tikkun*), suggests an "ethics of motion toward encounter, a willingness to situate one's self so as to be available to the call of others" (p. 5). While acknowledging the impossibility of undoing or unmaking histories of violence, suffering and destruction, a relational turning toward seeks what Haraway (2016) calls "partial recuperation".

17 I first came across 'fossicking' – a term used mainly in Australia, particularly for prospecting abandoned mine workings – in Brewster (2009). I find resonance also with Walter Benjamin's figuration, in the texts posthumously published as *Das Passagen-Werk* (*The Arcades Project*), of the materialist historian as collector (see Wohlfarth, 2006). A peripatetic ragpicker, gathering and reassembling what Benjamin (2002) calls the "refuse of history" (p. 461). Slowly, skilfully. "I needn't *say* anything. Merely show" Benjamin writes of his method of literary montage; to allow the "the rags, the refuse", *refused* by the master narratives of the archive proper, "to come into their own" (p. 460).

18 Using "the time is out of joint" from Shakespeare's *Hamlet* as a refrain, Derrida (1994) writes of a "disjointed or disadjusted now" (p. 3). This is a "time without *certain* joining or determinable conjunction" – "*disarticulated*, dislocated, dislodged" and "off course, beside itself" (p. 18). Articulate, from the Latin *articulare* (separated into joints, to say clearly). A well-formulated argument. Expression that is fluent and eloquent, lucid and capable. But I find myself at a loss for words; only halting, wavering utterings to offer.

19 Tide, from the Old English *tīd* (portion of time). Rising and falling tides are long-period waves responding to the gravitational pulls of the moon and sun. High (flood) tide is the crest of this tidal wave; low (ebb) tide the trough.

20 Grievability, Judith Butler (2009) poignantly summarises, "is a presupposition for the life that matters" (p. 14). See Haraway (2008) on *making killable* and Irus Braverman (2015) on the hierarchies enacted by endangered species lists and conservation strategies. In many respects, African penguins have become conservation flagship species while other seabirds – even endangered species like Bank cormorants, Cape cormorants and Cape gannets – do not enjoy the same privileged status. Cape fur seals, especially, have been vilified as threats to both commercial fishing and vulnerable seabird populations. In late-2021, as unprecedented numbers of emaciated dead and dying seals washed up on more frequented shores around the Western Cape, their precarious existences finally elicited more public attention.

21 From the Greek *oikos* (home) and *tonos* (stretching, tightening), ecotone shares the Proto-Indo-European root **ten-* (to stretch) with tension. Defined by ecologists as a "transition between two or more diverse communities", a "junction zone or tension belt" (Odum, 1971, p. 157), feminist scholars have expanded the concept to consider "contest, change, and co-construction" (Mortimer-Sandilands, 2004, p. 48). Here, I think-with contact zones (see Pratt, 2008) not only in relation to postcolonial studies of the shore, but also Haraway's generative (re)conceptualisation thereof as multispecies *naturalcultural* encounters, dynamic and fraught "mortal world-making entanglements" (2008, p. 4).

22 Translate, from the Latin *translatus* (carried or borne across).

23 See also Melody Jue (2020) on *amphibious scholarship* where, submerged, our terrestrial biases are exposed to "pressure, salinity, and coldness" (p. 5).

24 Whereas fixed, Cartesian cuts take ontological distinction and distance as inherent and foundational, the *agential* cuts enacted by intra-actions cut "together-apart" (Barad, 2014).

25 To seek to understand, to measure depth or take soundings. From the Old English *fæðm* (length of outstretched arms) and *fæðmian* (embrace, envelop, surround).

26 The Bluff (KwaZulu-Natal) and Algoa Bay (Eastern Cape) are both Whale Heritage Sites; the Cape Coast Whale Route stretches from Cape Town to Cape Agulhas and includes the annual Hermanus Whale Festival in Walker Bay. As conservation icons and ecotourism attractions, the image of whales as charismatic megafauna is often based on what Arne Kalland (2009) calls a generic "superwhale", combining traits from different species.

27 In proposing a *more-than-wet ontology*, Kimberley Peters and Philip Steinberg (2019) retain the importance of "thinking *through* and *from* the ocean's liquid materiality" but stress that the ocean is never "simply wet", a "basin of salt water" (pp. 294–295). Rather, it is always in excess – embedded in the expansive hydrosphere, coursing through bodies and saturating "stories, dreams and imaginings" (p. 294).

28 Here, Isabel Hofmeyr's conceptual framework of *hydrocolonialism* – spanning colonisation "by way of water", "of water", "through water" and "of the idea of water" (2022, pp. 15–16) – is invaluable. See Paul Carter (2009) on how the Enlightenment logic of representing the coast as a stable outline, a thin "continuous line that differentiates a mass of land from water", served as "indispensable prerequisite of [imperial] territorial expansion" (p. 8).

29 Oceanic examples of diffraction are particularly relevant to the South African coast with its few natural harbours, violent storms and enduring legacies of shoreline hardening, land reclamation and coastal mining. The Latin root of diffract – *diffringere* (to break apart) – evokes the new interference patterns emerging from the many forms of artificial break/water(s).

30 The nineteenth-century international guano trade epitomises ecological imperialism and capitalist commodification. Capitalism, Jason Moore (2015) argues, is an *ecological regime* where Nature (singular, capitalised) – as external and separate – becomes "something to be mapped, rationalized, quantified, and above all, *controlled*" (p. 70).

31 See Griselda Pollock's neologism *after-affects*, evoking the "temporal displacement of trauma" (2013, p. xxx) and impact of aesthetic encounters with "traces or residues of what could not be immediately represented" (p. 27). See van Eeden-Wharton (2023) on thinking-with expanded notions of *after*.

32 See Mentz (2017) on *seep-stained* and *seep ecology*.

33 Ever-moving and intermingling, ocean currents are of course not amenable to clearcut directives or boundaries. Perhaps it is more helpful to think of the confluence of the cold Benguela and the warm Agulhas currents as a shifting ecotone.

References

Alaimo, S. (2010). *Bodily natures: Science, environment, and the material self.* Indiana University Press.

Alaimo, S. (2016). *Exposed: Environmental politics and pleasures in posthuman times.* University of Minnesota Press.

Barad, K. (2007). *Meeting the universe halfway: Quantum physics and the entanglement of matter and meaning.* Duke University Press.

Barad, K. (2014). Diffracting diffraction: Cutting together-apart. *Parallax, 20*(3), 168–187. https://doi.org/10.1080/13534645.2014.927623.

Barad, K. (2017a). What flashes up: Theological-political-scientific fragments. In C. Keller & M.-J. Rubenstein (Eds.), *Entangled worlds: Religion, science, and new materialisms* (pp. 21–88). Fordham University Press.

Barad, K. (2017b). Troubling times/s and ecologies of nothingness: Re-turning, re-membering, and facing the incalculable. *New Formations, 92*(1), 56–86. https://doi.org/10.3898/NEWF:92.05.2017.

Benjamin, W. (2002). *The Arcades Project* (H. Eiland & K. McLaughlin, Trans.). Harvard University Press.

Braverman, I. (2015). En-listing life: Red is the color of threatened species lists. In K. Gillespie & R.-C. Collard (Eds.), *Critical animal geographies: Politics, intersections, and hierarchies in a multispecies world* (pp. 184–202). Routledge.

Brewster, A. (2009). Beachcombing: A Fossicker's guide to whiteness and indigenous sovereignty. In H. Smith & R. Dean (Eds.), *Practice-led research, research-led practice in the creative arts* (pp. 126–149). Edinburgh University Press.

Butler, J. (2009). *Frames of war: When is life grievable?* Verso.

Carson, R. (1951). *The sea around us.* Staples.

Carter, P. (2009). *Dark writing: Geography, performance, design.* University of Hawai'i Press.

Cohen, J. J. (2013). Grey. In J. J. Cohen (Ed.), *Prismatic ecology: Ecotheory beyond green* (pp. 270–289). University of Minnesota Press.

DeLoughrey, E. (2007). *Routes and roots: Navigating Caribbean and Pacific Island literatures.* University of Hawai'i Press.

DeLoughrey, E. (2019). *Allegories of the anthropocene.* Duke University Press.

Derrida, J. (1994). *Specters of Marx: The state of debt, the work of mourning, and the new international* (P. Kamuf, Trans.). Routledge.

Despret, V. (2004). The body we care for: Figures of anthropo-zoo-genesis. *Body & Society, 10*(2–3), 111–134. https://doi.org/10.1177/1357034X04042938.

Despret, V. (2013). Responding bodies and partial affinities in human-animal worlds. *Theory, Culture & Society, 30*(7–8), 51–76. https://doi.org/10.1177/0263276413496852.

Haraway, D. (1997). *Modest_Witness@Second_Millennium.FemaleMan© _Meets_ OncoMouseTM: Feminism and Technoscience.* Routledge.

Haraway, D. (2008). *When species meet.* University of Minnesota Press.

Haraway, D. (2016). *Staying with the trouble: Making kin in the Chthulucene.* Duke University Press.

Hofmeyr, I. (2022). *Dockside reading: Hydrocolonialism and the custom house.* Duke University Press.

Ingold, T. (2007). *Lines: A brief history.* Routledge.

Ingold, T. (2010). Footprints through the weather-world: Walking, breathing, knowing. *Journal of the Royal Anthropological Institute, 16*(1), 121–139. https://doi.org/10.1111/j.1467-9655.2010.01613.x.

Ingold, T. (2011). *Being alive: Essays on movement, knowledge and description.* Routledge.

Ingold, T. (2016). On human correspondence. *Journal of the Royal Anthropological Institute, 23*(1), 9–27. https://doi.org/10.1111/1467-9655.12541.

Ingold, T. (2018). *Anthropology and/as education.* Routledge.

Ingold, T. (2022). *Imagining for real: Essays on creation, attention and correspondence.* Routledge.

Jue, M. (2020). *Wild blue media: Thinking through seawater.* Duke University Press.

Kaiser, B. M., & Thiele, K. (2018). If you do well, carry! The difference of the humane: An interview with Bracha L. Ettinger. *PhiloSOPHIA, 8*(1), 101–125. https://doi.org/10.1353/phi.2018.0005.

Kalland, A. (2009). *Unveiling the whale: Discourses on whales and whaling.* Berghahn Books.

Le Guin, U. K. (1996). The carrier bag theory of fiction. In C. Glotfelty & H. Fromm (Eds.), *The ecocriticism reader: Landmarks in literary ecology* (pp. 149–154). University of Georgia Press.

Mellet, P. T. (2020). *The lie of 1652: A decolonised history of land.* Tafelberg.

Mentz, S. (2017). Seep. In J. J. Cohen & L. Duckert (Eds.), *Veer ecology: A companion for environmental thinking* (pp. 282–296). University of Minnesota Press.

Merriam-Webster English Dictionary. (n.d.). www.merriam-webster.com.

Merriam-Webster English Thesaurus. (n.d.). www.merriam-webster.com/thesaurus.

Moore, J. W. (2015). *Capitalism in the web of life: Ecology and the accumulation of capital.* Verso.

Mortimer-Sandilands, C. (2004). The marginal world. In J. A. Wainwright (Ed.), *Every grain of sand: Canadian perspectives on ecology and environment* (pp. 45–54). Wilfrid Laurier University Press.

Neimanis, A. (2017). *Bodies of water: Posthuman feminist phenomenology.* Bloomsbury Academic.

Neimanis, A., & Walker, R. L. (2014). Weathering: Climate change and the "thick time" of transcorporeality. *Hypatia: A Journal of Feminist Philosophy, 29*(3), 558–575. https://doi.org/10.1111/hypa.12064.

Nixon, R. (2011). *Slow violence and the environmentalism of the poor.* Harvard University Press.

Odum, E. P. (1971). *Fundamentals of ecology* (3rd ed.). W.B. Saunders.

Online Etymology Dictionary. (n.d.). www.etymonline.com/.

Peters, K., & Steinberg, P. (2019). The ocean in excess: Towards a more-than-wet ontology. *Dialogues in Human Geography, 9*(3), 293–307. https://doi.org/10.1177/204382061 9872886.

Plumwood, V. (2008). Shadow places and the politics of dwelling. *Australian Humanities Review, 44*(1), 139–150.

Pollock, G. (2013). *After-affects/after-images: Trauma and aesthetic transformation in the virtual feminist museum.* Manchester University Press.

Pratt, M. L. (2008). *Imperial eyes: Travel writing and transculturation* (2nd ed.). Routledge.

Price, E., & van Eeden-Wharton, A. (2023). Spiderly sympoiesis: Tensegral tentacularity and speculative clews. *Qualitative Inquiry, 29*(1), 179–199. https://doi.org/10.1177/10778004221099566.

Rose, D. B. (2011). *Wild dog dreaming: Love and extinction.* University of Virginia Press.

Rose, D. B. (2013). In the shadow of all this death. In J. Johnston & F. Probyn-Rapsey (Eds.), *Animal death* (pp. 1–20). Sydney University Press.

Samuelson, M., & Lavery, C. (2019). The oceanic south. *English Language Notes, 57*(1), 37–50. https://doi.org/10.1215/00138282-7309666.

Sinclair, I. (2003). *London orbital.* Penguin.

Tuana, N. (2008). Viscous porosity: Witnessing Katrina. In S. Alaimo & S. Hekman (Eds.), *Material feminisms* (pp. 188–213). Indiana University Press.

van Eeden-Wharton, A. (2019). Review: Walking methodologies in a more-than-human world: WalkingLab. *CriSTAL: Critical Studies in Teaching & Learning, 7*(1), 113–116. https://doi.org/10.14426/cristal.v7i1.187.

van Eeden-Wharton, A. (2020). Salt-water-bodies: From an atlas of loss. PhD dissertation, Stellenbosch University. http://hdl.handle.net/10019.1/108209.

van Eeden-Wharton, A. (2023). Ultramarine: On aftermaths, afterlives and afterimages. In K. Murris & V. Bozalek (Eds.), *In conversation with Karen Barad: Doings of agential realism* (pp. 105–126). Routledge.

Wohlfarth, I. (2006). Et cetera? The historian as chiffonnier. In B. Hanssen (Ed.), *Walter Benjamin and The Arcades Project* (pp. 12–32). Continuum.

Zylinska, J. (2016). Photomediations: An introduction. In K. Kuc & J. Zylinska (Eds.), *Photomediations: A reader* (pp. 7–17). Open Humanities Press.

7

INDIAN OCEAN SEA BEANS

Affective methods in museum archives

Kristy Stone

Before arriving in Madagascar I started to research the history of the island, looking for links with South Africa that would support my work on oceanic aesthetics. Most of the literature I found was either traditional anthropology very specific to certain regions or the vague mention of Malagasy slaves in the Cape. However, shortly after I arrived in Andoany (formerly Hell-ville) in Nosy Be, I became ill with an ear infection. I was feverish, exhausted, in pain and unable to hear most of what was happening around me. I found this illness distressing because I had planned to conduct research and was interested in finding sacred and powerful objects in local museums, but was physically unable. I was forced to slow down and, with great difficulty, to let go of my research plans.

One evening, walking along the beach, I started collecting sea beans that had washed up on shore. I picked up one of the beans and shook it, something rattled. This was an intriguing sensation – it felt like something was living, safely hidden inside the protective shell. The experience ignited my imagination, and became the guiding concept in my work. I remembered finding beans like this on the beaches in KwaZulu-Natal. Was this bean the link between South Africa and Madagascar I had been looking for? I was thinking about the movement of people and how these travelling plants – tied into a cyclical history – bear the physical traces of both land and sea. I was captivated by this bean and began researching it, finding several names, uses and histories associated with it.

(Author's journal entry, 22 April 2018, Andoany,
Madagascar field trip)

Ntindile (or *Entada rheedii*) sea beans are to be found throughout the Indian Ocean region. Their vines grow in mangroves, and their seeds, which grow inside enormous

DOI: 10.4324/9781003355199-7

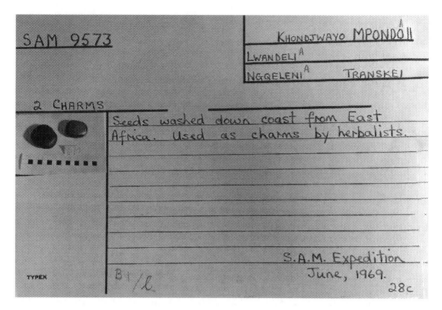

FIGURE 7.1   Catalogue Card, Iziko Social History Archives, Cape Town, South Africa (formerly S.A.M South African Museum). Photo: Kristy Stone.

pods, variably make their way to the sea where they can float for several years before washing up on near or distant shores. In this chapter, I discuss my interaction with a pair of beans held in the Iziko Social History Archive in Cape Town, South Africa. On the catalogue card (Figures 7.1) the beans are described as: "*2 charms. Transkei. South African Museum Expedition, June 1969*". My decision to work in ethnographic collections and to focus on objects classified as 'charms' is motivated by a concern that they are subject to a kind of ontological injustice within museum and archival practices. These objects, along with other 'everyday' items held in archival collections, continue to be discredited by the persistent use of colonial categorisations and bely a scientific arrogance that turns the metaphysical practices of Others into irrational 'beliefs' and superstitions – not to be taken seriously. The driving question with all of the museum objects I work with, is what does it mean for *me* to take these objects and their informing epistemes seriously? What does it mean to be affected, challenged, and changed through engagement with *objects of power* from different cultural or historical contexts?

Working with expanded theories of affect in the context of museums and archives – under the rubric of ocean as method – opens up several new ways of engaging with these types of collections.

The sea beans speak directly to the idea of nomadicy (Braidotti, 2011); of movement and exchange, and in so doing, destabilise land-based notions of identity and indigeneity. In museums, where objects tend to be thought of as static,

FIGURE 7.2   Sea beans collected in Nosy-Be, Madagascar. Photo: Kristy Stone.

categorised and stored out of circulation, the sea bean brings forth the opposite and invokes the heuristic of the ocean as a method (Figure 7.2). Following Clifford (2013), the oceanic method proposed here, is by no means a sovereign one, it is fluid, adaptable, and a continual creative experiment.[1] In this way, each object raises different questions, and the suitability of the method arises through a process of engagement – largely driven by the object itself (Manning, 2015; Hickey-Moody & Page, 2015).[2] The sea beans brought an unexpected richness of plant knowledge, texts, stories, and an oceanic life infused with the concepts of floating, archives, and sound. These diverse and, at times, disparate engagements are organised into six-story rushes, following Anna Tsing (2015, p. 37) who states that to, "… listen to and to tell a rush of stories is a method. And why not make the strong claim and call it a science, an addition to knowledge?"

In searching for a way of working with the bean and all the stories that it elicited, I found the writings of Anna Tsing (2015) most helpful, and particularly her concept of a rush of stories. A rush of stories is nonlinear, it is not a master narrative – history told from one person's perspective. It may also imply a convergence of several stories from multiple temporalities and of histories surfacing. There is a disorder in a rush, one that does not obey hierarchies, taxonomies or kinships. Rushing has a sense of urgency – what are the stories that are rushing to be told in our time?[3] Stories of dis-ease, looming ecological disaster, along with a return of the mythic and older ways of healing. Tsing argues that through capitalist investment, humans, and nonhumans have been made to stand alone, as mobile assets, and the entanglements of the living have been ignored (see Haraway 2016). Similarly, following Foucault, Monika Bakke (2016, p. 119) suggests in the premodern era, "a living being was characterised not only by its actual body features but also by all sorts of old and new stories involving it, such as travel, medical, literary, and philosophical narratives". Acknowledging an interconnectedness in life (past and present, nature/cultures) is fundamental to finding new ways of researching and knowledge making. When a rush of stories is considered a scientific method, we reclaim our capacity to honour experience, to be moved and to explore what mystifies us (Stengers, 2012). The following rush of stories – both directly and obliquely related to the sea bean – enact an oceanic method. The stories are gathered by more than just sea-bound content but by the properties of interconnectedness and the cyclical nature of memory and migration.

Rush 1: *Perim-kaku-valli*

Perim-kaku-valli, in Portuguese and Belgian Gairo; is a plant growing beyond Mangatti and other places; always green and having mature or immature fruits, are numbered among merchandise, because the use of beans which promotes the belly and vomiting …

(Van Rheede, 1688)

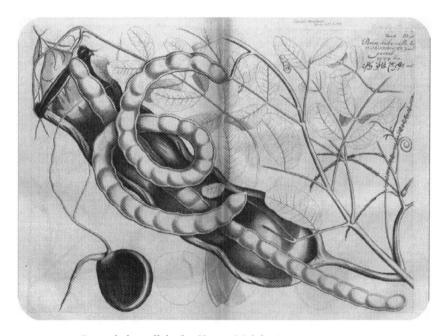

FIGURE 7.3 *Perim-kaku-valli* in the *Hortus Malabaricus*.

Perim-kaku-valli (Figure 7.3), as it is named in the *Hortus Malabaricus* was reclassified according to the Linnaean system as *Entada rheedii*, along with several other plants from the Malabar coast which were named for Hendrik Adriaan van Rheede tot Drakenstein (Lord of Mijdrecht). The genus *Entada* is derived from the Portuguese word *dentado*, meaning 'toothed'; describing the projection on the stems and leaves of some species (Hoveka, 2017).

Botanical Classifications:
Order: Fabales
Family: Fabaceae
Genus: *Entada*
Species: *E. rheedii*
Binomial name: *Entada rheedii* Spreng
Author: Spreng

Van Rheede was born into a noble family in Amsterdam in 1636 and appointed as the Dutch Governor of Malabar based in Cochin (Kerala, India) between 1670 and 1677. Shortly after his appointment as Governor Van Rheede began a private project of researching the plants of the Western Ghats resulting in the epic twelve-volumed *Hortus Malabaricus* (meaning 'Garden of Malabar') published in Amsterdam between 1678 and 1693.[4] With support from the King of Cochin, he assembled a team of approximately 200 people, including an advisory board of fifteen or sixteen scholars which included physicians, botanists, three Brahmin priests, an Ezhava physician, a Carmelite priest, and a Dutch minister (Manilal, 1980; Meeuse & Heniger, 1988).

Van Rheede believed the *Hortus Malabaricus* would contribute to the VOC knowledge of the flora and particularly medicinal plants and that it would be cheaper and more effective if the VOC made use of local plants for medicines (Heniger, 1980). The provision of medicine to their employees throughout the Malay Archipelago was a constant struggle for the VOC. The surgeon's shop in the castle in Batavia was the main supplier of medicines to passing ships and surgeons stationed in trading posts across the Dutch East Indies. Although most of the medicines were brought from Europe, many may have originated in India and by the time the medicines arrived in Batavia many of them had lost their efficacy. Van Rheede's research into the vegetation of Malabar was however, not supported by the Company, and as a result, the laboratory in Cochin he had set up in 1675 for pharmaceutical research was closed three years later by the High Government in Batavia (Heniger, 1980).

The 742 plants in the *Hortus Malabaricus* were collected and recorded in a period of less than three years between 1674 and 1676. The plants are described in great detail – the colour, smell, and taste of various parts of the plants are recorded. The description of the plants follows a strict schema: root, trunk or stem, leaf, flower, fruit, and seed. The shape and arrangement of leaves, the numbers and forms of petals, and stamens and pistils are shown. Information on habitat, seasonal flowering and fruiting is given. A collaboration of Europeans and Malabari, the *Hortus Malabaricus* gives the plant names in Malayalam (the language of Malabar), Konkani (the language of Brahmin priests), which are transcribed into Roman alphabet in Dutch or Portuguese and in most cases also into Arabic. As van Rheede acknowledges in the introduction, most of the information in the volumes about the medicinal powers of plants in the *Hortus Malabaricus* was provided by Itti Achuden, an Ezavah *vaidyan* (physician) also known as 'toddy-tappers' (makers of palm wine). Achuden, Ezhava the reader is told, drew much of his knowledge of plants and healing from inherited family manuscripts (Heniger, 1980).

Prior to British colonial rule, medicine in India was not a unified system; indigenous health care was practised by an ensemble of innumerable caste and social groups.[5] In the nineteenth century, following the introduction of Western biomedicine, Ayurveda came under pressure to prove itself as a 'Hindu science'. At this time many indigenous healing practices, including Ezhava medical systems in Kerala, were largely subsumed under the umbrella of Ayurveda and it is difficult to re-constitute this medical episteme as it was (Banerjee, 2012). After two decades of research, K.S. Manilal believes that the *Malabaricus* is the only existing record of Ezhava manuscripts, making the *Malabaricus* an invaluable source of indigenous knowledge (Cleetus, 2007). Malavika Binny (2015), however, contends this idea, arguing that the information has been distilled in such a way that it is bereft of any epistemic semblance, and that Ezhava traditions would not separate the medicinal uses of the plant from their magical properties. For Binny, the *Malabaricus* is largely a story of European expansionism and concerns for cultivating plants for commercialisation. Adding complexity to the questions of differing medical practices, it is worth noting that in Kerala, Ayurveda (a high-caste Brahmic tradition), and Unani (from Mappila Muslims in Kerala) are both theories of humoralism, and therefore, it is likely that the encounter with the dominant Indian medical philosophies would, in its broad outlines, have been recognisable to the Dutch (Banerjee, 2012, p. 29). By the seventeenth century, European botanists had worked out elaborate classification and hierarchical systems, however, it was not until 1753 that Linaé would set the standards for species and genus classifications – almost 100 years after the publication of the *Malabaricus*. The common system of medicine practised in Europe between the sixteenth and eighteenth centuries were largely drawn from ancient Greek-Arabic philosophies of alchemy and bodily humours, and it is likely that these informed van Rheede's understanding of illness and medicine.[6]

Rush 2: Evil eye talisman

"Amulets were worn by men, women and children throughout southern Europe in the 19th century. Before the development of modern medicine, fevers, cramps

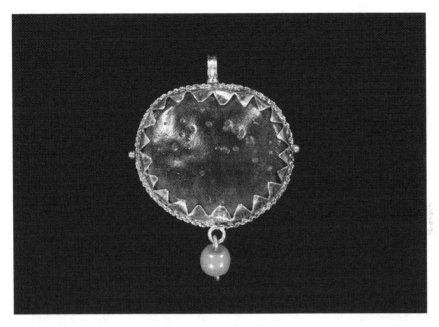

FIGURE 7.4 "Evil Eye Talismans" Spain circa 1800, Victoria and Albert Museum, London.

and toothache could be painful and dangerous. Many people believed that the supernatural powers embodied in an amulet could promote fertility and good health and offer protection against malign forces or the 'evil eye'" (Victoria and Albert Museum, 2009).

The Evil Eye talismans from Spain (Figure 7.4) remind us of Southern Europe's Islamic heritage and its ties to the Indian Ocean world, inviting us to consider the instability of the terms 'West' and 'Europe' – important in a discussion of 'Western' medicine. The Victoria and Albert (V&A) Museum's explanation of these 'talismans' is revealing of a blindspot in thinking about biomedicine as a history of progress. Terms such as 'folk medicine', 'magical', 'pre-logical', 'proto-scientific' are all based on the idea that Western medicine has evolved from 'belief' to science.[7] Non-Western or Western medical practices tend to be interpreted as early stages of modern medicine; shrouded in superstition and in which people had limited knowledge of the pharmacological properties of plants and animals (Good, 1993). When explaining the use of 'charms' Western museums may accept that there are personal and cultural interpretations of disease, but, disease itself is thought of as natural and therefore outside of culture (Good, 1993, p. 68). In this way, Enlightenment views of the 'salvation of science' still have great force in the domain of medicine as shown in the contemporary write up on the V&A Museum website (Good, 1993, p. 2).

The point here is not to set indigenous healing in opposition to biomedicine. To do so would be to assume that these are stable entities, and rely heavily on generalised and romanticised notions of indigeneity – as something that can be 'returned to' – and oversimplified notions of science. As the *Entada rheedii* sea bean shows, the history of medicine is polyphonic, involving networks of knowledge transfer and exchange, however, medical exchange is also implicated in colonial rule, imperial bio-prospecting and knowledge hierarchies and it is therefore necessary to reveal the persisting 'rules of practice' (Smith, 1999, p. 22).

Rush 3: Ntindile

I eat medicines that work in my body like matches to dry wood. I do not open my eyes. It is not with my eyes that I see. My ancestors see for me. I see in a dream.

(The Diviner Mahube to Kuper 1942: 167–168, in Sobiecki, 2008)

In KwaZulu-Natal the sea beans are called *ntindile* and used by sangomas to induce lucid dreaming for communication with ancestors (Figure 7.5).[8] Sangomas derive their power from the ancestors and trance, the use of divining bones, and dreams

FIGURE 7.5 Ntindile necklace bought from the Victoria Street Muthi Market, Durban, KwaZulu-Natal, South Africa. Photo: Kristy Stone.

serve as a means for the diviner to establish a direct link with ancestors who 'live' in the spirit world (Cumes, 2013, p. 59). Learning to interpret dreams is part of a diviner's training, and Zulu sangomas are described as "developing a soft head" that is "a house of dreams" (Hirst, 2005, p. 1). It is in dreams that ancestors often tell sangomas which plants to use for remedies and where to find them. Importantly, a plant's botanical classification does not automatically determine its powers to heal. While the plants used by sangomas may have isolatable pharmacological properties, the effectiveness of the *muti* is dependent on several other contributing factors that may be as important as the plant's species for example, the conditions of harvesting, time of day, area, stage of growth (Irigaray & Marder, 2016; Thornton, 2017; Ellis, 2018; Laplante, 2009). Whether or not these beans are picked directly from vines, or collected having been washed up on shore, may make a difference to their effectiveness. As a healer explained, when the *ntindile* bean washes up from the sea, it has come from the realm of the Sea People (*Abantu Baselwandle*) that is not accessible to humans. The bean has been part of this mysterious world and absorbing the energy of something outside of human knowing or experience. Medicine is not just about the physical act of taking something, it is also psychic and energetic. Even the act of finding the *ntindilie* bean can be the medicine if you are able to recognise that this bean is a gift from your ancestors. It is a gift because you are not entitled to it (pers. comm.).

Rush 4: African Dream Bean

Sold online as an aid to lucid dreaming, the African Dream Bean (Figure 7.6) is one of the many plant entheogens used by a subcultural group of researchers referred to as psychonauts ("sailors of the soul"). Psychonauts voluntarily subject themselves to altered states of consciousness in order to better understand the workings of the mind and for metaphysical understanding (see for example, Brown, 2016). Altered states of consciousness are achieved in several ways, and include the use of psychedelic drugs, dream aids, trance, meditation, and sensory deprivation. This form of self-experimentation using psychoactive drugs began in the early twentieth century with Western psychologists and other scientists interested in ideas of consciousness. Heinrich Klüver (1926) experimented with nitrous oxide, Aldous Huxley (1954) used mescaline (peyote), Albert Hoffman, John C. Lilly and Timothy Leary experimented with LSD, and Carlos Castenada worked with peyote, datura, and psilocybin. Today, leading psychiatrists, neuro-scientists, philosophical, and public thinkers advocate for the use of plant entheogens in their fields.

In this realm, plants that bring about altered states of consciousness are referred to as entheogens and "plant teachers". As Kenneth Tupper (2002) explains, the conundrum of classification of plant entheogens as drugs is an ontological problem. Due to the fact that many of the substances used (plant based and designer drugs) are deemed illegal, a new category of e-psychonauts has emerged on (mostly) private networks. Access to these forums is carefully restricted and it is here that

FIGURE 7.6   African Dream Bean. Image from The Dream Joint website: www.thedre
amjoint.com.

people share their 'trip results', and detailed instructions for the preparations of
various medicines and settings for intake. Since not all plant entheogens have been
classified as drugs, for example the African Dream Bean (*Entada rheedii*) and
African Dream Root (*Silene capensis*) there are several online shops that sell it to
the public. References to the bean can be found in forums where people share their
experiments and first-hand experiences. Many of these describe encountering an
existential intelligence (rather than a spiritual intelligence) which can be broadly
defined as a heightened ability to experience and attend to the cosmological
enigmas.[9] Psychedelic New Age spirituality, including psychonauts but particularly
the subgroup of neoshamans, have been criticised for the impact of entheogen
tourism and their appropriation of indigenous medicine and culture (Tupper, 2008).
The online forums of psychonauts however also represent a highly connected and
independent research community where experimentation is vividly narrated and
valued as contributing to the field of consciousness research.

Rush 5: Private Ntindile

In 1917, the *SS Mendi* set sail from Cape Town carrying 882 black men who had
joined the Commonwealth Labour Crew and were on their way to assist British

troops fighting in the First World War. En route to France, after a month at sea, the SS Mendi was struck by a cargo ship *SS Darro* travelling at high speed. The damage to the *SS Mendi* was severe, and the ship began to sink rapidly, and 607 Black men, 9 White men, and 33 crew members died in the icy waters. Private Ntindile body, like almost all of the drowned men, was not found, and his name appears on the *Hollybrook Memorial to the Missing*, Southampton, UK (South African Delville Wood Commemorative Museum Trust, 2017).

As part of the countrywide commemorations held in Atteridgeville on 21st February 2017 to mark the centenary of the sinking of the SS Mendi, military soldiers, residents, and school children in paid tribute to the men who lost their lives. Lebogang More, who had been trying to find the record of her great-grandfather's presence on the *SS Mendi*, explained that "He showed up in a very vivid dream – because at the time we did not know they were using the wrong name for him – he said he was one of the men who washed up in Britain and he said if you look into the records you will find that only the surname you will recognise, because the name that was used was wrong (Szabo, 2019)".[10]

As the *Mendi* was sinking, Reverend Isaac Wauchope Dyobha comforted the black soldiers by urging them to stand courageously together. Ending his speech with the following words, "Raise your cries brothers, for though they made us leave our weapons at home, our voices are left with our bodies" (Clothier, 1987). Following his rallying call, the men subsequently removed their boots and fearlessly began stomping, dancing the death drill as they went down with the ship. While there has been some debate as to whether the death dance did happen, equally, one might ask why this haunting myth is subject to this line of truth enquiry at all? As KaCanham asserts, what this story does is remind us to consider the many forced Oceanic crossings of black people, and to imagine how ships carrying slaves would have reverberated with dances, singing, and the cries of those who were reduced to human cargo (Hugo KaCanham, 2023). In Rev. Dyobha's moving sermon, he reminds the men facing their death on the *Mendi*, "your voices are left with your bodies". The soundscape of the middle passage is, in narrative accounts of captors, described as the "noise" of the slaves – cries, groans, shrieks, complaints – reverberating through the ship "reminded the captain and crew that their cargo was one that could think, feel, and act" (Skeehan, 2021). Danielle Skeehan (2021, also see Gilroy, 1956) suggests that in the colonial accounts of slave routes, we can listen for the sounds of histories sunk in the sea. The sea remembers those histories that are absent that were willfully omitted from the archives, it is "a reliable vault" (KaCanham, 2023). The sea, as described by KaCanham, is keeper of "tribal memory – a repository of black, enslaved and indigenous peoples memory – that refuses suppression". The ocean cleanses and can be used to combat evil, and is simultaneously the holder of historical trauma, therefore it is critical to making sense of black possession.

Conclusion: Returns

Engaging the idea of *sea as memory* in relation to Indian and Atlantic oceans, Baderoon explains that "slavery binds these two bodies of water, but the oceans are also a connecting tissue to memories of a life before and outside of slavery and the promise of return" (Baderoon, 2009, p. 95). "In this vision, the Atlantic and Indian Oceans are the oceans of middle passage, but also of cosmology, memory, and desire, tracked in the movement, language and culture of enslaved and dominated people" (Baderoon, 2009, p. 91). This kind of longing for return is contained in the following account written in 1775 by the French poet E. de Parny in Reunion describing the plight of Malagasy slaves:

> Their country (Madagascar) is two hundred leagues from here. They imagine themselves, however, listening to the cock's crow and recognising the smoking pipes of their comrades. Sometimes twelve or fifteen of them steal away, carrying a pirogue and give themselves up to the waves. They almost always lose their lives, and it is a small thing when one has lost one's freedom.
>
> *(Campbell, 2004, p. 63)*

FIGURE 7.7   The "charm" drawer, Iziko Social History Archives. Photo: Kristy Stone.

It was when I returned from Madagascar that I discovered the two *Entada rheedii* beans in the 'charm' drawer at Iziko Social History Archive (Figure 7.7). There is a chance that I had seen it before and had a subconscious memory of them. This is easier to accept than the idea there might be other forces at work. It is worth noting that the only information, other than the region they are from, is that they are charms. An entire ontology, related healing practices and intersecting stories reduced to a belief in 'charms'.

Following the Savoy and Sarr Report on the Restitution of African Cultural Heritage (2018), museums are showing a growing commitment to the return of African artworks and artefacts from European and North American museums (Hicks, 2020, 2021; Harris, 2022; Porterfield, 2022). Ciraj Rassool (2019) insists that while repatriation of objects is long overdue, and a meaningful move towards decolonisation, the return of objects does not cancel debts that arise from a colonial past. Decolonisation, as Rassool explains, is not a once-off event, it is a process of unsettling that cannot be rushed. Returns need to be understood as part of a process of establishing a new agenda, a new ethics, and new concepts of personhood – where the ontological boundaries between human and object cannot be presupposed (Legassick & Rasool, 2000).[11] While there is undoubted need for change in museum collection practices, the beans themselves complicate any attempts at return – who should they be returned to – are they objects, plants of the sea or land or ancestral items?

Plant medicines are activated by the drum beats, dancing, singing, and trance states of the healers. In the museum, the bean is stored in a silent room, in a dark object drawer. The room's temperature and humidity are regulated in order to keep a stable atmosphere. Sounds are outside, inside the museum archive it is silent – waiting – between resonances and echoes? I like to imagine the seed beginning to grow in its cupboard, taking root, extending out of objectness, and into living being. As one sangoma suggested, the objects of power in the Iziko Social History Archive need to be cleansed with sea water. Sea water, although the bearer of slavery, also cleanses, fortifies, and connects the living to the dead – a potent image for transformation. However, a cleansing with sea water is unlikely, given the museums' strict policies of object care, but in this way, again, we are introduced to the paradox of the museum's attempts at transformation. It is hoped that the rush of stories and oceanic methods here invoked, offer a creative and generative process of calling forth the layers of memory, history, and interconnection beyond archival drawers.

Notes

1 Drawing on James Clifford (2013, p. 37), "No sovereign method is available, only experiments working outside the frozen alternatives of local and global, structure and process, macro and micro, material and cultural". *Returns: Becoming Indigenous in the Twenty-first Century.*

2 Erin Manning (2015, p. 52) in her paper *Against Method* explains this way of working without a pre-existing method, is emerging as a new field called "research-creation" sometimes also referred to as art-based or practise-led research. There can be several ways of researching and making and the purpose of these can be varied and constantly changing. Research-creation produces new forms of knowledge, many of which are not intelligible within current understandings of what counts as knowledge. Manning discusses how the processes of artmaking activate and constitute new forms of knowledge, *in their own right*. These new forms of knowledge, therefore, not only require new forms of evaluation, they also, perhaps more importantly, need new ways of valuing the work we do. As Manning explains, by refusing the traditional disciplinary boundaries and obsession with control, prediction and master narratives, research creation is restless and willfully creative, it strives for a poetic release of energy in response to the world (2015, p. 18).

3 For more on a rush of stories see Donna Haraway, https://welcometolace.org/lace/a-rush-of-stories-screening/ and *Staying with the trouble: Making kin in the Chthulucene* (2016), pp. 34–37.

4 Van Rheede joined the Dutch East India Company (VOC) and served with Admiral Rijklof van Goens in several brutal campaigns between 1658 and 1663 against the Portuguese to gain control of the Malabar coast. Van Rheede was an amateur naturalist and his extensive botanical research was not officially sanctioned, causing him to receive much criticism within the VOC and particularly from his superior van Goen.

5 Kerala were the *Ezhava vaidyans* or 'toddy-tappers' who were low-caste physicians, and other medical traditions such as *marmacikitsa, kalari vaidyam* and *kathakali vaidyam*. So called 'tribal medicine' *lada vaidyam* was practiced by travelling low-caste physicians. In addition to these, *Unani* medicine practiced by Mappila Muslims also had a presence in Kerala. Ayurveda, a Brahmic tradition, was the domain of high-caste physicians and was practiced in several parts of India. Unani introduced by Mughals stems from a Greco-Roman system of medicine and influenced by traditional knowledge systems in Egypt, Syria, Iraq, and other Middle Eastern and Far East societies.

6 In the late seventeenth century, the two most notable European studies of plants in Asia were compiled by laymen – the *Hortus Malabaricus* by Hendrik Adriaan van Reede tot Drakenstein and *Herbarium Ambionese* by Georg Eberhard Rumphius. Although van Rheede does not give details of any medical philosophies it is useful to consider the theories of Rumphius – also a VOC official based in Ambon and a contemporary of Van Rheede. In *Herbarium Ambionese* Rumphius writes, for example, "that the leaves of overhanging mangrove trees turn into perches when they touch the water (de Beaufort 1959, p. 58)", throughout the book Rumphius refers to the "spontaneous generation of living matter" this being a basic principle of alchemy. The use of alchemical philosophy was not unusual at this time and alchemy, astrology, mysticism, and the occult formed part of Newton's early enquiries (Ellen, 2016, p. 15).

7 Western medicine, defined here as biomedicine, was developed from the nineteenth century microscopic research and germ theory, and explains the body via biology and the study of infectious disease through anatomy and physiology.

8 In South Africa the sea bean's names are *reuseseeboontjie, seeboontjie, boonbobbejaantou* (Afr.); *inkwindi, intindile, intindili, umbhone* (isiZulu).

9 In reference to Howard Gardner's theory of multiple intelligences (1983, 1999).

10 SS Mendi Memorial in Atteridgeville, Tshwane, South Africa. In the dream, More's grandfather explained that the name, Pinefas, given as his first name in the records, is not correct and that his name was in fact Josiah Magope More (Szabo, 2019)

11 North American and European museums have embarked on significant programmes to bring about the return of human remains – What is not being adequately addressed, however, is that in many cases, the scientific field workers who were collecting the human remains, were also, simultaneously, acquiring items of material culture. Although these

items have been separated from each other within the rubric museum classifications, Rassool insists that human remains and objects should be considered as ancestors (2022, p. 63).

References

Baderoon, G. (2009). The African oceans: Tracing the sea as memory in slavery in South African literature and culture. *Research in African Literatures, 40*(4), 89–107.

Bakke, M. (2016). Plant research. In I. van der Tuin (Ed.), *Gender: Nature*. Macmillan Reference USA.

Banerjee, M. (2012). Ayurvedic pharmaceuticals. In P. Bala (Ed.), *Contesting colonial authority: Medicine and indigenous responses in nineteenth and twentieth century India.* Lexington Books.

Binny, M. (2015). Plants, power and knowledge: An exploration of the Imperial Networks and the circuits of botanical knowledge and medical systems on the Western Coast of India against the backdrop of European expansionism. *Global Histories, 1*(1), 3–20. https://doi.org/10.17169/GHSJ.2015.33.

Braidotti, R. (2011). *Nomadic subjects: Embodiment and sexual difference in contemporary feminist theory* (2nd ed.) Columbia University Press.

Brown, D. J. (2016). *Dreaming wide awake: Lucid dreaming, shamanic healing and psychedelics.* Park Street Press.

Campbell, G. (2004). *Structure of slavery in Indian Ocean Africa and Asia.* Frank Cass.

Cleetus, B. (2007). Subaltern medicine and social mobility: The experience of Ezhava in Kerala. *Indian Anthropologist: Special issue on the Ethnography of Healing, 37*(1), 147–172.

Clifford, J. (2013). *Returns: Becoming indigenous in the twenty-first century.* Harvard University Press.

Clothier, N. (1987). *Black valour, the South African native labour contingent 1916–1918 and the sinking of the "Mendi".* University of Natal Press.

Cumes, D. (2013). South African indigenous healing: How it works. *Explore, 9*(1), 58–65. DOI: 10.1016/j.explore.2012.11.007.

Ellen, R. (2016). Is there a role for ontologies in understanding plant knowledge systems? *Journal of Ethnobiology, 36*(1), 10–28. DOI: 10.2993/0278-0771-36.1.10.

Ellis, W. (2018). Plant knowledge: transfer, shaping and states in plant practices. *Anthropology Southern Africa, 41*(2), 80–91. https://doi.org/10.1080/23323256.2018.1476165.

Gilroy, P. (1956). *Black Atlantic: Modernity and double consciousness.* Harvard University Press.

Good, B. (1993). *Medicine, rationality and experience: An anthropological experience.* Cambridge University Press.

Haraway, D. (2016). *Staying with the trouble: Making kin in the Chthulucene.* Duke University Press.

Harris, G. (2022, July 4). 'The Benin Bronzes are returning home': Germany and Nigeria sign historic restitution agreement. *The Art Newspaper.* www.theartnewspaper.com/2022/07/04/the-benin-bronzes-are-returning-home-germany-and-nigeria-sign-historic-restitution-agreement

Heniger, J. (1980). Van Reede's preface to vol. III and its significance. In K. S. Manilal (Ed.), *Botany and history of the Hortus Malabaricus.* Balkema.

Hickey-Moody, A., & Page, T. (2015). *Arts, pedagogy and social resistance: New materialisms*. Rowman and Littlefield Int.

Hicks, D. (2020). *Brutish Museums: The Benin Bronzes, colonial violence and cultural restitution*. Pluto Press.

Hicks, D. (2021). Towards the anticolonial museum. Museums in motion workshop series: Boasblogs. https://boasblogs.org/dcntr/towards-the-anticolonial-museum/

Hirst, M. (2005). Dreams and medicines: The perspectives of Xhosa diviners and novices in the Eastern Cape, South Africa. *The Indo-Pacific Journal of Phenomenology, 5*(2), 1–22. DOI: 10.1080/20797222.2005.11433901.

Hoveka, L. (2017, January). Entada *rheedii* Spreng http://pza.sanbi.org/entada-rheedii

Irigaray, L., & Marder, M. (2016). *Through vegetal being: Two philosophical perspectives*. Columbia University Press.

KaCanham, H. (2023). *Riotous deathscapes*. Duke University Press.

Laplante, J. (2009). South African roots towards global knowledge: Music or molecules? *Anthropology Southern Africa, 32*(1), 8–17. https://doi.org/10.1080/23323256. 2009.11499974.

Legassick, M., & Rassool, C. (2000). *Skeletons in the cupboard: South African Museums and the trade in human remains. 1907–1917*. South African Museum & McGregor Museum.

Manilal, K. S. (1980). *Botany and history of the Hortus Malabaricus*. Balkema.

Manning, E. (2015). Against method. In P. Vannini (Ed.), *Non-representational research methodologies: Re-envisioning research*. Routledge.

Meeuse, A. D. J., & Heniger, J. (1988). Hendrik Adriaan van Reede tot Drakenstein (1636–1691) and Hortus Malabaricus: A contribution to the history of Dutch colonial botany. *Taxon, 37*(2), 419. DOI: 10.2307/1222157.

Porterfield, C. (2022, April 21). Europe's museums, collectors are returning artifacts to countries of origin amid fresh scrutiny. *Forbes*. www.forbes.com/sites/carlieporterfield/ 2021/10/27/europes-museums-collectors-are-returning-artifacts-to-countries-of-origin-amid-fresh-scrutiny/?sh=734152fb675b

Rassool, C. (2019, November 1). *Rethinking the ethnographic in museums in South Africa and Germany: Mimicry, violence and the challenges of decolonization*. Haus der Kulturen der Welt (HKW). www.hkw.de/en/app/mediathek/video/76713

Rassool, C. (2022). Rethinking the ethnographic museum. *African Futures, 27*, 56–66. Brill: free online pdf. https://doi.org/10.1163/9789004471641_007.

Sarr, F., & Savoy, B. (2018). The restitution of African cultural heritage: Toward a new relational ethics. Ministère de la culture. www.about-africa.de/images/sonstiges/2018/ sarr_savoy_en.pdf.

Skeehan, D. (2021). Chapter 5: Black Atlantic acoustemologies and the maritime archive. https://books.openedition.org/obp/19303?lang=en

Smith, T. L. (1999). *Decolonising methodologies: Research and indigenous people*. Zed Books.

Sobiecki, J. F. (2008). A review of plants used in divination in southern Africa and their psychoactive effect. *Southern African Humanities, 20*, 333–351.

South African Delville Wood Commemorative Museum Trust. (2017). *Centenary retrospective: Sinking of the SS Mendis 1917–2017*. Gunners' Association (www.gunn ers.org.za).

Stengers, I. (2012). "Reclaiming animism" in *e-flux journal*. www.e-flux.com/journal/rec laiming-animism/

Szabo, J. (2019, March 3). Atteridgeville pays tribute to Mendi bravery. *SABC News.* www.sabcnews.com/sabcnews/atteridgeville-pays-tribute-to-mendi-bravery/

Thornton, R. (2017). *Healing the exposed being: A South African Ngoma tradition.* Wits University Press.

Tsing, A. L. (2015). *The mushroom at the end of the world: On the possibility of life in capitalist ruins.* Princeton University Press.

Tupper, K. (2002). Entheogens and existential intelligence: The use of plant teachers as cognitive tools. *Canadian Journal of Education/Revue canadienne de l'éducation, 27*(4), 499–516.

Tupper, K. (2008). The globalization of ayahuasca: Harm reduction or benefit maximization? *International Journal of Drug Policy, 19,* 297–303.

Van Rheede, H. A. (1688). *Hortus Malabaricus Volume 8: Concerning various genera of fruit-bearing and leguminous herbs.* Sumptibus Johannis van Someren, et Joannis van Dyck: Amsterdam. https://archive.org/details/mobot31753003370076

Victoria and Albert museum. (2009, June). *Collections: Amulet.* http://collections.vam.ac.uk/item/O373962/amulet-unknown/

8

LIFE AND DEATH IN AN ANCIENT SEA

Zayaan Khan

Life and death in an ancient sea

Based in Cape Town, South Africa, this is a collection of anecdotal stories of the sea appreciated from the terrestrial limitations of my body and the immeasurable space that memory holds to transcend this. I have learnt that the ocean has a profound capacity for grief, but compounding realities of colonial invasion, ecocide and capitalistic belittling of life have created a critical point in our collective healing, stemming from what Quijano calls the "colonial power matrix" (Quijano, 2007). Poet Toni Stuart reminded me (personal communications, January 2021) of how the COVID-19 lockdown in 2020 prevented us from experiencing our rituals so deeply connected to land and especially ocean,[1] and so I share some of these moments, exposing deeply private practices I tend not to share, but am moved to bear witness to the possibilities retrieving these practices may hold, for our collective deep timescales. I am telling stories of ocean through the senses we experience the world through, navigating ourselves by starlight and the spectrum of life and death, the big ways that both sides of this spectrum somehow hold us through all the tribulations we experience. This navigation also firmly relies on contextualising our sense of spacetime and gently reminding ourselves of the prehistoric time frame of the sea and life itself.

Let us begin this story roughly one hundred years ago. Our family is a blend of many; in some lines, we have always been here along this peninsula that sticks out like the smallest toe of a giant continent, stretching as if seeking the South Pole. In other lines, we can say we have been here at the Cape for four generations, from what we have been told. The story of my father's grandfather is about a pair of sailor brothers who left Northern Afghanistan, one who jumped ship when it docked at Cape Town, while the other carried on to the United States, not knowing

DOI: 10.4324/9781003355199-8

his brother had disembarked. This brother, my great-grandfather, worked in a dairy and brewery, perfecting the art of ginger beer, and eventually opening a business selling bottled soda, first by wheelbarrow and then by horse and cart with his sons, who eventually inherited the business. They lived and worked at the northern foot of Devil's Peak, a walk up from Woodstock Beach, where the children (my father being the youngest) could easily access the beach by walking straight downhill to while away the days. This beach no longer stands and has been forcibly removed to make way for industry; a lot of the land is now ironically used for boatbuilding and repairs, particularly along what is now called Beach Road as a reminder of where the beach once stood. The word "reclamation" is used in this instance; land is "reclaimed" from watery bodies, here in Woodstock, and all along the coast across the northern bay, what is now called the Foreshore. This continues further around the mountain, along the Mouille Point promenade, where the walkway rises above the sea and in some places quite deep into the water table. Walking any of the rocky shore along this part of the bay, even with the many years of pollutants washing through from the city, the rocks teem with life and one can only wonder what the promenade buried. This zone was backfilled with mostly household and builders' rubbish, as it covers quite a height in many areas; so many of the rocks gone, so much of this liminal ecotone instantly buried alive, mummified under refuse, then lawned or paved over to counter "often stagnant rock pools and in effect reclaim this area for future gardening and a generally more user-friendly public open space" (Büttgens & O'Donoghue, 2015, p. 39). This thin ecological transition zone is host to countless vegetable and animal bodies, born into the space that is mostly submerged under briny waters, as well as lying dry for hours on end when the tide moves out. This word, reclaim, feels filled with so much more death than life that a word like 'forfeit' feels more fitting.

Death is not new to the ocean; nor is life, for that matter, but let us begin at the end. It is at this Mouille Point promenade, at the small Three Anchor Bay beach, that writer Ingrid Jonker chose to walk into the sea under the cloak of darkness, seemingly filled with grief and having finally succeeding in what she had attempted before, "to finish everything" (Herbst, 1965, para 1). The ocean here has welcomed death for those who choose it, offering a final resting space as a respectable respite from the harshness of life. For those who do not choose how they die, some are able to choose the ocean as their final resting place, in what is known as a full-body burial at sea. LA Times journalist, Deborah Netburn, describes some stories of people choosing the sea as burial rites. She shares one story of a woman who did not want to be cremated when she finally succumbed to cancer, but chose to be placed in a shroud and released into the sea after having her body stay at home for a few days before her burial. A family explained that her son jumped in with his mother as she was released and watched her body sink. Their family friend commented on this moment, seeing "his warm body, floating above her cold one" (Netburn, 2022, n.p.) as a poignant moment none of them will ever forget.

The Atlantic Ocean has stories of death so innumerable, and many so horrific, that the stories must come with a warning entitled, The Trans-Atlantic Slave Trade. These ship journeys between Africa and the Americas saw millions transported and many died en route, their bodies thrown overboard, sometimes already deceased, but in many cases still alive. The stories that live on in the memories of the descendants of the witnesses describe the horrors of children, of the sick, of pregnant people, all drowned at the cruel hands of white supremacist workers of the first multi-national corporations. I actively choose to remember these people who were buried alive at sea and seek to bring healing in my connection to their watery graveyard, from the shallow waters in which I immerse. Artist Thania Petersen's remarkable embroidered triptych work, *Drowned Bodies Never Die* (Petersen, 2022), is an ode to this, in the sewing of innumerable threads to create an intricate tapestry of woven story "about the Indian Ocean and the people and stories it holds", Petersen shares with me in a Whatsapp chat. The triptych depicts stories of migration between her ancestral homes across the Indian Ocean woven through myth and legend, using powerful ongoing motifs that the artist employs in her work such as land and sea, the passion gap[2] and traditional garb. Petersen describes our knowing of memory as something that will "never die", it is the "personification of memory" and speaks to the ways in which our ancestors exist alive in our memories. Peterson believes that memories are also inherited and the steady fashion in which they ebb and flow in and out of our remembering is in the same way that the waves come ashore, there is a steady reliability, "the ocean just keeps bringing our memories back to us, the ocean stores memory but [also] moves it and releases it" (T. Petersen. Personal communication, 21 March 2023).

The sea is a space that sees so many deaths, both within the watery body and without – the atmospheric terrestrial environment. I started working with death as part of my process in 2015 by journeying through a deep and multi-dimensional depressive state (Khan, 2021), and learning what I could in workshops and courses held around death and *janaazah*[3] processes. Death unfolded into a spectrum of such diversity seen through many lenses. The many ways death arrives to us, all of us who live; what big death (perhaps an eland) means compared to small death (maybe an insect or tiny spider) compounded by the varying environments, materialities and timescales. How death presents, whether before or after meeting ocean, can tell us stories of those ultimate times where life and death merge and submerge. The closest we may get to this space while in life may be in the subconscious slumber that brings dreaming.

Building methodologies from dreaming has pushed my work beyond the fictional realm into a space from which I am able to draw from reliably. Accepting that I am being guided and understanding that my path is already made, brings me a lot of ease and peace, especially with deeper healing work. This land, this planet, has been alive for so many solar returns that the souls departed must be thick beyond this physical world. It makes sense to hear what they say since they speak loudest beyond the veils. When we are born into systems inherited from colonial severing, meaning so many of our ways of knowing have been usurped and replaced with colonial and imperial ideals, we are lifted with our familial traditions and rituals and seek out the retrieval[4] and reclamation of knowledge that has been made extinct through the genocides and epistemicides of our people. Dreams, through their subconscious and vividly animated appeal, become fertile spaces for ideas and stories to live into the conscious spaces (Khan, 2021). Terrestrial animals visit me in my dreams, sometimes many at once and often in recognition; they see me, I see them. Yet, so far, with ocean, it's always me witnessing them, cautious not to disturb their freedom. I arrive at the ocean to see animals visiting too, and I become a silent spectator, not wanting to alarm anyone, but drink in the dream joys that are denied to so many. I once dreamt a family of rhinos came out of the sea from a swim, babies playing alongside their parents, being pushed onto shore in the waves, all giddy and skipping their way out of the waves. Rhinos who knew freedom in excess. I could feel their exhilaration at the freezing waters and loud thundering oceans and the immediate calm that comes after. Another dream saw me trek across the dunes, again and again, up and down over the soft sand. Eventually, at the last hump before the shoreline, I saw a cheetah sitting elegantly, tail flicking, gazing at the sea, looking up and down the beach at whomever else may go there. There's something about the cultural freedom of expression experienced by others (not just humans) that, when placed at the beach, drives this concept home. So often, animals are relegated to national parks and sites of conservation as a method of control, through the waves of colonial rule here in South West Africa (Campbell, 1897) that continues until today. Most notably, hunting and the subsequent laws dominating these acts, dispossessing indigenous freedoms and secured animals (and people) as property, to be hunted, effectively disappearing from the landscapes in a relatively short period (Couzens, 2001). These atrocities have had such resounding effects that the thought of lions visiting the sea, or owls catching moles in the dunes, or cobras cooling off, or families of mongoose fishing in the rockpools, now seems unimaginable. The dreams act like memories from the ancient future, things that were, that I may never have witnessed, but which could remain true, asking me to bear witness to their possibility. I feel a strength in my work is to be this witness for the invisible things, to take these possibilities and celebrate them, to mourn them and honour them, remember them and make offerings as part of this practice.

The dreams come because of the immense death that has been, death in big ecocidal ways and small individual ways. I think about all I have witnessed washed up in the shoreline on beach walks in the city; so many jellyfish and blue bottles, fish, sharks, penguins (once, a beheaded penguin), seals, porcupine parts, birds, insects, egg sacs, sea sponge, coral, the innumerable cities that grow in the holdfasts of kelp. It reminds me of the vastness of the ocean as a holding space for death, for those who choose it and those who did not. The ocean stands in mercy, the place that is the ultimate solution – both to practically solve and draw out healing, while also being the solvent to the dissolved solute of all that has ever existed, the billennia of life and death. Through the grand rotation and revolution of earth, our winds and water pathways ensure that the seas become the final resting place of all, through being blown in or leaching through the ground. I think about the memory of water, especially having travelled through our mycelial, leafy and animal bodies (both in live and deceased states) that must saturate every drop of rain and ultimately become part of this grand oceanic solution. To go back in ocean time, to a time before seas when land masses were all under water, allows us to see what a solution ocean may be. For so much of Earth's history, the atmosphere was noxious, compared to the oxygenated nitrogen-rich atmosphere we thrive on, and that has driven evolutionary processes from the ancient cyanobacteria to today.

A recent paper speaks to a "possible link between Earth's rotation rate and oxygenation" (Klatt et al., 2021), where a shift in the rotation of the planet supported a surge in oxygen, what's known as the Great Oxidation Event. The increase in daylight created more photosynthetic opportunity for cyanobacteria, which laid a substantial foundation for subsequent biological evolution, for billions of years. At some point, great rains commenced and fell for thousands of years, diluting the salts from the land, creating one ocean mass (thus a time long before the movement of waters into separate seas). The saltiness imbibed its way into everything in life, an essence of our tears and sweat, our amniotic fluid, semen and mucus, a fundamental ingredient to our lives, so much a part of us and so vital to everything that lives, including the land from where it came.

I think along the lines of fermentation, of ocean as the original brine, of fermenting at sea compared to fermenting terrestrially. I began fermenting food with brine billions of years old, such ancient solution that it is life beyond every invisible and microscopic thing. The Atlantic here, near where I live is approximately 3.5%[5] (NASA's Earth Observatory, 2012) salt to ancient water solution, and I encourage its use as fermenting agent only if important steps are taken to clean and clear the water, explained towards the end of this piece. The ocean is a space of ultimate *umami*, the Japanese word meaning "essence of deliciousness", which I suspect has something to do with the ocean being such a solution; plant and protein and mineral bodies diluted over the infinite generations. Greek philosopher Empedocles spoke to the origins of seawater, saying the "sea is the sweat of the earth" (Fairbanks, 1898). He was also founder of the four classical elements earth, air, fire and water, which he distinguished by mythical names; Hades, Hera, Zeus and Nestis, but instead of Nestis being just water as we have assumed all these years, Empedocles tells us that Nestis "moisten[ed] mortal springs with tears" (Fairbanks, 1898) – somehow, salt stays more connected with water than land.

Early Greek philosophers pondered the saltiness of the seas, and its nature, origin, materiality and mythology. It was Aristotle who described the flavoured quality of the sea: "Why is the sea salty and bitter? Is it because the juices in the sea are numerous? For saltness and bitterness appear at the same time" (Shkvorets, n.d., p. 1). This taste of the sea is easily sensed as an approach from land: the air quality changes, we can taste the salt on the wind as it calls us. The Greek philosophers distinguished taste in only four parts: salt, sweet, bitter and sour, yet I would argue that the bitterness that puzzled Aristotle is in fact a sea that lays on the spectrum of salt and bitter and sweet, a deep *umami*. This flavour I can also connect to the experience of harvesting salt from kelp, the big *Ecklonia maxima* that creates the underwater forests so connected to our land and seascape. The thick flavour of this kelp can be overwhelming compared to the similar but subtler flavour of other kelp, such as the Kombu family, from the Laminaria species. This harvested kelp salt reminds me of what I can only imagine the taste of merman milt[6] to be, a very particular kind of *umami*, staggering in its savouriness that moves quickly into bitter.

The sea has offered deep refuge for the rituals needed to give thanks or call for aid, and always as an antidote to mourning. The immense memory that the water holds, suspended between salts and plankton, seems to hold just that much more every time I plea. Upon reaching a hefty pregnancy in the heat of summer, the sea formed new meaning as it held me buoyant and cool, my tiny but heavy unborn baby immediately at ease and the symptomatic pains and discomfort brought on by pregnancy were instantly lifted. Being so weightless and cooled in the heat of summer made me mourn for the gravid elephants, rhinos, warthogs and hyenas, all the larger animals depleted by colonial regimes and forced inland, not able to easily access the beaches to release their tension and tired bodies to the sea.

Being so pregnant at sea, I sensed the ocean as fertile, a space where so much reproduction takes place, reminding me of countless jars of whizzing, burping, bubbling ferments, where trillions of lives (Rezac et al., 2018) are born over a short time. I remember the excitement of the final days of that pregnancy, of my dreams being so powerful, bringing respite to the fatigue I was experiencing. We took a last walk as a family of two, full moon had just passed and I was sure birth was imminent. I fell asleep after the walk, a deep sleep, and found myself in big dream waves, close enough to shore and feeling free, the weight of the pregnancy held by the sea. I bobbed in the sunrise and sunset sky and could hear the gushing of the waves, the rumbles and sprays and sheer exhilaration of the water being so much bigger than me, even though I was the biggest I would ever be. The sound engulfed me and seemed to be coming from inside me and woke me up, moments before my own whole ocean erupted and came gushing out of me, signalling the arrival of our son.

Once, with a group ceremony, we turned to the wild sea at *Dappat se Gat*, a beach with alcoves, caves and many stories to tell. The ocean demanded I ask forgiveness; it washed over me again and again, the sea wild and angry, but not angry with me. Telling me to ask for forgiveness again and again, to feel the shame at the atrocities so casually acted out over the years, to continue to tell the stories and do the work it takes towards healing. I sat in the cave and released that shame, salty tears mixing with salty sea on me, salty mucus running down my lips, and out of my mouth as I wept. The sea roared, but with kindness, bellowing against the back of the cave where I was collapsed, ringing in my ears and enveloping the whole of me, the rest of the group disappearing for what seemed like hours. The sea has infinite space, it seems, and the sea does not forget.

On another day, in a quiet way and as part of a much bigger ritual process, we offered white eggs to the calm sea, asking for guidance and calling in community for future works. Just two of us sat and watched the eggs drop into the sea and roll around with the eddy of the wave, their perfect forms looking like treasures with the anemones and urchins. We marvelled and imagined what would happen to these eggs, would they be eaten, by who and how? Would they get hidden and disintegrate?

In seal pup season of 2021, a friend went to visit West Coast National Park and was horrified to see how many dead seals were on the beach, and how many of them were young. He was visibly shaken as he described seeing the dead bodies and the puzzle as to what could be causing this. Flagging down a ranger, he was told that most likely there was just not enough food in the sea. Subsequent research led by Dr Tess Gridley[7] has shown it could be a variety of factors, and it is common to find many of the seal bodies emaciated, or at least with far less body fat than expected. Depleting fish populations are a stark reminder that ecocide is not something relegated to colonial times but is connected to neoliberal policy as "colonial economic policy has always been neoliberal with respect to two important economic spheres, public finance and international trade" (Menon, 2019, para 6). Understanding fish as commodifiable stocks and the destructions of habitats has caused death to ocean ecosystems on a level we are not able to comprehend.[8]

One big factor likely contributing to the large death toll of the seals is the presence of *Pseudo-nitzschia* diatom and their neurotoxin-producing domoic acid. It takes a healthy dose of artistic license to connect the diatom, a young millions of years old, to a super-ancestor like cyanobacteria, which are billions of years old, but the connection is plausible, and what are the diffusions between life here on this planet but time and environment?[9] Dead seals continue to wash ashore along the west coast. On a beach walk, I came across a seal skeleton, a few metres from the parking lot but hidden under sand, only noticeable because of the change in colour and texture of sand due to the decomposition of flesh. I was called to collect as much of this skeleton as I could, not yet certain why, but with clarity that I needed to. This bag sat in my home for a few months into my pregnancy until I had a dream that someone had left a big refuse bag full of narcotics at my gate and at the door from my bedroom into the garden; I was being framed, and it felt like a warning to protect the sacred space of our home immediately. I woke up thinking of the bag of bones and how they needed to be repatriated and began a cleansing ritual that took the greater part of the day and put plans into action to move the bones.

The fateful day arrived and was coupled with a celebration of self and becoming mother now for the second time – a moment not afforded to me as my firstborn happened during the initial Lockdown of 2020. I gathered with dear friends at the sea, we burned plants as an ancestral and spirit offering and gave the ashes with our intentions to the sea. We stood in a semi-circle and as the bowl of ashes was passed around, a big pod of dolphins and seals swam past us southward, where I would later be offering the bones. There were at least 40 individuals, but probably many more. It was a poignant moment; unexpected, but as if they were with us, so close they were to the tidal pool where we all stood half-submerged.

I then moved down the coast to Cape Point for a research trip with dear friends and I, heavily pregnant, went to the sea and offered some breastmilk, watching the white mingling in the eddy of the waves, announcing myself and my intention to offer the bones, and to say I knew of the immense loss they were experiencing, to say I am in the time of caring and nursing my young, my belly protruding as a submission. At this moment, my soul was indeed the biggest part of me, bigger than my belly ever could be, but coupled with this, way beyond the 120 days since conception, I was officially carrying two souls,[10] so all the offerings I could make would speak louder and travel further, especially when given to the sea. It is a moment burned into my memory: the sea accepted the bones so wholeheartedly and rose up quickly to me, almost as if to swallow me too. The tide changed after that, immediately dissipating the calm but I heard acceptance, I heard acknowledgement. My friends, watching from above, witnessed this moment with some concern as soon the area in which I had stood to make the offering became covered in ocean again.

This sense of seeing and knowing, the deep listening to ocean and being witness to the vast and heightened diversity the ocean holds, I began to question why we do not hear about ocean water as a source for indigenous foods. In 2016, when the City of Cape Town was approaching Day Zero[11] and people were saving water from every drop of rain and easing off on the hygiene that water brings, I began to interrogate my water use and thought about how I could mitigate this by using seawater as I lived so close to shore. I started to soak my beans and pulses in seawater, instead of adding salt to freshwater and of course, using seawater as a tool in fermentation. This habit has lived on and I must caution that because life comes from the sea, the sea is extremely full of life, so when harvesting oceanwater for consumption, know that there will most likely be phytoplankton and zooplankton that reside, suspended invisible, and this water must be treated to render it stable to work with. Yes, this means that the processing of this water is a form of plankton deathmaking, as death is an essential part of our continued consumption in health and so we must do so in honour. To process this water, harvest it from clean environments, strain it twice through a fine filter to eliminate fine sands, grit and microplastics, thereafter let it boil steadily for at least ten minutes, then cool. I have used this with great success over the last seven years with many human bodies as workshop students, eaters and creators. To live with the ocean in a vessel, fermenting over the weeks that the recipe takes to develop allows for the slow building of community – both the visibles and invisibles in the jar and the building of community outside of the jar, the flies and people curious to the bubbles, smells and whizzes.

Notes

1 Lockdown was a government issued stay-at-home order including closing down public spaces such as beaches and parks.
2 The common practice of removing the front teeth common in so-called coloured communities of the Cape.
3 Islamic funeral rites.
4 Thank you, Abri de Swart, for the use of this word in this context.
5 known through my own repetitive sea salt refining practice of coastal surface waters, confirmed via NASA's Earth observatory, a measure of salt.
6 Fish sperm.
7 Not yet published at the time of writing but please see news article: https://maritime-executive.com/editorials/what-is-killing-south-africa-s-seals
8 With thanks to conservationist Carika van Zyl who taught me that ocean baselines arrived far too late to fully comprehend the vastness of ocean populations, and thus their depletion.
9 See Behrenfeld et al. (2021) for a similar vein but for diatoms. Also to imagine the stories that these two life forms, diatoms and cyanobacteria, evolved by being so saturated at sea with one another.
10 As is our Islamic belief, the soul enters the foetus 120 days after conception
11 Severe drought experienced in the city in that time saw a campaign urging residents to spare water, dubbed "Day Zero" when the taps would potentially run dry.

References

Behrenfeld, M. J., Halsey, K. H., Boss, E., Karp-Boss, L., Milligan, A. J., & Peers, G. (2021). Thoughts on the evolution and ecological niche of diatoms. *Ecological Monographs, 91*(3):e01457. DOI: 10.1002/ecm.1457. https://esajournals.onlinelibrary.wiley.com/doi/full/10.1002/ecm.1457

Büttgens, P., & O'Donoghue, B. (2015). *Heritage Impact Assessment Sea Point Promenade, Sea Point, Cape Town, Erven 153, 151, 604, 837, 838, 1061, 1141, 1143, 1197 and 1198.* City of Cape Town Spatial Planning and Urban Design Department, Energy, Environmental and Spatial Planning Directorate. p39. https://sahris.sahra.org.za/sites/default/files/heritagereports/HIA%20SP%20MP%20Prom%20Final%20Rev%20 1%2020150324.pdf

Campbell, C. T. (1897). *British South Africa; a history of the colony of the Cape of Good Hope from its conquest 1795 to the settlement of Albany by the British emigration of 1819 [A.D. 1795–A.D. 1825].* John Haddon.

Couzens, E. (2001). *The influence of English poaching laws on South African poaching laws* [Dissertation, Joint Degree between the Universities of Natal (Pietermaritzburg), South Africa and Nottingham, England]. Research online. https://researchspace.ukzn.ac.za/bitstream/handle/10413/5776/Couzens_Edmund_2001.pdf?sequence=1&isAllowed=y

Earth Observatory, NASA. (2012). A measure of salt. https://earthobservatory.nasa.gov/images/78250/a-measure-of-salt

Fairbanks, A. (Ed.). (1898). *Empedokles – Fragments and commentary; The first philosophers of Greece.* K. Paul, Trench, Trübner & Co. https://history.hanover.edu/texts/presoc/emp.html#book1

Herbst, T. (1965, July 25). On the Brink. *Sunday Times, Sunday Express.* https://sthp.saha.org.za/memorial/articles/on_the_brink.htm

Khan, Z. (2021). *DeathLife*. Pool Library. https://drive.google.com/file/d/1OCd6kjm_QQ-CVzgf3s-vMc1FnPDng2Uu/view

Klatt, J. M., Chennu, A., Arbic, B. K., Biddanda, B. A. & Dick, G. J. (2021). Possible link between Earth's rotation rate and oxygenation. *Nature Geoscience, 14*, 564–570. https://doi.org/10.1038/s41561-021-00784-3.

Menon, R. (2019, January 11). Neoliberalism or neocolonialism? Evaluating neoliberalism as a policy prescription for convergence. *Developing Economics*. https://developingeconomics.org/2019/01/11/neoliberalism-or-neocolonialism-evaluating-neoliberalism-as-a-policy-prescription-for-convergence/#comments

Netburn, D. (2022). LA Times Today: Why people pick the ocean as their final resting place. *Los Angeles Times, 16 May 2022*. Retrieved May 31, 2023, from www.latimes.com/california/burial-at-sea-latt-123

Petersen, T. (2022). *Drowned bodies never die*. Embroidery Triptych.

Petersen, T. (2023). Personal communication, 21 March 2023.

Quijano, A. (2007). Coloniality and modernity/rationality. *Cultural Studies, 21*(2–3), 168–178.

Rezac, S., Kok Car, R., Heermann, M., & Hutkins, R. (2018). Fermented foods as a dietary source of live organisms. *Frontiers in Microbiology, 9*. www.frontiersin.org/articles/10.3389/fmicb.2018.01785

Shkvorets, I. (n.d.) Early determination of salinity: From ancient concepts to challenger results. Salinometry: Info-site about the determination of seawater salinity. Retrieved May 31, 2023, from https://salinometry.com/early-determination-of-salinity-from-ancient-concepts-to-challenger-results/

9

RELATIONAL BODIES OF MEMORY, TIME AND PLACE

Hauntings in salty Camissa waters

Joanne Peers

Sea-Place[1]

A long and far drive, not very often. A hot car.
Eventually cold clear water, brown bodies everywhere.
Excited that in Apartheid, I can take my three children to places. Even though
it's not the whites only beach which we drive past or the whites only tidal
pool which comes next, it's the lagoon, it is still the ocean water.
We have a good time.
I remember the feelings sitting there with you in the water.
I feel proud of myself for being able to be in the water with my little girl.
The lycra red costume creeps and carries sand.
So many houses, no place to stay for the night, we travel back home.
Sleeping, salty, sandy bodies on the backseat, mending in time.

In increasing numbers people not classified as White visit Cape Town and its environs. It is difficult for them and even for Capetonians to know where they may go without offending some law or ordinance or regulation. It is even more difficult for them to know where they may go for entertainment, sport, and recreation.

(Wollheim, 1969, p. v)

Introduction

South Africa is haunted. Disorderly ghostly matter/s surface, sink and drift in the ocean and shorelines. The sites of Camissa, ǁ*khamis sa*, translated as "place

DOI: 10.4324/9781003355199-9

FIGURE 9.1 1969/1985/2022. Photo: Joanne Peers' family archive.

of sweet waters"[2], carry the history of colonisation and apartheid, characterised by segregation and exclusions. Camissa is not separate from global waters and land but always already a part of entangled violence of settler colonialism, land dispossession, slavery, transnational labour exploitation, extractivism and omnicides (McKittrick, 2006; Sharpe, 2016). One of the many violences expressed in law in South Africa was The Separate Amenities Act[3] in 1953 which built spatial borders, separating the land, water and relations between nature and black and brown bodies (see Figure 9.1). The presence of these borders and forced separation is a violent history that continues to wash up in the present and breathes into time, memory and space (Hofmeyr, 2019; Shefer, 2021; Shefer & Bozalek, 2022). Bodies digest, excrete and perspire with memories of colonial histories which forms part of the hydrogeological (Neimanis, 2017). With this in mind, this chapter washes over linear structure and presents a surge of multi-directional waves of time, space and memory. I trace the multiple temporalities that seep into my body through the watery memories of childhood, through my womb as a place of life and labour in my early twenties and into my salty hair. I find myself floating in False Bay, a part of Camissa, as a doctoral student in ~~environmental~~[4] education. Experiences and inheritances of racism, the folding, unfolding and refolding of time uncover ghostly memories that float around as I pursue my PhD research. Applying a diffractive and hauntological hydrofeminist lens, this chapter surfaces injustices and violence[CE: violences] of the past/present/future through embodied engagements with ocean/s and memory.

Relational bodies

Sea-Place

The spirit hovers over the deep
What memories sing in the crevices of the surface?
Where do they go when they rise?
Who makes the bodies evaporate?
Who listens to the marks of condensation on skins?
When does the weight make it re-turn a precipitation?

Bodies being pulled, reclassified, removed.
Dragging waves pulling bodies deep into the darkness.
Hands stretching but the water doesn't flow over them.
Breath is taken. The waves demolish the walls.
These porous skins speak of these questions and tell these stories.
Bodies erased. Bodies buried under the surface of colonialism.

She is 9, she is on a bus, my pa is the conductor, she gets onto the train with
her mommy and 3 siblings and all their baggage and watermelon. They are
breaking the law.
I am 38, I get into my car and I am not breaking the law.
I am a stranger, I am asked multiple times "Where do you come from?'

She is 9, she can't swim. She doesn't remember the tidal pool wall.
I am 38 and I can swim in a pool. I am petrified of the tidal pool wall.

FIGURE 9.2   Genesis/1957/2018/2022. Photo: Joanne Peers' family archive.

She is 9, she sits far away from the tidal pool. She is wet. She doesn't stay long
because they see her and her family. She is back on the train.
I am 38, I stand on the borderlands of the tidal pool where the water meets the
wall. I go underwater. I stay and keep going back. I keep swimming towards
the wall.

The ones we no longer see, they are there and here.
They glisten with a saline shimmer.
The ones to come are calling.
My mommy, my body, more than two bodies
I swim because we can't keep drowning.

My journey in water is wild with fear and misunderstanding and yet I keep finding
myself in the ocean. As I struggle to trust the backwash pulling me into the expanse
of the ocean, my spiritual sensibilities are awakened. As I notice the skins and
wetsuits that speak about my difference, exclusions and access makes my palms
sweaty. I am unclear about what to do with my fears and equally feel like the
salty water welcomes my embodied complexities and questions (see **Sea-Place**).
Do the wetsuits hold the memory of access to salty water for the bodies that have
never been separated from the sea? I find it hard to breathe. I search for a place
where the noise softens and reveals a map for calmer waters. I turn towards my
research hoping I will find a language for the complex stories of bodies, land and
water. I read and listen to different concepts and don't find a cognitive grasp or
language to write or express my voice or thoughts. As I make way into deep ocean
waters, I am taken up by Compostist Feminist scholar Donna Haraway's (1997)
development of the metaphor of diffraction. I have heard this word diffraction so
many times in reading groups, papers and seminars. In the waves and sensorial
world of cold ocean waters, I become attuned to a growing expression of this
concept of diffraction. It is gradual and slow.

Haraway (1997, p. 16) proposes diffraction as "an optical metaphor for the effort
to make a difference in the world", one which disrupts the practice of making copies
of originals and sameness. Diffraction concerns itself with patterns of interference
and differences. For Haraway, diffraction records "the history of interaction,
interference, reinforcement, and difference" (2000, p. 101). This concept begins to
appear between the pattern of the tidal pool wall and the water. Karen Barad takes
Haraway's work with diffraction into the world of physics with the bending and
changing of waves (2007, p. 80). Continuing in this line of exploring, Barad (2007)
argues that, "surfers know this phenomenon well, since they are sometimes able to
catch really nice waves on the other side of a large boulder sitting offshore" (2007,
p. 80). I have come to experience this myself when I am freediving and I rely on the
way that boulders and kelp forests interfere with the waves which creates diffractive
patterns. When diving, like in Figure 9.2, I am able to manoeuvre myself so that
I travel to shore or to places in the water within the pattern that is created in the
meeting of water, light, waves, kelp and boulders. Barad (2007, p. 80) explains this

phenomenon as "literally riding the diffraction pattern". Diffraction happens when waves of any kind and interference occur under specific conditions. Barad presents a number of other everyday examples, like swirling of colours on a soap bubble, a layer of oil on a puddle of water or even the way that colours change on birds, butterflies or other creatures depending on the observer's position (2007, p. 80). The phenomenon of diffraction deliberately ruptures and interferes as it performs as waves within the tides of my research process. I come to understand diffraction as reading theory, concepts, bodies, experiences or events through one another.

In the kelp forest the water, kelp, salt, boulders, jellyfish, sand and brittlestars seem to dance diffractively and relationally. In other words, they are not entities or contained bodies alongside one another or bound by physical position or skins but connected across space and time (Neimanis, 2020). Thinking-with Astrida Neimanis (2017, p. 65), I embrace bodies as "neither stagnant, nor separate, nor zipped up in some kind of impermeable sac of skin". Bodies are vital sites of experimentation "rather than a fleshy container or an essentialized object that can be definitively known" (Fullagar & Taylor, 2022, p. 38). I find buoyancy in Haraway's (1990, p. 220) question, "why should bodies end at the skin?" Feminist materialist theories and concepts emphasise unbounded and porous fleshy borders which draws attention to sensorial moves and modalities (Sharpe, 2016; Nxumalo, 2020; McKittrick 2006, 2021). These movements include swimming, diving, dancing, researching, stirring, walking, remembering, sweating and painting; movements that contaminate bounded notions of bodies. Bodies are relational beings dispersed, diffracted and materially threaded through one another. Most significantly for my brown porous skin, I am able to breathe using diffraction as a tool to unzip my body as a bounded subject or individual (Judge, 2021; Murris & Peers, 2022).

I refuse to be zipped up in the in/visibility that accrues to brown bodies and draw on Neimanis' (2017, p. 63) disruption of the perceived notions of bodies as individual subjects that are 'zipped up'. I come to notice the entanglement with bodies in relation to difference, loss, wetsuits, access, place, time and memory. My choice not to wear a wetsuit cannot be reduced to a tactile defence as the zipping up of the thick rubbery skin is a closure and form of containment. A tight black costly second skin, pulling over, rolling on my skin, tightening my limbs and pressing my organs. The wetsuit suffocates my skin and restrictively makes me sweat. I am reminded of Sarah Ahmed's "sweaty concept" which she explains as "one that comes out of a description of a body that is not at home in the world" (Ahmed, 2014, n.p.). With Ahmed, my difficult bodily experiences are a part of the effort and labour that drenches my writing process, especially when tidying up texts and using texts to write bodily stories (Ahmed, 2014). My palms are sweating as I type. My body responds to the wetsuit by resisting its grip and releasing the anticipation of sweatiness because there are too many other sweaty encounters for my brown skin to live through. Researching diffractively breaks the teeth of the zip in its forceful attempts to zip skins of bodies – or at least how Western philosophers have positioned bodies of all kinds: individualised and bounded. The notion of unbounded relational subjects helps me remember and listen with my skin to the ungraspable entanglements with other bodies. Thinking-with bodies as relational and unbounded has become a method for me to wade through haunted waters and diffraction as a methodology where questions leak and drip to make murky the perceived transparent waters of research. In her PhD research, Judge (2021, p. 45) diffractively opens pores and space for the watery concepts to breathe and together we sediment:

> …a world where brown bodies, othered through climates of singularity in the legacies of the anti-black apartheid regime, seek out how to become porous so as to breath better with oceanic multiplicity. This seeking of porousness within climates of breathlessness moves within the trouble of singularity and antiblackness posited by Sharpe, finding ways to world away from the trajectories of singularity. Even in climates of singularity, where the othered ocean is moved toward the black hole of non-life along with othered bodies of blackness, Peers' pores work toward finding breath. This is done through relations within the multiplicity of what is othered by singularity.
>
> *(Judge, 2021, p. 45)*

Hauntings in salty waters

Sea-Place

> *a time to scatter stones and a time to gather them,*
> *a time to embrace and a time to refrain*
> *a time to love and a time to hate[5],*
> *A cold swim with shells under my feet, food in little bakkies in a basket and towel under me. My cup with the etching of my initials JKH under it balances on the tickling grass. The tracing of white salty lines shimmer on my drying skin. My skin is browning more from the rays of the sun. Darker and darker, more golden and more symbolic of its exclusion.*
> *a time to keep and a time to throw away,*
>
> *a time to search and a time to give up[6],*
> *Child me: Daddy, why are we here on the grass, why aren't we down there on the sand with the other people?*
> *Daddy: It's sandy there. We are better here on the grass because the sand won't get into our food.*
> *a time to be silent and a time to speak,*
> *a time for war and a time for peace.[7]*

I am ten, I am 1990, I am coloured, I am not allowed on this sandy beach, I am not allowed in this tidal pool. All around is a time to keep, I did not notice the

FIGURE 9.3 Before time/2022/1820/1990. Photo: Cape archives.

*time thrown away until years later. This story is multiple; it belongs to more
than me.*

*a time to mourn and a time to dance,
a time to tear and a time to mend*[8]*,*

Settler colonialism is the system that determines certain bodies as killable and
exiles them in chronological time to the past. For Eve Tuck and Ree (2013)
these ghosts are not left behind, they are living in the bodies of the present and
that continue to move through time in the bodies of future generations. "Settler
colonialism is the management of those who have been made killable, once and
future ghosts—those that had been destroyed, but also those that are generated
in every generation" (Tuck & Ree, 2013, p. 642). Camissa reminds me that these
ghosts are not only human bodies but include tidal pools, houses, rubble, signposts,
sandy beaches, railway lines and societies (Zembylas et al., 2020; Judge, 2021;
Tuck & Ree, 2013). Ghosts carry the memory of loss and erasure to haunt the world
in its materiality. Ghosts are breathing and swirling in the world. Jacques Derrida
suggests "hauntology" as a spectral domain where life and death are originally
entangled (1994/2006). What vibrates is what might yet have been; imagining
possibilities for living and dying otherwise. Hauntology for Derrida (1994/2006,
p. viii) is "an ongoing conversation with the ghosts of the past; the aim of this

conversation is to invent a different future rather than fixing the past". The gesture of hauntological thinking offers a thickness to the meshwork of entangled lines and invites us to consider new imaginaries of the past/present/future (McKittrick, 2006; Sharpe, 2016). This concept of hauntology comes into being through the indeterminate relationship between now and then, absent and present, alive and dead. Furthermore, it is embedded in the legacy of living in post-Apartheid South Africa (Muthien & Bam, 2021, pp. 3–15; Judge, 2021). For Tuck and Ree, haunting is "the relentless remembering and reminding that will not be appeased by settler society's assurances of innocence and reconciliation. Haunting is both acute and general; individuals are haunted, but so are societies" (2013, p. 642). The ghosts dance across the borders of linear time; the time to dance and time to mourn is not in sequence (see **Sea-Place**). Haunting lies precisely in its refusal to contain, define or express the closure of a time to speak and time to remain silent. My writing drifts in the salty waters where "social life, settler colonialism, and haunting are inextricably bound; each ensures there are always more ghosts to return" (Tuck & Ree, 2013, p. 642). Haunting is not focussed on perceptions, or a hope of reconciliation, haunting concerns itself with acts of resistance and resolution. I re-turn to Derrida's assertion that "justice" or "justice-to-come" requires learning from ghosts and in order to do so, we have to be pulled by and open to their voices and receptive to their messages (1994/2006, p. 221). In other words, our "historical expression, oral history, community perspectives, imagination, nuance, and interpretation" with-in Camissa demands a radical listening and responding as an important entanglement to restorative memory (Camissa Museum, 2022). The past and history is not left behind but rather its materiality is felt in our bodies. How then can "learning to live with ghosts" in Camissa, haunted by racial and spatialized exclusions, uncover invisible questions of erasure and displacement and their relations with memory and place (Derrida, 1994/2006, p. viii)? I respond to this question by re-turning[9] to collective memory and remembering what we have been forced to forget.

In Barad's posthumanism, the past is not simply given, and re-membering is not a subjective activity of the human mind, nor are ghosts only human. Re-membering, a dis/embodied reconfiguring of past and future, is larger than any individual, because past events are neither singular, nor locatable, and leave traces. Memories can never simply be erased, overwritten or recovered, because the past is not "closed" or "finished" "then" bleeds through "now" (Barad, 2018, p. 224). Memory is not a straightforward recollection of the past (Franklin-Phipps & Murris, 2022). As I wander around in Camissa I recognise the insufficiency of memory defined as being in the past. I collect the ways that articulate and register "fluid, embodied, partial, and shifting" (Davies & Gannon, 2006; Morrison, 1987). All memories don't matter equally in remembering the past, "some people's memories matter so little it's almost as they do not even have them" (Franklin-Phipps & Murris, 2022, p. 86). The past is not simply given and the act of remembering is not a subjective activity of the human mind. Memory is not a linear record of a fixed past that can be ever fully or simply erased, written over, or recovered, but we re-member childhoods as an embodied reconfiguring of past and future that is larger than any individual (Barad, 2007). Memory is a pattern of sedimented enfoldings of iterative intra-activity.[10] In other words, it is written into the fabric of the world. Camissa 'holds' the memory of all traces; or rather, the world is its memory (enfolded materialisation). I find comfort in memory not owned by me or as a property of mine nor as a property of my parents, grandparents, great grandparents, but as a material condition and written into our flesh and the flesh of other more-than-human bodies (Barad, 2017b, p. 49). Who and what is able to remember? To re-turn? To restore? To breathe, to resist, to undrown? (Gumbs, 2020). I consider these questions in my entanglement with apartheid and post-apartheid South Africa. I respond by tracing relations with time, memory, space and the ghosts (human and more-than-human) of South African's apartheid and colonial past.

Bodies of memories

My interest in imagining different ways of remembering[11] and following ghosts in Camissa has sparked my interest in finding out more about figurations (Bam, 2021, p. 106). In my earlier introductions to figurations, through feminist posthuman scholars such as Donna Haraway, Astrida Neimanis and Karen Barad, I was pulled in by the ways that figurations play de(con)structively with language, speak, describe the world and tell vibrant stories that sounded like the performativity of ghosts. The more I followed the allure that seeped in whenever I was in the presence of figurations in literature, the deeper I sank into the fullness of other features of figurations. I remember the pull and push in similar ways to floating in a tidal pool and feeling the pull and push of waves.

Figurations afford me an opportunity to see theory, practice, creativity and my faith as an ongoing worlding. Figurations are bodies that move, breathe and act beyond human notions of organising matter and bodies into systems (Braidotti, 2019; Haraway, 2019; Neimanis, 2017). Figurations produce other forms of knowledge which float through research and time. When it comes to research, theory does not precede practice or vice versa, but is a form of doing (Barad & Gandorfer, 2021). For Rosi Braidotti, figurations are conceptual beings which do not define the human condition, instead they offer an indeterminate, complex and ongoing process of subject formation (Braidotti, 2019, p. 36). The more I have explored different views and makings of figurations, the more excited I have become about the invitation to think, notice and witness unusual ways of thinking about the world. I swim in watery worlds with Astrida Neimanis and her idea that figurations are alternative concepts or bodies to think with and are present, "semi-formed and literally at our fingertips, awaiting activation" (Neimanis, 2017, p. 5). This does not mean that figurations are in the world waiting to be discovered, instead they arise and come into existence through specific conditions.[12] The material world becomes more dynamic and entanglements more lively through figurations as bodies or concepts in the world. In my research endeavours figurations have waded into my thoughts, ideas, writing, swimming and making which has created new imaginative and dramatic possibilities for relational research.[13]

Figurations teach me that there is no outside that I can go to in my writing, no way of going outside of a chapter and diving into the next one. Figurations act against the theories of creating organised structures of hierarchical order that place the human above the sea or gender below land or any concept in a linear form. This performative way of writing and creating research lures my body into an unbounded multiplicity of matter, bodies, figurations, language, propositions and visual stories. I am sensitive to the many dynamic moments that absorb into my skin and how I need to continuously think about the bodies reading with and through my writing. Figurations invite themselves into my PhD, speak differently, ask unfamiliar questions and write themselves into existence.

In this chapter, I introduce you, the reader, to the figuration of **Sea-Place**. **Sea-Place** is entangled with Camissa, which includes its people (human and more-than-human), water and land, and cannot be defined by colour, features, race, ethnicity, colonial borders, constructed binaries and boundaries (Camissa Museum, 2022). **Sea-Place** draws on the presence, dynamism and performativity of Camissa as a "common experience of facing and rising above systemic adversity and a range of crimes against humanity–colonialism, slavery, ethnocide and genocide, forced removals, de-Africanisation and Apartheid" (Camissa Museum, 2022). I am implicated in this figuration, in my entangled relation with the water, place, race and bodies in South Africa. I see my implicatedness with **Sea-Place** as a move towards vulnerability through welcoming my personal experiences, theories and memories into writing. Figurations are a form of protest against and a response to haunted knowledges about bodies and historical acts on bodies. With the marks and cracks on my body I dive deeper into forms of response-ability in relation to time, place, memory and research in the chapters that follow. Response-ability means enabling responses and not holding to the idea of making meaning from the outside (Braidotti, 2019; Barad, 2007; Neimanis, 2017). I slow down in the presence of **Sea-Place** as I write with it, in order to keep reading bodies (e.g. my children, dogs, researchers, water, my mommy, supervisor, friends, community) immersed in the performative doings of figurations.

Sea-Place

Forced underground, the Camissa River still flows, lingers, burrows and rages, so do the bodies[14]. Flowing below the borders.

Neither eagle nor serpent, but both. And like the ocean, neither animal respects borders.[15]

"In one spot it was through the agency of the big moles of Camissa [change of term added] that I discovered rather considerable traces on the surface. Their

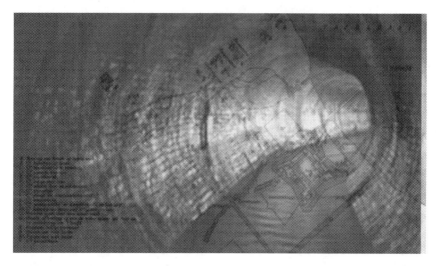

FIGURE 9.4   1900/2013/2020. Photo: Camissa website.

burrows had undermined the sand everywhere, and each burrow appeared to have contributed in its excavation some chip or flake or shard which spoke of prehistoric occupation.[16]"

Sandy dunes revealing watermarks and sites of unusual artefacts and occupation. The moles burrowing beneath the perceived land and sea divide and breaking the divide wide open. A breaking of the shoreline or beach and land divide.

There will be swarms of living things wherever the water of this river flows. Fish will abound in the Dead Sea, for its waters will become fresh. Life will flourish wherever this water flows.[17]

*This is **Sea-Place***[18]

Sea-Place continuously dislocates itself from being bounded by sea or place. It cannot be defined in geographical terms or through the movement of the sea. Instead, it is a figuration that moves through the relations of sea and place which includes the material presence of bodies, ghosts, time and memory. Figurations are tricksters in that they blur the lines and boundaries of definitive ways of knowing and thinking-with concepts (Haraway, 1988). The practice of troubling concepts like land and sea is central to this figuration. It dilutes the human-centric knowledge of understanding the world and offers newer forms of thinking about ways of knowing **Sea-Place** as a figuration that moves beyond the humanist organising of matter and bodies into systems so that other forms of knowledge float through research and time (Haraway, 1988; Tsing, 2015; Neimanis, 2017). It is more concerned with the generative relations and less interested in determinate responses to relations.

As a figuration, **Sea-Place** shifts the stable nature of research stories and murkies the singular ways of thinking about the world. As I re-member **Sea-Place** and travel with-in time, a restorying of memory as embodied and unbounded unfolds (Barad, 2017a; Murris & Kohan, 2021). Memory of racial segregation is a moment in time and at the very same time it lives on forever. The **Sea-Place** stories and experiences cascade and flow through time, which is not about direction of flow but an entanglement of now, then or rather nowandthen. Time in this way is reworked and includes the generations before (not only my parents) and the generations to come (not only my childhood).

Sea-Place questions times' measure and participation in the goings on of learning and knowledge and of what stories we tell ourselves about relations. It also disrupts what it means to be a human (or a collective of humans) 'with' memories–moving as a fleshy unit 'in' space and 'through' time (the modernist notion of the self with, for example, individual agency and rights). Instead, living as porous human bodies without bodily boundaries implies that it is impossible to write 'a' history (e.g. of philosophies of time or an autobiography) objectively in the traditional sense as this would involve power-producing dualisms between self and world.

As a relational body, my skin, like **Sea-Place,** is open to absorption and recognising bodies as leaky. As I re-turn to memories and events in time, my brown skin follows. At times my skin is achy and at other times it is wrinkly, on many occasions it feels tender and it reminds me of how present I am within this writing process. The brown colour is an optical metaphor that diffracts with my writing and sensitivities in this process (Barad, 2007; Haraway, 2000). I am opening up the doing, hearing and sensing otherwise of who I am be-coming as a researcher. **Sea-Place** creatively illustrates ways in which my practice of playing and manoeuvring images, narrating dialogues with my parents, responding to scriptures and engaging with theoretical ideas are part of the creative process of be-coming researcher. **Sea-Place** invites different practices and is a part of the research making as it offers a space to make, remake, slow down the rushing of determinate ideas about time, memory and place.

Sea-Place and my experience of wild ocean water and exclusions then and now. In the case of forced removals of people, place, space and beaches in Camissa, hauntology responds to the ghosts of apartheid, colonialism, racism, and oppression that haunt our time. The ghosts which I am thinking-with are not only in human relations, but the relations that include other species (rockpool creatures) and places (tidal pools and beaches). These relational hauntings entangle, fold and reconfigure humans and more-than-humans.

Sea-Place

"I knew you before I formed you in your mother's womb."[19]

We park where it is open, no price needing to be paid. We are at the park, we can see the water, hear the sea, feel the amniotic waters. Our skins are prickly

FIGURE 9.5 2022/Gestation time/1980. Photo: Joanne Peers' family archive.

with the salty breeze. You are my third, the whole of the street waits to know if
you are a girl. Layers of fabric brushing the forming womb. You swim before
you breathe.

the tiny spaces between the words & footnotes
or the bibliography marked expert scarce the range
flesh and bone don't work that way
blood is even more tricky, defiant of historical text
here at the Cape somebody distilled you down to rape
managed the magma & roughage transported on rivers,
seas, across stone and sand to this thing
Coloured
It didn't carry sweet in the name
Coloured means secret
You live in the great sea of old ships with bloody
secrets chained up in silent memory…
Single stories dirty the air where the lords of history
have cut-throat passions
Coloured…
Nothing about it came cheap

She is the blood of untimely history
is a woman spread legs akimbo across Buuren and
Katzenellenvogen, they say
She is a devastated monologue on a ghost river tongue…
Where water murmurs from the clouds the name, Camissa
She is many skins of the ||Ammaqua…
Her name is Krotoa
Her name is Sarah, Susanna, Pieternella,
Johanna, Amosijn
Her name is Angola, Timor, China, Mozambique
Her name is Ethiopia
Camissa
is the tides that rolled in from every side of our great mountain
and river collecting blood and words
from the stone tablet of Hoerikwaggo's Rosetta
from Thoathoa to the Keiskamma, over land, over sea
to this place
come the children of ||Hui !GAeb
to unburden their stories from labels aggressive with….
this is a story as old as all stories as we shake the devil from our eyes
we love, we lust, we birth, we war, we move, we eat, we live, we die
this is our story
the story of all stories
|coab (blood)
We are the story[20].

Conclusion

Just as the Camissa River was covered over by layers and layers of city superstructure, but still flows vigorously below the surface, so too has been the identity and cultural heritage of the people born of Camissa. But like the river, our hearts beat strong and we are reclaiming Camissa and healing. One of the layers that has weighed heaviest in smothering the real story has been the term 'COLOURED' rooted in colonial and Apartheid racism.

(Mellet, n.d., n.p.)

Sea-Place is about situating myself in multiple temporalities which enfold, knot, entangle, complexify lines and slow down the very nature of ontological conclusions. Through temporal and spatial diffraction time leaks as I am always moving, swimming, thinking, considering, affecting and being affected which adds disturbances and interruptions in my research journey (Barad, 2007, 2011, 2020). This writing is not a representation of a moment from the past or revisiting **Sea-Place** as a bounded location locked in time. Writing with **Sea-Place** now is not an event in time but a coming together of voices, stories and memory (see **Sea-Place** above; Heeger, 2021a, 2021b). In order for me to do justice to **Sea-Place** as an entanglement with Camissa I have to listen with my skin as it reads the stories and memories of my mother, poet, scripture, water and ghostly matter. I have to refuse the understanding of concepts of memory, research, theory, family, relationality and response-ability as separate concepts (Barad, 2007; Judge, 2021). This chapter is a performance of entanglements of ocean breeze, thoughts, porous bodies, memories and struggle. I am reminded about the intensity of its performance as the writing forces me to leave the keyboard and rush to wild salty water. I cling to the collection of re-storying of Camissa, the voyage towards greeting the ghosts and bodies who keep the tides from standing still. I feel the lycra red swimming costume, the way it would creep along my sandy skin when it dried in the sun. I wade in the places of oral memories of my mother and strangers to keep me afloat. My faith and spirituality is unbounded and continues to grow in embodied waves, "this is our story | the story of all stories" (Heeger, 2021a, 2021b).

Notes

1   **Sea-Place** is figuration. It is imagined and actually brown. Working within the limitations of black ink on white pages for published books. Running through these restrictions **Sea-Place** bends and leans itself inside the writing of this chapter and presents its form in *italics* and at times in **bold**.
2   Camissa, meaning 'place of sweet waters', was the Khoi people's name for Cape Town. The city once had four rivers, including the Camissa River, and 36 springs, all of which were channelled underground and drained out to the sea as the city expanded. **Camissa** is the creolised form of ‖*khamis sa*, meaning **"sweet water for all"** in Kora the Khoe-language of the Cape. It refers to the river that flows from the *!areb* (mountain) *Huri‖amma‡kx'oa* (rising from the sea – Table Mountain) down to *huri‖amma* (the sea) (‖amma also means water). This river system has over 40 tributaries and springs. Today the river runs beneath the city of Cape Town. Symbolically, Camissa represents **life** because without water, life cannot be sustained. More generally, ‖*khamis sa* is the Kora name used for fresh-water rivers across Africa (2022, Camissa Museum).
3   "Amenities such as beaches, parks, playgrounds, recreation halls and theatres which at one time might have been open to everybody irrespective of colour are today segregated and are available for use according to the race of the user" (Wollheim, 1969, p. v).
4   Crossing out environmental by putting a line through the text is not about erasing the presence of environmental education rather it draws attention to the categorisation of environmental education as a bounded subject within education.
5   New Living Translation (1996, Eccl. 3:1).
6   Ibid.
7   Ibid.
8   Ibid.
9   Karen Barad explains the difference between 'returning' and 're-turning' through the familiar visual metaphors of reflection and diffraction. Returning is associated with reflection (how light returns from where it came once it hits the mirror), while re-turning is about diffracting (Barad, 2014, pp. 184–185). Thus, if returning implies a going back in time to what once was in linear time, re-turning in research involves always already being entangled with/in a world that is not at a distance.

10 For Barad, intra-action "signifies the mutual constitution of infinitely entangled agencies", unlike the concept of interaction (Barad, 2007, p. 333). Interaction starts with things in relation to one another, whereas intra-action starts with relations.

11 An entanglement of being, becoming, researching, learning, encountering and thinking.

12 "All figurations are localised and hence immanent to specific conditions; for example, the nomadic subjects, or the cyborg, are no mere metaphors, but material and semiotic signposts for specific geo-political and historical locations. As such, they express grounded complex singularities, not universal claims" (Braidotti, 2011, p. 34).

13 "In some ways a figuration is the dramatisation of processes of becoming, without referring to a normative model of subjectivity, let alone a universal one" (Braidotti, 2011, p. 34).

14 The Khoe and the enslaved became the cornerstones of a new creole African population who would, from 1911, be formally classified as 'Coloured'. Camissa Africans cannot be defined by colour, features, ethnicity, or race but by a common experience of facing and rising above systemic adversity and a range of crimes against humanity – colonialism, slavery, ethnocide and genocide, forced removals, de-Africanisation and Apartheid. Just like the Camissa River was forced underground, so were the Camissa Africans (Camissa Museum, 2022).

15 Gloria Anzaldúa (1987, p. 62).

16 Gooch (1882, p. 159).

17 New Living Translation (1996, Ezekial 47:9).

18 Sea-Place drifts beyond the confines of my PhD and this chapter through Judge's eloquent expansion. Reconceptualising "the notion of linings by reconstructing the human as ontologically unbounded." I do this through "a description of "seaplace", wherein [my] "porous brown body" rejects categories of singularity that "haunt" [me] from Apartheid's racial divisions. Here, seaplace is conceived of and embraced as a zone for entangled bodies that exist through 'leaking time', wherein bodies are not silenced as they exist through space, time and matter" (Peers, in Judge, 2022, p. 34).

19 New Living Translation (1996, Jer. 1:5).

20 Excerpt from Khadija Tracey Heeger's poem 'Camissa' (2021b).

References

Ahmed, S. (2014). Sweaty concepts. *feministkilljoys*. https://feministkilljoys.com/2014/02/22/sweaty-concepts/

Anzaldúa, G. (1987). *Borderlands/La Frontera: The New Mestiza*. Aunt Lute Books.

Bam, J. (2021). Feminism-cide and epistemicide of Cape herstoriography through the lens of the ecology of indigenous plants. In *Rethinking Africa: Indigenous Women Reinterpret Southern Africa's Pasts* (pp. 103–120). Fanele.

Barad, K. (2007). *Meeting the universe halfway: Quantum physics and the entanglement of matter and meaning*. Duke University Press.

Barad, K. (2014). Diffracting diffraction: Cutting together-apart. *Parallax, 20*(3): 168–187.

Barad, K. (2017a). What flashes up: Theological-political-scientific fragments chapter. In C. Keller & M. Rubenstein (Eds.), *Entangled worlds: Religion, science, and new materialisms* (pp. 21–88). Fordham University.

Barad, K. (2017b). No small matter: Mushroom clouds, ecologies of nothingness and strange topologies of spacetimemattering. In A. Tsing, H. Swanson, E. Gan, & N. Bubandt (Eds.), *Arts of living on a damaged planet*. University of Minnesota Press.

Barad, K. (2018). *Troubling time/s and ecologies of nothingness: Re-turning, re-membering, and facing the incalculable*. New Formations.

Barad, K., & Gandorfer, D. (2021). Political desirings: Yearnings for mattering (,) differently. *Theory & Event, 24*(1), 14–66.

Braidotti, R. (2011). *Nomadic theory: The portable Rosi Braidotti.* Columbia University Press.

Braidotti, R. (2019). A theoretical framework for the critical posthumanities. *Theory, Culture and Society, 36*(6), 31–61.

Camissa Museum. (2022). What is the Meaning of Camissa? *Camissa Museum.* https://camissamuseum.co.za/index.php/orientation/meaning-of-camissa

Davies, B., & Gannon, S. (2006). *Doing collective biography: Investigating the production of subjectivity.* Open University Press.

Derrida, J. (1994/2006). *Specters of Marx: The state of the debt, the work of mourning and the new international.* Routledge.

Franklin-Phipps, A., & Murris, K. (2022). Memory. In K. Murris (Ed.), *A glossary for §§doing postqualitative, new materialist and critical posthumanist research across disciplines* (pp. 86–87). Routledge.

Fullagar, S., & Taylor, C. A. (2022). Body. In K. Murris (Ed.), *A glossary for doing postqualitative, new materialist and critical posthumanist research across disciplines* (pp. 38–39). Routledge.

Gooch, W. D. (1882). The stone age of South Africa. *The Journal of the Anthropological Institute of Great Britain and Ireland, 11*, pp. 124–183. Royal Anthropological Institute of Great Britain and Ireland.

Gumbs, A. P. (2020). *Undrowned: Black feminist lessons from marine mammals.* Emergent Strategy, *2.* AK Press.

Haraway, D. (1988). Situated knowledges: The science question in feminism as a site of discourse on the privilege of partial perspective. *Feminist Studies, 14*(3), 575–599.

Haraway, D. (1990). *Simians, cyborgs, and women: The reinvention of nature.* Routledge.

Haraway, D. (1997). *Modest_Witness@Second_Millennium. FemaleMan_Meets_OncoMouse: Feminism and Technoscience.* Routledge.

Haraway, D. (2000). *How like a leaf: An interview with Thyrza Nichols Goodeve.* Routledge.

Haraway, D. (2019). Reflections on the plantationocene: a conversation with Donna Haraway and Anna Tsing moderated by Gregg Mitman. *Edge Effects,* University of Wisconsin-Madison. https://edgeeffects.net/wp-content/uploads/2019/06/Plantationoce neReflections_Haraway_Tsing.pdf

Heeger, K. T. (2021a). Camissa. *Launch of Camissa Museum Online.* https://camissamus eum.co.za/index.php/7-tributaries/tributes-of-poet-descendants/khadija-tracey-heeger-coloured

Heeger, K. T. (2021b). Camissa. In B. Muthien & J. Bam (Eds.), *Rethinking Africa: Indigenous women reinterpret Southern Africa's pasts* (p. 123). Fanele.

Hofmeyr, I. (2019). Provisional notes on hydrocolonialism. *English Language Notes, 57*(1), 11–20.

Judge, M. (2021). *The re-orienting ocean: A creative praxis that rearranges human-ocean relations.* Unpublished Doctoral Dissertation, University of Witwatersrand.

McKittrick, K. (2006). *Demonic grounds: Black women and the cartographies of struggle.* Regents of the University of Minnesota.

McKittrick, K. (2021). *Dear science and other stories.* Duke University Press.

Mellet, P. T. (n.d.) The seven steps in cape identity. Asirawan Siam Healing House and SA-Thai Slave Heritage Reflection Centre. https://slideplayer.com/slide/13512891/

Morrison, T. (1987). *Beloved.* Alfred A. Knopf.

Murris, K., & Kohan, W. (2021). Troubling troubled school time: Posthuman multiple temporalities. *International Journal of Qualitative Studies in Education, 34*(7), 581–597.

Murris, K., & Peers. J. (2022). Go-Pro(blem)s and possibilities: Keeping the child human of colour in play in an interview. *Contemporary Issues in Early Childhood,* Special Issue. DOI: 10.1177/14639491221117219.

Muthien, B., & Bam, J. (Eds.). (2021). *Rethinking Africa: Indigenous women reinterpret Southern Africa's pasts.* Fanele.

Neimanis, A. (2017). *Bodies of water: Posthuman feminist phenomenology.* Bloomsbury Academic.

Neimanis, A. (2020). We are all at sea: Practice, ethics, and poetics of "hydrocommons" Astrida Neimanis, RIBOCA2—2nd Riga International Biennial of Contemporary Art 2020. *Mousse Magazine.*

New Living Translation. (1996). *Holy bible.* Tyndale House Foundation.

Nxumalo, F. (2020). Place-based disruptions of humanism, coloniality and anti-blackness in early childhood education. *Critical Studies in Teaching and Learning, 8,* 34–49.

Peers, J. (2021). *Rel*ational Bodies of Memory, Time and Place: Race in Salty Waters. Paper presented at *Hydrofeminism and wild engagements with ocean/s: Towards a justice-to-come in South African contexts* Colloquium, Simonstown, Cape Town, 19 August 2021.

Sharpe, C. (2016). *In the wake: On blackness and being.* Duke University Press.

Shefer, T. (2021). Sea hauntings and haunted seas for embodied place-space-mattering for social justice scholarship. In V. Bozalek, M. Zembylas, D. Holscher, & S. Motala (Eds.), *Higher education hauntologies: Speaking with ghosts for a justice-to-come* (pp. 76–87). Routledge.

Shefer, T., & Bozalek, V. (2022). Wild swimming methodologies for decolonial feminist justice-to-come scholarship. *Feminist Review, 130*(1), 26–43. https://doi.org/ 10.1177%2F01417789211069351

Tsing, A. L. (2015). *The mushroom at the end of the world: On the possibility of life in capitalist ruins.* Princeton University Press.

Tuck, E., & Ree, C. (2013). Exemplar chapter 33: A glossary of haunting. In S. H. Jones, T.E. Adams, & C. Ellis (Eds.), *Handbook of autoethnography* (pp. 639–658). Left Coast Press, Inc.

Wollheim, O. D. Dr. (1969). Introduction. In S. M. Parks (Ed.), *A guide to Cape Town for coloured people.* South African Institute of Race Relations.

Zembylas, M., Bozalek, V., & Motala, S. (2020). A pedagogy of hauntology: Decolonizing the curriculum with GIS. *Capacious: Journal for Emerging Affect Inquiry, 2*(1–2), 26–48.

10

OCEANIC SWIMMING-WRITING-THINKING FOR JUSTICE-TO-COME SCHOLARSHIP

Tamara Shefer, Vivienne Bozalek and Nike Romano

Diving-in

We plunged into our swimming in the ocean practice at the same time that we were working on a project of reconceptualising higher education as part of larger efforts to transform the university. It was also around the pre-COVID time of student activism in South Africa (2015–2018), and the revitalising of decolonial, feminist and queer challenges to normative traditions of scholarship. We were reading feminist new materialist, indigenous and decolonial feminist and posthumanist writings. We were experimenting with alternative embodied and relational pedagogical praxis and forms of research, in efforts to resist dominant representational and extractivist traditions of research (Smith, 1999; Tuck & Yang, 2014).

Our swimming-writing sessions take place throughout the year. We generally meet in the early morning, at St James tidal pool or at Windmill Beach, beaches on the False Bay side of the Cape Peninsula. Our intention is to take our thoughts for a swim, in order to explore how this opens us possibilities for doing academia differently. We put in place a series of enabling constraints that "create specific conditions for creative interaction where something is set to happen, but there is no pre-conceived notion of exactly what the outcome will be or should be" (Massumi, 2015, p. 73).

After brief greetings we gear up. With GoPro and cameras, and wearing masks and snorkels, we immerse ourselves in the ocean. Swimming happens differently each time; on mornings when the water is murky we abandon our masks and bob on the water's surface. On these days birds, cloud formations and sounds carried through air permeate our writings. Sometimes our swims coincide with the low tide in which case our proximity to creatures is much closer and we are able to observe and learn from them without the constant need to come up for air.

DOI: 10.4324/9781003355199-10

During the winter months, the waters are rough, we are tossed about, entangled with kelp, brushing up against rocks, our skin punctured (and punctuated) by urchins. On these days we are disoriented, adrift, our bodies awash with icy salty foam. Like flotsam and jetsam, we emerge from the water onto the shore and hasten towards the coffee shop where we immediately begin to write together on a shared google document. Fresh from the sea, our swimming experiences spill over into our writing. Writing together is an extension of our swimming encounters, our thoughts flow into the shared pool of words. We start with choosing a colour for our text, our choices affected by the swimming event. We write until our words run dry and then, when we are ready to, we read our pieces aloud to each other.

In our desire to share our learnings, we were not sure how to give shape and form to these encounters. How might we do this without limiting the experience? Would it be possible to invite others to dive into the depths with us in ways that create ripple effects of further becomings-with writing and swimming? We set about creating our film as an invitation to others to engage with our practice.[1] The experimental piece comprises a montage of shared readings and writings, diffracted through underwater images, videos and found artifacts that give life to some of our memories and histories.

This chapter is located within two intersecting projects: the critique of the neoliberal racial capitalist academy which remains haunted and shaped by the symbolic and material violences of coloniality, neoliberal capitalism and patriarchy, as well as its firm location in a human-exceptionalist and human-centred paradigm; and global and local efforts for a justice-to-come scholarship that locates human inequalities and injustices in the current environmental crises, acknowledging also the entanglements of global racial capitalism and its rootedness in western coloniality, in the damages and losses to the planet, humans and other species.

Our experimental practice is deeply located in this imperative to *make a difference* in our scholarship in current times of pressing environmental challenges. Anthropocentric ontologies, epistemologies, ethics and politics are prevalent in academia, and have invariably led to dead ends in terms of accounting for our current condition of living on a damaged planet (Carstens & Bozalek, 2021; Tsing et al., 2017; Haraway, 2016). The centrality and exceptionalism of the human, as well as eurowestern individualist logic are taken for granted in much academic writing.

Following an overview of our theoretical framings, we share excerpts from our swimming-thinking-writings that surfaced in relation to the entangled problems of the academy, and anthropogenic damages to the planet and all its inhabitants, including its watery seaspaces.

Reading

A key part of our swimming-thinking praxis is its location in reading scholarly, literary and artistic work.[2] As such we are thinking with a number of bodies of knowledge, some directly related to reconceptualising scholarship and others engaged with ecofeminist and other justice-to-come literatures. As we noted in our introduction, colonial logics, neoliberalism and bureaucratic cultures have either been endemic to, or further seeped into higher education, resulting in the proliferation of managerialism in increasingly corporatised, for-profit universities. COVID-19, which resulted in many universities closing down their face-to-face operations of teaching and research, provided a breathing space to interrogate previous taken-for-granted assumptions.

Increasingly, scholars are proposing and experimenting with Slow[3] scholarly practices, relational ontologies, immanent critique (Manning, 2016; Massumi, 2015) and diffractive methodologies (Barad, 2007, 2014, 2017; Barad & Gandorfer, 2021; Bozalek & Zembylas, 2017) which disrupt the neoliberal combative and individualistic practices of mainstream higher education. There is an increased focus on knowledges generated through embodied artmaking practices towards an alternative ethical praxis of knowledge making and sharing, that is not only directed at 'outputs' but at process. Slow scholarship is one example of doing academia differently through resisting the driving forces of neoliberalism (Harmes et al., 2017). In swimming-thinking-writing, the Slow amphibious scholarship emerges in the buoyancy offered to us as land mammals who are guests to the sea, a drifting with ideas which surface during and after salty immersion, in the thrill of the unknown as we collaboratively traverse wild watery scapes and blank google pages.

Our work is further informed by and located in a feminist eco-materialist approach which incorporates concerns of planetary and social justice. These transversal concerns of social and ecological, ethical and political, ontological and epistemological necessitate a diffractive approach to our swimming, thinking and writing, as experimental practices which generate new insights. Such an approach incorporates the capacity to listen and apprehend our response, our response-ability, to the omnicide of the multispecies world (Ghosh, 2021), which has emanated from colonial extractivism, one consequence of which was the global COVID-19 pandemic. State responses to COVID-19 incorporated various forms of attempted mastery of the virus through regulatory regimes, a fraught and failed endeavour of dealing with deadly matter, always favouring some groups of humans at the expense of others (Bozalek & Pease, 2021). Notably our swimming-reading-writing was practised in the midst of the pandemic, under strict lockdown rules enacted in the South African context, with the asymmetries which were starkly apparent during that time. COVID-19 was an affecting force which propelled us to seek solace in the sociality of seaswimming, all the while painfully conscious of the danger of human breath and the transmission of the virus through microscopic airscapes (Arthur, 2021).

Our work is particularly indebted to hauntological thinking. Hauntology, a neologism invented by French philosopher, Jacques Derrida, is a play on the word 'ontology' – a similar pronunciation in French, refers to inhabiting multiple temporalities simultaneously. In hauntology, we are visited by the uncanniness of the past, which are not necessarily confined to human ghosts but include land, houses and other material phenomena (see Barad, 2017; Sharpe, 2016; Talbayev, 2023; Zembylas et al., 2021, for more on the materiality of ghosts). Ghosts which haunt our seascapes, leave spooky traces of saturated colonial and settler crimes of drowned human bodies (McKittrick, 2006; Gordon, 2008; Glissant, 1990; Sharpe, 2016), disorientate, make, unmake and remake our collective capacities to confront the historicities of multispecies extinctions and oceanic ruins in the thick present. A key part of our project is to confront such necropolitical violences (Mbembe, 2019) in multiple pasts, presents and imagined futures in the seas and their littoral zones (Gan et al., 2017).

Since we were thinking in/with oceans, and deeply aware of our watery bodies and their permeability to planetary and other watery bodies, we were particularly drawn to an increasing number of scholars who are thinking with water and oceans (for example, Boon et al., 2018; Chen et al., 2013; Christian & Wong, 2016; Gumbs, 2020; Ingersoll, 2016; Jue, 2020; Neimanis, 2012, 2013, 2017; Probyn, 2016, 2023). Astrida Neimanis' hydrofeminist thinking was particularly instructive and resonated strongly with our project. Neimanis (2013, p. 27) argues the value of feminist figurations for the ways in which "they powerfully incite an imaginative political space". She proposes the feminist figuration of the "body of water" as responding to a "particular problematic" at a particular moment in time, as she elaborates (2013, p. 27–28):

In purely descriptive terms, we *are* bodies of water, but we also reside within and as part of a fragile global hydrocommons, where water – the lifeblood of humans and all other bodies on this planet – is increasingly contaminated, commodified and dangerously reorganised. In some cases, water's capacity to sustain life is seriously imperilled. It is this hydro-ecological context in which I am inextricably embedded that draws me, with a heightened sense of urgency, to the figuration of the body of water right now.

Neimanis' (2013, p. 28) hope is that the bodies of water figuration will disrupt the cartesian divides that humans live by, the 'cut we make between our human waters and ecological ones', thus realising our entanglements with ecological damage and therefore our response-ability. She (2013, p. 28) suggests that

imagining ourselves as irreducibly watery, as literally part of a global hydrocommons, we might locate new creative resources for engaging in more just and thoughtful relations with the myriad bodies of water with whom we share this planet.

Our swimmings together enact Neimanis' feminist figuration of becoming bodies of water, whereby we think/move through embodiment differently. Becoming a body of water further ushers a challenge to phallocentric Western humanist valorisations of Man as idealised, discrete and self-sufficient, ruler of the world. Not to be confused with metaphor, watery embodiment dives deeper than superficial essentialisations of biological sexual difference between masculine and feminine, gestating instead "new feminist concepts and practices into existence" (Neimanis, 2012, p. 102). In the water, our sense of embodied individualised selves dissolves, our porous skin becoming conduits of watery slippages through which things move within and through, beyond human control. No longer discrete, our fluid bodies are moved by and move with affective currents, at once displacing and being displaced within continual indeterminate flows. Drifting and adrift we explore "aqueous understandings of body and community" in ways that do not reproduce extractivist logics and practices at the expense of the more-than-human world (Neimanis, 2012, p. 107).

Our swimming-writing together is an embodied, speculative and non-representational research and creative practice. In it we explore processes of co-creation with the more-than-human world in order to trouble the waters of normative pedagogies and standardised research outputs. We swim with Erin Manning's understanding of research-creation that troubles 'business as usual' notions of pedagogy as a transmission of knowledge from expert knowers to "those to be brought up to standard" (2022, 173). Manning (2022, p. 173) writes, "It's about swimming with the creative flow of concepts' emergence, being fed and led by it, and inflecting it in return [...] research-creation processes teach us what a body can do as we go about doing it". Linked to this is her theorisation of the hyphen as the differential between making and thinking that makes a difference in the creation of new knowledge (2020, p. 228). In our swimming-writing practice, research-creation finds expression through experimental bodily ways of thinking whereby knowing, doing and being emerge in ongoing and open-ended ways that are both generative and transformative of how inquiry is done and how inquiry might become.

Thinking-with our narratives

In what follows are excerpts of our writings in emerging themes that speak to what matters in our project.

Academic toxicities

Since we were thinking about the university as part of our critical, feminist and decolonial approach to scholarship, it is not surprising that our discomfort with the institution and its violences frequently surfaced in our writings. Viv, for example, who had recently retired and was no longer office-bound, though still engaged with much scholarly work, wrote:

> Swimming every day (more than I did when I was going into work at the university) and being away from those tedious toxic rule-obsessed meetings,

I feel more and more impatient with things that I was coerced to do and should feel liberated from, but don't always.

Tamara narrated her growing dissatisfaction with normative expectations of the academy and how its consumerist and technicist traditions are shown up while swimming, as are the fraught contexts of our scholarly critique. Yet, swimming also brings a glimmer of hope, a sense that the seas contribute to a radical revisioning through the figuration of waves and their constructive (or destructive) possibilities of cleansing and reshaping:

I increasingly fear that I am losing my curiosity for academic language, that I would rather just be in this body and mind and heart, and live simply and ethically than to write about it, or attempt to bring it into a legible format. But how else does one contribute to making a difference without packaging it for human consumption and affirmation? Which inevitably implicates one in the very logics that we critique and reject. Caught between fraught pulls and tensions, the tides and currents, the inevitable sight and sensibility of being human and yet wishing to make a difference – to make a splash, or be splashed or be a splash – a splash that disturbs the normativity and its violences, that brings fresh salt and water and organisms and life and colour and beauty into the pool, to re-fresh and to sustain, to make and re-make, to keep the flow and harmonies, before another flash, or splash, sometimes maybe even a crash is necessary …

Some of the complexities of academic life and its continued intersecting inequalities of power, authority and privilege also surfaced, exposing some uncomfortable and shameful experiences, such as the irony of deploying the privileged status of professor to raise funds for students. In this respect, Tamara, as owner of a funded research project that provides postgraduate scholarships shared the contested location of such privilege and authority, the inevitable relations of patronage, given the hauntings of past exclusions and inequalities in and through the university:

At times in my research projects, I sense an ambivalence towards me as the owner of the research funds, as a white middle class established academic with power through the largesse of funds and other social privileges. How I always feel both appreciated and yet perhaps disliked and resented for the patronage that is endemic to the professor-student relationship especially when it is cut across by raced and classed divides and the particularities of South African histories.

The sharing of discomfort in the position of financial and academic authority also however opens the possibility for realising situatedness and implicatedness in larger inequalities and violences. The thresholds encountered in the sea open up different thresholds, and our responsibility for the violences of past, present and future in South Africa and globally.

Confronting the violences of past, present, future

Our swimming in the sea frequently triggered thoughts of the entanglement of ocean with violences of South African pasts and what so many have written about (Hofmeyr, 2019; Putuma, 2017;[4] Shefer, 2021; Shefer & Bozalek, 2022), including other pieces in this book (see Hugo, Khan, Peers, Martin) in remembering the way the hauntings of coloniality, slavery and apartheid figure in the sea. As Elspeth Probyn (2023, n.p.) comments about white-settler engagements with oceans:

> It is a seemingly easy proposition with an obvious response: jump or dive in. However, as a white-settler researcher, these acts are far from straightforward. To do so unthinkingly could constitute violence against the past and present of so many: those Africans whose bones lie on the seafloor an enduring if invisible testimony to slavery, those whose bodies are twisted by the atrocious labour practices that plague much of the global fishing industries; those whose homes and lives are being swallowed by rising seas; those of the First Nations excluded from their sea countries by settler governments in Australia and elsewhere.

Nike for example, writing about her home beach, remembers the atrocities of apartheid forced removals and legislated segregation that were very specific to post 1948–1990s decades of apartheid:

> Swimming is a life skill that white South African children learnt at school. The beaches were spaces of privileged open access. I grew up in Camps Bay, a little seaside village back then, a white suburb on the Atlantic ocean that is now one of the trendy tourist destinations in Cape Town. In 1985 I remember the so-called crowd control fences that were erected overnight … whites only beaches … markers of apartheid violences, of structural enforcement of segregation. Back then, the only people of colour were the ice cream vendors trudging up and down in the baking sun trying to entice white parents to buy.

Not only did such images and memories of apartheid violences surface, but so too did our privileged irresponsibility (Tronto, 2013) and the imperative to face such privileges and be response-able:

> When Viv and I wrote the paper on swimming, there was a line that Viv wrote about us 'as settlers' and my body and heart rebelled and resisted … 'no, this is not me'. My defensive narrative spills out of me: I am only second generation South African, I am of Jewish descent, my family arrived as peasants, escaping

pogroms and a holocaust that wiped out any relatives who were not in another distant land. I carry around the sharp image of my great grandmother and great aunt, the latter only about 16 years old, standing briefly, breathing hard with fear into cold air, around a mass grave, before being shot into it. Me, a settler? No, I am of refugee stock, my grandmother came out on a boat between the two wars. And yet Jews became white in many parts of the world and perpetuate these unresolved violences on others and share in the fruits of colonial exploitation and bolster an entire nation-state founded on violence. And yes, I need to face the shivering after emerging from the cold sea, the discomforting and uncomfortable bodily quivers that are the result of the threshold encounter, facing myself as SETTLER.

(Tamara)

While confronting hauntings of the past, temporalities were also blurred as we faced, both figuratively and literally, the hauntings of present and future with respect to the anthropocentric damages of coloniality that are entangled in the present-future (Ghosh, 2021). Such writings were often inspired by actual material pollutants encountered, or recent news about these that filtered into our underwater imaginaries, as articulated by Viv:

Yesterday it was hectic trying to get into the pool with the waves crashing and I realised that the sea is not to be taken for granted or played with as I was dashed against and on the rock in the middle of the pool and for a while couldn't get off it …. I was also thinking about the sewage leak at Fish Hoek into the sea yesterday due to load shedding and wondered if it could possibly be reaching us here. It is so distressing what is happening to the sea and how humans can think that they can get rid of their debris and shit into the sea and it will just disappear without consequences.

Making sense of COVID

As previously mentioned, our shared swimming-writing-thinking encounters took place during the COVID-19 pandemic and much of our writing is infused with the threat of the virus and its impact on life as we knew it. The South African government enforced a harsh lockdown which at times prohibited people from leaving their homes. At times this felt overwhelming, as Viv writes:

I've been feeling quite dispirited of late as I feel that there's nothing special to look forward to. The future is so uncertain we don't know how things will pan out. The first time I got a fright in this way about the precarity of life was during the water shortage in Cape Town. Suddenly the things I took so much for granted were no longer possible. The disconcerting thing about life now is that things are so unpredictable. We are so used to planning our lives and looking forward to this and that, but it doesn't seem possible at the moment.

We were also banned from visiting beaches and swimming in the sea for a period. However, when we could engage in swimming-together, and even sometimes alone, then sharing together, provided some comfort from the isolation – both in engaging with each other, but also through encounters with the ocean and marine species. The narratives below articulate ways in which swimming offers comfort and shifts dystopic sensibilities:

> In the time of COVID the swimming together is especially a balm for the extraordinariness of isolation and the entrapment in home, city, nation-state. The swimming and the writing dissolves the alienation, accesses a moment of freedom and community, if only for a stolen moment. [Tamara]
>
> For the last year I've either been at home locked down with my family or somewhere in the sea along the False Bay coast. It's quite discombobulating between being anchored at home and adrift in the sea … when my body is in the water the space between my body and the water melts away and the water becomes the space between, and a matrix as in 'binder' or 'glue' of connection, or is the water the body of which my body becomes a part? My mind has moved on to our Covid way of life. The sea is safe, it is Covid free, it has become a refuge, another world that is virus free.
>
> *(Nike)*

Thinking with the sea during COVID-19 also gave us the opportunity to appreciate the way in in which the virus has surfaced inequality and indeed, exacerbated inequalities, as Nike shared:

> This virus more than anything has highlighted how privilege works. Talking to the students on Monday I recognized how vulnerable they are … public transport, high density living, no safe refuge like the house I live in, the car I drive in. I wonder how many of them and or members of their families are already immuno-compromised. What will this virus do to social relations? How to be still in all of this uncertainty, how to hold the uncertainty, how to carry it? Ettinger distinguishes containment as fixed and *carriance* as fluid. It seems to be a better fit. Perhaps that's the difference between the pool and the ocean, although the pool is tidal, the walls are fixed.

Octopoid sensibilities

A powerful source of inspiration in our oceanic swimming emerged out of our encounters with more-than-human marine creatures. Alexis Pauline Gumbs' (2020) meditations on marine mammals as a Black feminist project have been especially inspiring for us: She thinks with marine mammals who refuse to be controlled by humans by becoming fugitive in the surveilled and colonised ocean. She asks: "What becomes possible when we are immersed in the queerness of forms of life that dominant systems cannot chart, reward, or even understand?" (Gumbs, 2020, p. 109).

Some time before 'My octopus teacher'[5] rose to fame, we found the octopus figuration particularly engaging and stretching, as did other swimmer-scholars we swim with (see Carstens & Roberts, this edition; Bozalek & Hölscher, 2023; also see Imbler, 2022). Thinking with Probyn's (2016) 'methodology of encounter', we found ourselves deeply engaged with the marine species we encountered and the octopus featured strongly in our affective imaginaries. We found that the octopus as a complex critter offers affordances for thinking about different ways of being human-in-relation. Viv shares:

I am grey[6] today after the octopus I was observing for so long. Grey makes one more imperceptible on the page – an octopus move. Although grey is misleading as the four octopuses we saw were all such different colors and shapes, becoming with anything they moved towards or what flowed in their paths. At one time the octopus was green and indistinguishable from the kelp which wrapped around its body, then the color of the sand with the tentacles – reaching reaching. One, and then two, towards sandy-coloured fish. Fish-octopus intra-action coming and going, reaching and darting away. As humans we always try and make sense or interpret what is happening here. How will we ever be sure whether the octopus was hunting the fish, playing with the fish or engaging in some sort of mutual communication? I wonder what they make of these big hulkish humans circling them like sharks? Whether it is just a mild irritation or when the humans come too close, whether they are seen as a threat? Here I am trying to interpret or anthropomorphise the feelings of the octopus, just after castigating that type of behavior … but we humans are full of contradiction – swaying this way and that, justifying our moves along the way.

Engagements with the ocean and its marine inhabitants in general also disrupted a range of (western) human spatio-temporal conventions, such as 'clock time' which dictates our work in the university (Barad, 2017, 2019). As Nike articulates this:

… a highlight for me was finding myself surrounded by thousands of small silver fish moving in sync with one another, one and all glittering, swaying, shifting, shimmering along. At times they would turn back and swim through each other like waves diffracting through one another, with minimal effort and no collisions, almost magnetic-like forces repelling and therefore never actually touching. I'm hearing Barad again: we never actually touch, there's always that space that is always in between. I wonder what it would be like to write at the beach. I often wish we could linger there longer. We are either in the water or writing on our computer on a table somewhere else. What would it be like to linger in the littoral zone? To move between the sea and the beach, our bodies both in and out of the water.

Further, our embodiment and realisation of the possibility of vulnerable encounters with the sea and others opened up a respectful sense of our subjective precarities:

In the sea, we cannot *not* be embodied, we are in our body, floating, moving and vibrantly sensate, both deeply aware of our self in the sea, yet also melting, seeping into the surrounds, both a body and an entanglement. Different temporarility and space, our usual clock time suspended, we are surprised when so many minutes have passed. And we surface questioning the regulated lives we take as normal. We float through kelp, just above the sparking tendrils of anemones and urchins poised to pierce our skin if we are not vigilant. We are never sure what might swim our way. Suddenly a dark large creature surfaces, it could be a threat, but it is a seal, only playful and curious. In wonder and awe, we face our subjective precarity ....

(Tamara)

Our methodology of encounter also shakes up the illusion of our cartesian selves, challenging many aspects of what humans assume are normal and correct, and exposes our relationalities and response-abilities. As Viv writes:

Water is a creator of bonds and relationships. My world is extending, expanding and morphing further and further through seaswimming. Swimming is extending human relationships, it is also extending my relationship with water, sand, rocks, anemones sea stars. I'm learning how to avoid the prickles and negotiate my way through and around creatures in the water. I'm also getting a sense of how different the same watery space can be depending on the tide, the wind, the rain, the sun, the season.

And Tamara's experience of the disruption of the mind-body dualism:

Slow swimming, it can only be Slow as one needs to watch, to see, to feel. And the splash is only at the point of our joining a new element. Arriving and leaving. A moment of disruption, a moment of troubling the smooth surfaces, of opening up new imaginaries, very old sensations but shifting the current into something new. Not something we haven't known before in our individual or collective sensibility, but a re-turn and a woking moment. The splashes then are our splashes, but we also open ourselves to the splashes already there – the wave crashes over the pool's edge and diffracts across the surface and we are in that, on the surface and below, and our vision shifts again – new imagery, new openings, new possibilities. In the moments underwater, before my breath leaves me, I am in awe, but I am also not in my normal disguise as an individualised entity, it is both scary and exhilarating.

Coming up for air

We have shared one example of an experimental watery methodology for doing academia differently towards a scholarship for a justice-to-come. The question that readily surfaces in the output-driven academy is 'so what?' (Selwyn, 2014). At the risk of being technicist since neat packaging is not our intention, we are suggesting that swimming-floating-playing in/with ocean/s offers diverse possibilities for engaging immanent critique and imagining alternative scholarly endeavours. Our writings provide possibilities for ourselves and others to think-with the sea as a capacious and complex space for a radical revisioning of what it means to know and become.

Encrusted with ocean bacteria, shivering with cold, and awash with images of luminescent underwater spaces, our writings enact further swimming-together, moving us to engage with what matters. Our relational encounters with more-than-human species have sharpened our response-ability to challenge damages to the ocean and larger Manthropocentric (Hultman & Pulé, 2020) ecological violences. Our skin porous to fluid temporalities, we confront apartheid hauntings and colonial violences so saturated in the oceans. We swim with the precarities of pandemic times, entangled with current ecological disasters, embedded in (post) colonial capitalist extractivism, while also taking succour from our swimming-together in troubled times.

Acknowledgements

Appreciation to the National Research Foundation of South Africa for 'Doing academia differently' (Grant number 120845) and the Andrew W. Mellon Foundation funded project 'New imaginaries for an intersectional critical humanities project on gender and sexual justice' (Grant number G-31700714). We also acknowledge the constructive engagements of the reviewers.

Notes

1   See www.youtube.com/watch?v=vMDu1YTKDhw&t=18s&ab_channel=NikeRomano.
2   Our Slow reading is often a pleasurable part of our swimming workshops, where we live and swim together for a few days, and have engaged in collectively reading out loud from a range of texts before or after a swim. Some of us also engage in regular reading groups centred on one book or volume at a time.
3   As elaborated further below, Slow is not about the speed or slowness of linear temporality, but about queering time (Bozalek, 2017, 2021). Carl Honore of the Slow movement referred to Slow as tempo giusto meaning the right speed (Gearhart & Chambers, 2019, p. 9). Slow is also not about returning to some idyllic period.

4 See www.youtube.com/watch?v=8dfq3C8GNrE, Koleka Putuma reads 'Water'. Accessed 2 December 2022.
5 My Octopus Teacher (2020) is an award-winning Netflix documentary that documents an encounter between filmmaker Craig Foster and an octopus in a Cape Town kelp forest, told from his perspective (of course).
6 We wrote in different colours in our shared google doc to express moods etc.

References

Arthur, M. (2021). Foreword. In V. Bozalek & B. Pease (Eds.), *Post-anthropocentric social work: Critical posthuman and new materialist perspectives* (pp. xvi–xviii). Routledge.

Barad, K. (2007). *Meeting the universe halfway: Quantum physics and the entanglement of matter and meaning*. Duke University Press.

Barad, K. (2014). Diffracting diffraction: Cutting together-apart. *Parallax, 20*(3), 168–187. DOI: 10.1080/13534645.2014.927623.

Barad, K. (2017). What flashes up: Theological-political-scientific fragments. In C. Keller & M-J. Rubenstein (Eds.), *Entangled worlds: Religion, science and new materialisms* (pp. 21–88). Fordham University Press.

Barad, K. (2019). After the end of the world: Entangled nuclear colonialisms, matters of force, and the material force of justice. *Theory & Event, 22*(3), 524–550.

Barad, K., & Gandorfer, D. (2021). Political desirings: Yearnings for mattering (,) differently. *Theory & Event, 24*(1), 14–66.

Boon, S., Butler, L., & Jefferies, D. (2018). *Autoethnography and feminist theory at the water's edge: Unsettled islands*. Palgrave Macmillan.

Bozalek, V. (2017). Slow scholarship in writing retreats: A diffractive methodology for response-able pedagogies. *South African Journal of Higher Education, 31*(2), 40–57.

Bozalek, V. (2021). Slow scholarship: Propositions for the extended curriculum programme. *Education as Change*, 25, https://doi.org/10.25159/1947-9417/904

Bozalek, V., & Hölscher, D. (2023). Reconfiguring social work ethics with posthuman and post-anthropocentric imaginaries. In D. Hölscher, R. Hugman, D. McAuliffe (Eds.), *Social work theory and ethics*. Social Work. Springer. https://doi.org/10.1007/978-981-16-3059-0_20-1

Bozalek, V., & Pease, B. (2021). Preface. In V. Bozalek & B. Pease (Eds.), *Post-anthropocentric social work: Critical posthuman and new materialist perspectives* (pp. xix–xxiv). Routledge.

Bozalek, V., & Zembylas, M. (2017). Diffraction or reflection? Sketching the contours of two methodologies in educational research. *International Journal of Qualitative Studies in Education, 30*(2), 111–127.

Carstens, D., & Bozalek, V. (2021). Understanding displacement, (forced) migration and historical trauma: The contribution of feminist new materialism. *Ethics and Social Welfare, 15*(1), 68–83. DOI: 10.1080/17496535.2021.1881029

Chen, C., MacLeod, J., & Neimanis, A. (Eds.) (2013). *Thinking with water*. McGill-Queens University Press.

Christian, D., & Wong, R. (Eds.) (2016). *Downstream: Reimagining water*. Wilfred Laurier University Press.

Gan, E., Tsing, A., Swanson, H., & Bubant, N. (2017). In A. Tsing, H. Swanson, E. Gan, & N. Bubant (Eds.), *Arts of living on a damaged planet: Monsters and the arts of living* (pp. G1–G14). University of Minnesota Press.

Gearhart, S. S., & Chambers, J. (2019). Introduction: Contextualising speed and slowness in higher education. In S. S. Gearhart & J. Chambers (Eds.), *Reversing the cult of speed in higher education: The slow movement in the arts and humanities* (pp. 1–36). Routledge.

Ghosh, A. (2021). *The nutmeg's curse: Parables for a planet in crisis.* John Murray.

Glissant, E. (1990). *Poetics of relation* (Transl. B. Wing). University of Michigan Press.

Gordon, A. F. (2008). *Ghostly matters: Haunting and the sociological imagination.* University of Minnesota Press.

Gumbs, A. P. (2020). *Undrowned: Black feminist lessons from marine mammals.* AK Press.

Haraway, D. (2016). *Staying with the trouble: Making kin in the Chthulucene.* Duke University Press.

Harmes, M. K., Danaher, P. A., & Riddle, S. (2017). Partaking of pleasure: Regenerating the working lives of university academics. In S. Riddle, M. K. Harmes, & P. A. Danaher (Eds.), *Producing pleasure in the contemporary university* (pp. 1–12). Sense Publishers.

Hofmeyr, I. (2019). Provisional notes on hydrocolonialism. *English Language Notes, 57*(1), pp. 11–20.

Hultman, M., & Pulé, P. (2020). Ecological masculinities: A response to the Manthropocene question? In L. Gottzén, U. Mellström, & T. Shefer (Eds.), *The international handbook of masculinity studies* (pp. 477–487). Routledge.

Imbler, S. (2022). *My life in sea creatures: A young queer science writer's reflections on identity and the ocean.* Random House.

Ingersoll, K. A. (2016). *Waves of knowing: A seascape epistemology.* Duke University Press.

Jue, M. (2020). *Wild blue media: Thinking through sea water.* Duke University Press.

Manning, E. (2016). *The minor gesture.* Duke University Press.

Manning, E. (2022). *Out of the clear.* Minor Compositions, Open Humanities Press.

Massumi, B. (2015). *The politics of affect.* Polity Press.

Mbembe, A. (2019). *Necropolitics.* Duke University Press.

McKittrick, K. (2006). *Demonic grounds: Black women and cartographies of struggle.* University of Minnesota Press.

Neimanis, A. (2012). Hydrofeminism: Or, on becoming a body of water. In H. Gunkel, C. Nigianni, & F. Söderbäck (Eds.), *Undutiful daughters: Mobilizing future concepts, bodies and subjectivities in feminist thought and practice* (pp. 94–115). Palgrave Macmillan.

Neimanis, A. (2013). Feminist subjectivity, watered. *Feminist Review, 103,* 23–41.

Neimanis, A. (2017). *Bodies of water: Posthuman feminist phenomenology.* Bloomsbury Academic.

Probyn, E. (2016). *Eating the ocean.* Duke University Press.

Probyn, E. (2023). How to enter the ocean: Submersion. Extracting the Ocean: Analytical Practices. Retrieved June 11, 2023, from https://extractingtheocean.org/analytical-practices/how-to-enter-the-ocean-submersion/

Putuma, K. (2017). *Collective amnesia.* uHlanga.

Selwyn, N. (2014). 'So What?' … a question that every journal article needs to answer. *Learning, Media and Technology, 39*(1), 1–5. DOI: 10.1080/17439884.2013.848454

Sharpe, C. (2016). *In the wake: On blackness and being.* Duke University Press.

Shefer, T. (2021). Sea hauntings and haunted seas for embodied place-space-mattering for social justice scholarship. In V. Bozalek, M. Zembylas, S. Motala, & D. Holscher (Eds.), *Higher education hauntologies: Speaking with ghosts for a justice-to-come.* Routledge.

Shefer, T., & Bozalek, B. (2022). Wild swimming methodologies for decolonial feminist justice-to-come scholarship. *Feminist Review, 130*(1), 26–43. DOI: 10.1177/01417789211069351

Smith, L. T. (1999). *Decolonizing methodologies: Research and indigenous peoples*. Zed.

Talbayev, E. T. (2023). Hydropower: Residual dwelling between live and nonlife. *Angelaki: Journal of the Theoretical Humanities, 28*(1), 9–21.

Tronto, J. (2013). *Caring democracy: Markets, equality, and justice*. New York University Press.

Tsing, A., Swanson, H., Gan, E., & Bubant, N. (Eds.) (2017). *Arts of living on a damaged planet: Monsters and the arts of living*. University of Minnesota Press.

Tuck, E., & Yang, K. W. (2014). R-words: Refusing research. In D. Paris & M. T. Winn (Eds.), *Humanizing research: Decolonizing qualitative inquiry with youth and communities* (pp. 223–248). SAGE.

Zembylas, M., Bozalek, V., & Motala, S. (2021). A pedagogy of hauntology: Decolonising the curriculum with GIS. In V. Bozalek, M. Zembylas, S. Motala, & D. Hölscher (Eds.), *Higher education hauntologies: Living with ghosts for a justice-to-come* (pp. 11–28). Routledge.

11

DIFFRACTING FORESTS

Making home in a (post)apartheid city

Barry Lewis

Introduction

In this chapter, I use a diffractive methodology to investigate the Zinc Forest as a worlding process (Haraway, 2008), while thinking with the oceanic Kelp Forests such as those found in the Great African Kelp Forests in Cape Town. Worlding: Things that exist in the world are not just things, they are phenomena, they can be seen as multiple expressions of themselves, something which generates, something that is rooted in histories but also part of the making of new things. It is a be/coming state (Barad, 2007), not just emphasising epistemologies, but ontologies that exist in the now (being) but are also becoming for a time to come. My intent is to expand an understanding of the nature of the Zinc Forest as a worlding process, a process taking root, growing, and constantly forming, reforming and becoming. At no point in this research is there any proposition that I am working with posthuman methodologies to help make the Zinc Forest a better place to live. Rather, this diffractive inquiry aims to re-conceptualise and redefine how we think about/with informal communities to understand the nature of place-making and the forming of home.

In thinking-with posthuman philosophy, I propose the following: The city is not a tree, it is a forest. Never singular or isolated, but always multiple and entangled. And yet, in the (post)apartheid version of this forest, it is still subject to the power of the (isolating) historical policies and doctrines of division. Is the notion of 'home' even possible in such a landscape? How can designers of the city (e.g. architects, engineers and planners) work in more expansive ways to make a home in the city when the tendrils of apartheid policies are still be/coming? Amira Osman has stated in a public presentation at a design festival.

DOI: 10.4324/9781003355199-11

Nothing presented in South Africa has ever been as powerful as what the apartheid planners suggested. We need to re-imagine African cities as livable and lovable cities.

(Osman, 2019, n.p.)

By taking Osman's observations seriously, this study seeks to challenge the notion of 'separateness' in the spatial landscape of Cape Town and assist in conceptualising a more authentic and expansive notion of home and a sense of belonging. The study also introduces the concept of worlding (Haraway, 2008) and uses a diffractive methodology in putting the Zinc Forest in conversation with the Kelp Forest. In addition, the study uses Barad's (2007) notion of agential realism in investigating how worlding and relations between humans and more-than-humans in this landscape can assist in co-creating places of belonging: 'They longed for another place called home where they could recapture their past and dream other futures' (Hamdi, 2004, p. 59).

Apartheid's spatial planning legacy in the (post)apartheid city has '…crippled the ability of South Africa's cities to offer a decent urban life to the majority of their citizens. The spatial planning which characterised apartheid has seen to that' (Mabin, 2001, p. 17). Such cities have continued to build themselves in the manner in which they were originally conceived, along definitive lines of separation and

FIGURE 11.1   Silvertown, Khayelitsha. Photo: Barry Lewis.

disconnect. City designers like myself find our/themselves functioning in this separated and segregated house-making realm, especially when it comes to the developments of new communities in/through/beyond the Upgrade of Informal Settlements Programme (UISP[1]). The fruit of such projects looks like Silvertown, Khayelitsha (Figure 11.1), a community with houses on small plots, in rows separated by roads which double as play spaces for the children. Power and agency lie with the designers of the city who are 'employing' parameters (history, policy or other) to suit a singular/linear agenda that manifests a perpetuating of the apartheid city. This is a praxis that silently believes that we are separate from the multiple 'worldings' (Haraway, 2016, p. 76) that exist in the city, even the more-than-human worlds, and where planners (specific to the Silvertown project) have been heard to have said: 'But I've seen the children play in the streets Barry and they look like they are having fun...' Or as Turner remarked, '...architects and planners ... are confronted with a rapidly rising consciousness of their incompetence to decide for others what is best for them' (Turner, 1976, p. 11). It matters, therefore, that we think differently about relations in the making of home in the city, for a justice-to-come (Derrida, 1994; Barad, 2007). As Hamdi points out: 'Those who pursue housing find themselves without architecture, and those who pursue careers often find themselves without reason' (Hamdi, 2004, p. 168).

Forests as worldings

This research uses posthuman thinking, and draws on Haraway's concept of worlding (Haraway, 2000) and Haraway/Barad's notion of diffraction (Haraway, 2000, 2016; Barad, 2007). These concepts offer new ways of doing research which lean towards alternative knowledge and towards a justice-to-come (Derrida, 1994; Barad, 2007) and consequently what flourishing in the (post)apartheid city could be.

As a white, male designer, originally from the United Kingdom, I am implicated in the making and continual making of this (post)apartheid city. Thus, it is imperative I pay attention to my implicated responsibility and potential response-ability (Barad, 2007, 2010) both in my research and in the work I do as an architect/builder. In particular, how to 'stay with the *human* trouble' (Rose, 2017, p. 55). As such, I am interested in thinking differently about the methodologies used to build home and have chosen to explore the concept of worlding, as conceived by Haraway (2008). Worlding (as previously stated): Things that exist in the world are not just things, they are phenomena (Barad 2007, 2010; Haraway 2008), and they have multiple expressions of themselves. The research interprets worlding as something which generates, something that is rooted to past histories but also forms part of the making of new iterations. It is a be/coming state (Barad, 2007), not just emphasising epistemologies, but ontologies that exist in the now (being) but are also becoming for a time to come. Worlding understands the relations of humans alongside more-than-humans, as if we are not disconnected from the world in which we live: '...art, science worldings as sympoietic practices for living on a damaged planet' (Haraway 2016, p. 67).

FIGURE 11.2   Wave 1, The Zinc Forest. Photo: Barry Lewis.

The Zinc Forest is a worlding (Figure 11.2). As Vuyani Vellem states, 'The proliferation of the Zinc Forest is the prophetic building of the city' (Vellem, 2016, n.p.). Homes are being fought for, rebuilt, recreated and formed at every moment in the informal community. This occurs without apology and without consent where humans are doing, making and building home in the city, regardless of owning the land or formal building procedures. It is a relational process of homemaking, a building with/together. But more than this, it is a site of learning because there have been no shack-making manuals created.

I draw on Barad's notion of indeterminacy:

> Ontological indeterminacy, a radical openness, an infinity of possibilities, is at the core of mattering. How strange that indeterminacy, in its infinite openness, is the condition for the possibility of all structures in their dynamically reconfiguring in/stabilities.
>
> *(Barad, 2015, p. 16)*

The Zinc Forest is a site of indeterminacy, perpetually troubling linear and logical conventions of space, time and matter (Barad 2007) and 'involves a kind of sideways slippage along barely visible fault lines rather than the traditional scholarly labor of excavation' (Wigley, 1997, p. 3). It carries within it the histories of injustice and as such the 'start' of the Zinc Forest is not conveniently demarcated at the point when a human starts to build their shack. Barad's words resonate:

> If the indeterminate nature of existence by its nature teeters on the cusp of stability and instability, of determinacy and indeterminacy, of possibility and impossibility, then the dynamic relationality between continuity and discontinuity is crucial to the open-ended becoming of the world which resists a causality as much as determinism.
>
> *(Barad, 2007, p. 182)*

If we, as designers, pay attention to the Zinc Forest, we notice that there are complex infrastructures that enable forms of order and governance. Some systems are so closely connected to the realities of poverty that they are rejected by the Zinc Forest community, despite their clear and apparent significance. Building 'bit by bit' (translated: *ulangisa nganyenganye)* is an embodied praxis which ensures that no home stays the same; it is always changing, improving and adjusting to enviro-econo-socio (and other) parameters. All done without borrowing from a financial institution. In a comparable way, the Kelp Forest is a worlding. The Great African

FIGURE 11.3   Wave 2, holdfast. Photo: Barry Lewis.

Kelp Forest as an example of a growing and be/coming phenomenon, subject to the swell and surge of a sometimes-hostile, sometimes-violent environment. At the base of the kelp is the holdfast (Figure 11.3), a webbed rooted system that connects the stipe and blade to the sea bed.[2] Kelp is an algae and so this rooted base sits on top of the rocks. I am a freediver, and as I dive into this oceanic wonderland this hold fast fixes my gaze and I cannot remove the idea that this phenomenon somehow speaks directly to the Zinc Forest in some way. It came to the attention of Dr Nasreen Peer from Stellenbosch University that there has been very little research done in regards to the holdfast in South Africa, and she is leading an exploration into the holdfast phenomenon (Personal Communication, 2023). From the outside, it looks like a solid definitive mass, but on the inside they have discovered more than 90 different species all growing and existing and be/coming. The study affirms the holdfast as an example of a *nurturing habitat*.

Diffracting worlds

The concept of worlding includes the post-qualitative methodology of diffraction. For Haraway, 'diffraction is a narrative, graphic, psychological, spiritual, and political technology for making consequential meanings (Haraway, 2000, p. 102), 'an optical metaphor for the effort to make a difference in the world' (Haraway, 1997, p. 16).

Diffraction can be described when two pebbles are thrown into a pond and the waves from each submersion collide with the other to make a new pattern. It differs from reflection which is when light, heat or sound gets thrown back from whence it came via a body or surface. Diffraction is a worlding process that pays attention to new patterns that are created in and through relationships. Worlding is a matter of relations between human and more-than-human (e.g. zinc, sand). Diffraction patterns pull designers of the city into a conversation with things that are normatively excluded from the design process (e.g. more-than-human worlds). If we understand the notion of worlding through the methodology of diffraction, phenomena are being read through one another which means the agency gets distributed across time, history, architect, brittlestar, planner, indigenous knowledge, material, umqombothi,[3] facilitator, holdfast, the kraal, or even the song. It becomes a de-centring praxis, a protest, a momentary pause in the perpetual making of the apartheid city. The professional's office cannot be the epicentre of homemaking, in fact, it has been proved through instances like Silvertown – where 'community making' looks like copy and pasting small box houses – that it is not.

For Haraway 'understanding the world is about living inside stories. There's no place to be in the world outside of stories' (Haraway, 2000, p. 107). The story of the Zinc Forest and the Kelp Forest is with/in the world. Thinking with these two forests in the world draws the forests together into a worlding process instead of separate entities with no relation to one another. Diffraction enables a more just way of reading and relating these forests through one another.

In the next section of this chapter, I trace the diffractive patterns that emanate from two forest stories. I alternate between a conversation (which starts with a quote in relation to the start of a brittlestar's life) with Dr Nasreen Peer[4] relating to holdfasts and the juvenile beings that are be/coming within, and excerpts from a recording with a colleague called Andile Bonkolo. 'Zibha' (his nickname) lives in a community called Sweet Home Farm in Philippi, a Zinc Forest I had the privilege of working in for ten years between 2009 and 2019. In the video clip he speaks of a notional fragile egg (which symbolises his life), and the rules required to keep this egg from dropping.

Diffracting waves as a world-making process

'When the gonads are ripe, they discharge in the bursae, probably by rupturing the bursal wall, and the sex cells are carried out of the body in the ventilating water current. Fertilisation and development take place in the sea in many species, but brooding is common. The bursae are commonly used as brood chambers, as in the common *Axiognathus squamata* (*Amphipholis squamata*), but the female of some viviparous species gestates her eggs in the ovary or coelom. Development takes place within the mother until the juvenile stage is reached when the young crawl out of the bursal slits. In most brooding species only a few young occur in each bursa' (Ruppert, 2014, p. 895).

> Zibha: 'Our lives in Sweet Home are like eggs, which you are given in your hand…the Lord gives you an egg as your soul and your life, you know, you are in control of it for a little bit of time you know. So you have to control yourself, how you walk, don't drop the egg, if you drop the egg it's like the moment you die. As soon as you go straight to the other road, bad way, and then you meet a death by your own hand, sometimes by your own hand, your own doings. You can't come back to life again. That's why I say you must watch over the egg, like being careful, you must hold it gently, you know, don't slip and fall…too many things'.

We identify little threads of constants: Is it possible that brittlestars, or any other species exist or grow in other pockets within the channel? In rocks, caves or other plant life? It is possible. I have a preponderance of the notion of meaning, as if the holdfast 'holds' some special meaning because of what is being manifested in and through it. It is enough however that life has been proven to exist at all, given the view from the outside which might suggest otherwise. It is a community of beings, a city, a kraal[5]. A situatedness of life not disconnected from the other versions of nurturing habitats that surround it, or indeed the Zinc Forest. What happens when a group of holdfasts gather together, what exchanges happen in that space? How do they communicate with each other? The notions of scale and separateness have been dispelled. The 90 species of beings are inextricably linked together in the way

FIGURE 11.4   A holdfast and Zinc Forest diffractive pattern. Artwork: Barry Lewis.

that multiple holdfasts are, in the way that the Zinc/Kelp Forests are. Nothing exists in isolation or separateness, and this applies to size and scale also (Figure 11.4).

> Zibha: 'To be safe you must watch over yourself, change your ways or change your friends to save yourself. Don't walk at night, to save yourself, everything, you know, is to watch over yourself. The meaning of the egg is like life because that egg gives life to something else that is going to be…good or bad. Out of the egg it will come anything. Even me now, its like I live in a poor community…I have nothing, don't have a car, fat bank account, and all these things…but I'm still grateful because I'm still alive, walking, drinking, with the same people, everyone is the same without the things of this world, we are all the same but we don't see it. I'm still alive, the greatest blessing, the Lord knows why. But I'm happy, I'm glad to be alive at this time in this moment now, sharing my story with you…it's the greatest gift, I'm still alive'

How is it possible that a baby brittlestar can start life in its mother, travel along the bursal slit then find its way to the holdfast? And yet it can be found existing there in a juvenile state. How did the mother know that the holdfast was a nurturing habitat? Does it give off a chemical cue? Is there something else already dwelling in it that gives off a chemical cue? Or did it find its way there by chance? Either way, the baby brittlestar exists and grows and be/comes in the holdfast, along with

FIGURE 11.5   A holdfast and the egg. Artwork: Barry Lewis.

the likes of 90 other species. The holdfast is a site of indeterminacy. It looks static but it is always be/coming we just get to choose what we are paying attention to at any given time. Life and species grow in and within it, while itself grows. Or dies (Figure 11.5).

Making home in the Zinc Forest

When we diffract the holdfast through the Zinc Forest graphically we start to make decisions about what gets included, which lines have hard edges and which sections get blurred or multiplied. Certain things get foregrounded (possibly for the first time) and other things get excluded all together. What are we paying attention to? I have to understand my implicateness in this diffractive pattern observing, which includes politics of position and power. Cutting-together-apart is a deeply political activity, one which must pay attention to the fact that we are unbounded beings, and our skin is not a separator of entities because even our skin is porous. Within this epistemological understanding, our ontological be/coming is therefore rooted to a perpetual instability, where previously simplified lines are contaminated by indeterminate worlds that inextricably feel like they have never met, but in truth have never been apart. Our understanding of how we build home in the city becomes tidal, forever changing, but always subject to the environment in which we choose to make observations. What does stability even mean? It challenges the very notion of architecture and architect as conceiver of ideas for projects. Even the *concept* as an origin or starting point must be challenged.

What are the conditions for generating potential? Massumi talks about affect as a version of hope:

> Once again it's all about the openness of situations and how we can live that openness. And you have to remember that the way we live it is always entirely embodied, and that is never entirely personal – it's never all contained in our emotions and conscious thoughts. That's a way of saying it's not just about us, in isolation. In affect, we are never alone. That's because affects in Spinoza's definition are basically ways of connecting, to others and to other situations. They are our angle of participation in processes larger than ourselves. With intensified affect comes a stronger sense of embeddedness in a larger field of life – a heightened sense of belonging, with other people and to other places.
>
> *(Massumi, 2015, p. 6)*

A heightened sense of belonging, with other people and to other places; to other worlds, and most certainly to more-than-human worlds. In the disembodied city maybe our endeavour to make places of belonging can only take root when we subjugate the notion that we lie separate to the worldings that are happening around us, and that the worlds are separate in any way (which includes the notions of scale). Guide/lines exist for staying alive in the Zinc/Kelp Forests, the fragility and potential of the egg so painfully evident. Juvenile forms of life are found, exist, be/come and somehow thrive in these nurturing habitats without us knowing the details of the how and why. Maybe a form of instability is simply knowing that a baby brittlestar exists in the holdfast, and not knowing anything more.

Maybe it is also imperative that in order for this 'intensified affect' to take place – that leads to a heightened sense of belonging – that certain enabling constraints exist. In and through the Zinc/Kelp Forests the constraints for this be/coming are extensive and entirely necessary. It is in the detail of material accumulation that someone needing a home starts to rely on the wider community for assistance. No one ever builds alone in the Zinc Forest. Maybe there's a reason why the holdfast becomes a nurturing habitat, and that is because multiple species are needed to exist together, in order for this intensified affect to take hold.

Conclusion

Diffraction as a methodology re-conceptualises and re-defines the nature of placemaking. The forming of home cannot be removed or separated from the past. Diffractive patterns emanate from stories, images, processes and infrastructures. In the (post)apartheid city which reminds humans that they do not belong, we need new ways of understanding how the city is becoming, and how we are becoming as part of it. If we have any desire to build, as Osman states, 'livable and lovable cities' (2019, n.p.) we need to pay attention to the relations in the world and not erase them. The opportunity to build with humans who have traditionally been forgotten, along with histories, architecture, indigenous knowledge, brittlestars, holdfasts, umqombothi, facilitators, the kraal in and through the Zinc/Kelp Forests has major implications for how we design and build a home in the city. It also helps us re-configure our understanding of the building site. It is more than just a place where we build a piece of the city; it is a site of relations where we conceive and build together, a site of learning and also a site of healing.

Notes

1 From Part 3 of the Department of Human Settlements, National Housing Code – Incremental Interventions.
2 The Kelp is made of three elements; the blades (which can be seen on the surface of the water), the stipes (which are the stalk-like trunks of the plant) and the holdfasts (that connect the plant to the substrata). 'The huge sporophyte plants are long-lived and form extensive underwater forests. They have sturdy, root-like holdfasts and long stalks or stipes that support the blades' (Griffiths, 2016, p. 386).
3 The name for Xhosa beer.
4 Dr Peer is the leader of the holdfast study happening at Stellenbosch University.
5 Kraal: A traditional (rural) African village/homestead typically enclosed by a fence.

References

Barad, K. (2007). *Meeting the universe halfway*. Duke University Press.
Barad, K. (2015). *What is the measure of nothingness? Infinity, virtuality, justice.* Erschienen im Hatje Cantz Verlag.
Griffiths, C. L. (2016). *Two oceans. A guide to the marine life of southern Africa.* Struik Nature.
Hamdi, N. (2004). *Small change. About the art of practice and the limits of planning in cities.* Earthscan.
Haraway D. J. (2000). *How like a leaf: An interview with Thyrza Nichols Goodeve.* Routledge.
Haraway, D. J. (2008). *When species meet.* University of Minnesota Press.
Haraway, D. J. (2016). *Staying with the trouble. Making Kin in the Chthulucene.* Duke University Press.
Mabin, A. (2001). What's left of reconstruction – The rise and fall of a planning ideology. In *Proceedings of the South African planning history study group, millenium conference, May 2000* (pp. 16–29). University of Natal, Durban.
Massumi, B. (2015). *The politics of affect.* Polity Press.
Osman, A. (2019, February 26). *Resilience thinking for the next generation of designers @ the #cocreate Design Festival 2019.* Retrieved May 31, 2023, from http://amiraosman. co.za/2019/03/19/resilience-thinking-for-the-next-generation-of-designers-the-cocreate-design-festival-2019/.

Rose, D. B. (2017). Shimmer: When all you love is being trashed. In A. L Tsing, H. A. Swanson, E. Gan & N. Bubandt (Eds.), *Arts of living on a damaged planet: Ghosts and monsters of the anthropocene* (pp. G51–G63). Minnesota Press.

Ruppert, E. E. (2014). *Invertebrate zoology: A functional evolutionary approach.* Cengage Publication.

Turner, J. (1976). *Housing by people. Towards autonomy in building environments.* Marion Boyars.

Vellem, V. (2016, August 6). *Epistemological dialogue as prophetic: A black theological perspective on the land issue.* Scriptura. Retrieved May 31, 2023, from http://dx.doi.org/10.7833/115-0-1201

Wigley, M. (1997). *The architecture of deconstruction, Derrida's haunt.* MIT.

12

GRANDMOTHERS OF THE SEA

Stories and lessons from five Xhosa ocean elders

Buhle Francis and Dylan McGarry

> *As a child, I saw myself as a child of the ocean, as part of the ocean and grew up knowing that my source of livelihood and income was the ocean – so I had to look after it … I hope one day we will be able to go to the ocean as we used to so that we perform those rituals that our forefathers did to make species visible.*

These are the words of Gogo Nomalibongwe, a grandmother living in the Eastern Cape of South Africa, along with four other Grandmothers who have experienced the harsh dichotomies of soul-nourishing kinship and unspeakable hardship and trauma in relation to the ocean. As children living in a world where they had free and unadulterated access to the ocean, they have a life and associated wisdom that spans through a shifting political and social landscape of South Africa. Wisdom that offers a coherency and continuum of knowledge. One that surpasses any contemporary marine sociologist or marine scientist that we have encountered. Despite this wisdom and expertise, they remain unseen. Now, as elderly women, they articulate the quality of their lives and the impact of the legacy of direct and structural racism and economic expansion in South Africa on their relationality to the sea. In this chapter, these Grandmothers give clear testimonies and sophisticated analyses, in their own voices, of their relationality with the ocean across political, economic, social, ecological and spiritual nexus.

Since 2019, we have been working with coastal women in the Eastern Cape region of South Africa and have befriended five Xhosa Grandmothers, who have become our teachers and mentors, not just for us but for an entire emergent social and ecological justice movement. Their knowledge and expertise are formidable, and we have learned of the dynamic leadership and strength that women of the Eastern Cape coast offer, despite many obstacles and challenges thrown at them. In our collaboration to support self-organising, yet government-mandated fishing

DOI: 10.4324/9781003355199-12

cooperatives, we have uncovered some particular insights around constraints and enablers to meaningful collaborative and inclusive bottom-up ocean governance. With the co-development of new capacities and new livelihood projects through our work in the Coastal Justice Network,[1] we have gained trust and critical insights into the experiences and concerns of woman's cooperatives and collectives along our coast. In these relationships, we have come to learn that for a participative, inclusive and equitable ocean decision-making process to be established in the Eastern Cape, and the country at large, the expertise and leadership of women (particularly these Grandmothers) is critical. In this chapter, we simply open a window into the lifeworlds of five Grandmothers who derive their livelihoods and identities from the sea. We offer the field of hydrofeminism a political, cultural and historical analysis as conducted by these Grandmothers, to enrich our ocean literacy, meaning making and support more inclusive ocean decision-making. These Grandmothers bring together a feminist sensibility with an ecology of the ocean (Neimanis, 2012) that is utterly unique and politically essential.

The Eastern Cape is considered one of the largest and at the same time poorest of the nine provinces in South Africa (Bantwini, 2010). It was formed in 1994 and Xhosa people are a majority in the province. The majority of livelihoods are supported by small-scale livestock farming and the traditional livelihoods reliant on and with the ocean. The Eastern Cape has suffered a long history of exclusions and forced removals during the Apartheid regime, along with older political and ideological schisms that emerged during the 1856–1857 Xhosa Cattle-Killings[2] which separated coastal and inland communities against each other (Bank, 2002). With coastal communities inclined to more traditional ways of life, and less access to development opportunities, there is also a weaker influence of colonialism. Bank (2002) suggests that these pre-existing cultural differences between coastal and inland families became highly politicised in the 1950s, and again during the post-freedom betterment period where households struggled for resources and development opportunities. Regardless, events like the cattle killings and apartheid's group areas undoubtedly played a significant role in shaping coastal people's approach to social justice (Mahlatsi, 2018), and these Grandmothers provide heart-breaking personal evidence of this idea.

To worsen their situation, in a society that has had to struggle for resources and development for over 160 years, within an inherently unique African patriarchal system of inheritance and decision making (Erwin & Marks, 2021), women are often rendered silent and excluded from most decision-making and governance. We would argue that this exclusion is felt more heavily in the marine livelihood space, where fishing is predominately dominated by men, unlike farming where there are diverse labour divisions within agricultural practices.

In our witnessing with marine users, the barriers to accessing the oceans, both through imposed physical and legislative mechanisms have become more entrenched, especially since the impact of COVID-19, something Gogo Margaret testifies to below. This inability to fight a system that has for decades been designed to make it impossible to return to their childhood experiences of oneness with and of the sea – has seen the gradual erosion of an important contextual and embodied hydrofeminist set of principles and knowledge that is unique to Grandmothers of the Eastern Cape.

In this chapter, we seek to surface the experiential realities of these hydrofeminists leaders, who unlike the 'hero' myth deconstructed by Ursula Le Guin (2020), are the ones that raise the heroes, they are the receptive carers and carriers of a different knowledge and approach to ocean governance and literacy, and deserve much, much more airtime.

Methodology

As the lead author is fluent in traditional Xhosa, we have carried out an unadulterated approach to exploring the personal experiences of the five Grandmothers in their indigenous language, with minimal edits. Conducting interviews with each woman, we build a contextual profile of each woman's context and situation through many informal conversations and visits, along with establishing informed consent, and ongoing call-and-response negotiation of ethical praxis. We then followed with a formal open-ended interview with the five generative questions which include: (i) Who taught you how to fish and harvest?; (ii) What's your first memory or most interesting experience with the ocean?; (iii) In what way have you been excluded from ocean decision making and how has this exclusion affected your livelihood; and as well as finally, (v) What is your hope for the ocean? These generative questions opened up a bigger conversation about these women's relationship around/ with the ocean. We share below each grandmother's stories which have been translated into English.

Gogo Margaret's story

Fishing has been running in my family for generations after generations as it is a livelihood that my parents survived on and it was passed to me and my siblings. I have known about fishing from the tender age of seven years old. My brothers were fishermen, and growing up in such an environment was normal during our times as the ocean was a stone 's throw away. However, at the time of growing up our parents had to separate the chores which were for girls and those that were for boys, so while boys were taught how to go into the ocean water and catch fish – I was taught how to catch and harvest seaweeds and abalone. Seaweed was abundant in the ocean rocks, and one would find these rocks at the edge of the ocean whereas abalone would also be abundant in the shallow coastal waters. Over the school holidays in Hamburg, we will get several visitors coming to camp at the Caravan Park. These visitors were coming to fish and relax at the beach and they became our customers. Those were good memories.

Ever since the Government made us into Kiwane Fishing Cooperative it has been a struggle after the other with no tangible benefits. We have recently been granted the right to Squid Fishing (an expansion of what we can catch) – though everything is new, that will change our lives because we have other species in our basket as well. I have not been consulted on anything about the ocean space, yet I am the custodian of the ocean. My government has made several decisions without my input. The Government decides for me! Worse now with the COVID-19 pandemic – I hear that there are "online meetings" of which I have never been part and decisions are made there without anyone bothering to inform me or query why people like me are not present. This pains me a lot! The decision-makers sit in their boardrooms and craft these policies – they have all the reasons to justify, why they failed to access me and/or how they consulted me, but for some reason, I failed to attend. *But* in the same voice when they have decided on what they have agreed upon, they have means to reach me to ensure that I comply! What is that? Is that genuine? For example, the Government will tell us about the species that are being banned from harvesting because for some reason are meant to be conserved and/or are at risk or under threat. They do not consider my knowledge of how we have always preserved and ensured the sustainability of that very species for hundreds of years.

Remember, fishing and harvesting have always been there in our families and our forefathers practised it and they never ran out of species for they knew and we know how to fish sustainably. However, it is the Government and its commercialisation that is doing all the nonsense in the ocean and we the poor people suffer for the decisions they make for us. If they would ask me, I would tell them how to harvest and where to harvest for I know about the diverse species of the ocean.

Look at the issue of the Draft Management Plan for the Amathole Marine Protected Areas (MPA) – if it was not for the Coastal Justice Network, we would not have been part of it; we were already left out and only joined at the tail end of it.

In addition to all this poor consultation, you are then informed that you can fish from this site to that site, for example, from Keiskamma River to Chalumna River – that is a very short distance and it is poorly occupied by those species we want. However, the reality is that someone decides for me while calculating kilometres using the internet, with no idea of what is viable on the ground. I was not part of that decision, because someone trusted and relied on their Geographical Information System more than I! Let me tell you; I know what species are available, I know and understand their ecology, and I know in which areas within the ocean waters they prefer to inhabit! These species they think are becoming extinct, I know where they are because the ocean talks to me and I understand what it says! You cannot talk to Google in your office, be it in Pretoria or Cape Town or even nearby from East London and think that you know more than I do – never!

The very "abalone" which they have monopolised, commercialised to others and prohibited and banned and limited me to access it – it is my baby! I understand its behavioural trend more than them! I was born into it and I grew up in it and survived out of it and still share the same space with it! I did not read about it from Google!

That is me. I can spend the whole day giving you examples of injustices that I meet as a Coastal Villager. I have no say in the permits that I am given – absolutely nothing! I do not even know what criteria are used to come up with these quotas (basket) that we are given – no one asked me about it. Even the seasons are decided in offices without my knowledge or input. Now that I have to rely upon a permit which is seasonal – that excludes me to access my livelihood! It is not good! I am the one who should decide on seasons because to me and others, we understand in our unique way what the ocean is saying during the half-moon, during the quarter moon, during the new moon and so on. The ocean waves are just not mere ocean waves to us – but they are something more – they are something important to us! Think of someone looking at a Google calendar and deciding on what I should fish when, where and how (sick)!

This is my livelihood that someone is messing with! Then I should comply with that decision – how does this work? As the people that live in the Coastal areas, we should be part of the decision-makers because it is our livelihood that is under threat. It is us that can bring those species allegedly becoming extinct to the shores of the ocean. We are people that talk reality, people that know the science of the ocean in our special way – We do not rely on them and not internet delusions – that is a fallacy!

I hope to see the ocean going back to what it was when we were growing up. We had lots of sea species which were easier to be accessed and indeed a variety as well. Now we find plastics in our oceans! Plastic which we do not know where it comes from. Sometimes we see huge vessels that we are not even so sure what it is doing and all this affects me. The ocean is my livelihood and I look up to it to improve myself and other community members. Ensuring that it is healthy – remains my hope and a top priority.

Gogo Nofoto Demise

I was born, grew up here and I still live here in my parents' homestead which is adjacent to the ocean. Born living adjacent to the ocean influenced my upbringing and livelihood as I grew up seeing my parents and neighbours going to the ocean to fish. So, I can say not only my parents taught me to fish, but also my neighbourhood in Phozi. My family shaped me into a better fisherwoman. I was introduced to fishing at a very young age, and I cannot remember the age though, it was in the late 50s. I was taught to fish/harvest abalone and seaweed. At the time when we got involved, it was mainly for home consumption, but over time we came to know and meet buyers that were visiting our area in search of either seaweed and/or abalone, that way our interest intensified as we started to make a good income. Making money out of abalone at a tender age was very exciting and adventurous as a young person. It motivated me to work hard each time we go to the ocean and I developed a passion for abalone harvesting, a skill I still survive on today.

Recently, I became part of a recognised cooperative, an initiative which the Government assisted in putting place. Though since the formation, we have never realised anything, it would appear that our prayers are being answered as we are now beginning to see the light in the dark tunnel. We recently signed a deal with one commercial company which has paid us a lump sum for the year and we have each managed to earn at least about 11,500 and as we speak, I am tiling up my house – this is very interesting. My dream has always been to come out of this Rondavel house and build something modern that my family will remember me for. I have not been consulted on anything about the Government or anyone on anything, let alone the ocean.

The Government, from time to time tells us about the permits, and about what areas are targeted for protected areas. They play on my behalf, without me! It is so painful that we are excluded from everything. We have an area called Christmas Rock; in this place, cars are not allowed – so once we harvest the seaweed we have to walk a long distance to access the cars and we were not part of that decision. This exclusion sets a bad example. We collect seaweed for a white businesswoman[3] based in the district, and to think that she even decides on what to pay, which to us sounds like a joke, but it is happening – we can never leave her even though the deals are so bad and poor because half a loaf is still better than nothing. We have no voice, she decides on what to pay us and we are voiceless to negotiate for our kgs which she buys at R7,50/kg. We find ourselves in unfavourable deals because of a lack of consultation and respect.

There is a verse in the bible which teaches us about doing things in the dark/hidden and thinking/assuming that it will remain like that forever … it is impossible! One day such things will come out! We are not educated, so I guess it becomes easier for us to be overlooked. We are now living in an era where everything (harvesting of ocean species) requires one to access a permit to access the ocean; and permits, by their nature of being permits, are exclusive and we find our livelihood being limited through the permit conditions. While I understand the scope of permits there comes a time when I sometimes fail to find logic in them. Imagine I have to have a permit to go to the ocean and catch a small amount of fish to cook, I have to have a permit to harvest seaweed, I have to have a permit to be allowed to harvest abalone and trust me the process of getting a permit is a mountain task! The permits are not easily processed – we have to wait for a long time and remember we will be needing to feed our families while someone is delaying processing the permits. What options are there for us? It is someone who sits somewhere in a government office and decides what species I am allowed to harvest when and how, while I am there and being overlooked and undermined. That same someone forgets that the ocean has always been my livelihood. What I see and dislike in other areas such as the Tsitsikamma is also somehow here coming with the proposed Amathole district Marine Protected

Area (MPA). To me, the ocean is "*Honey*". It is my pot of honey. Honey is nice, but once spoiled it becomes undesirable! So, the same with my ocean – once it is not looked after it does not produce the way it should. I hope to see everyone doing their bit of responsibility in cleaning the ocean. It pains me so much to go there and see the litter. We see plastic floating and sometimes it comes from the boats and vessels that utilise the ocean. People just dump things in the ocean without second thoughts which is very bad.

Gogo Nomalibongwe

I am the founder member of the Siyaphambili Co-operative which was successfully registered in 2018. I was born in Hamburg and grew up playing in the ocean and fishing from the ocean without any restrictions, I was free. As a child, I saw myself as a child of the ocean as part of the ocean and grew up knowing that my source of livelihood and income was the ocean, so I had to look after it. These are the memories I hold dearly as well as catching various species with my mother and selling them to others. My mother taught me how to fish and collect other species within the ocean.

Now, all that is gone – it was taken away from us when the permit holder arrangement was introduced by the Government. I can no longer fish and support my children. As you can see, I am wearing a cleaner's uniform, and I work as a cleaner temporarily in various holiday houses. For me to go to the ocean, I need to have at least a permit and I am told that a permit will also be specified on the type of species that I can fish, seeing I had no choice, I then complied and applied for the permit, but by the time I received it the permit had already expired, it took that long to arrive. I submitted a second application and until today, it has been years nothing has been received – these are the free Government permits that we should apply for but are not easily accessed.

I have never been any part of any decision-making. We do not know what is happening within the cooperative as well as at the National. It appears the plan of establishing is not clear from the Government's perspective. All I know is that nothing is happening. The meetings were last held before lockdown so as we do not know where we stand or if there will be any progress it is very quiet. That is exclusion! We have never participated in any form of ocean governance, especially on issues that require decision making such as the MPAs which have such a huge impact on our lives as well as in which ocean species we are eligible to harvest. Our exclusion and non-access to the ocean make it difficult to assist in removing the litter that we see floating such as plastics. I am hoping that the ocean can be what it used to be. We were able to go there uninterrupted and at the ocean, we will find a variety of choices of species that are no longer visible currently. Above all, we would clean the surroundings and ensure that was is litter free. So, I hope one day we will be able to go to the ocean as we used to so that we perform those rituals that our forefathers did to make species visible.

Gogo Charlotte

I was installed as a Chief, representing the Griqua Royal house over five years ago. We have not been accepted as the first house. We are the official group that can meet with the Government to deliberate on a variety of issues. I was born and grew up in Cape Town but moved to the Eastern Cape, and importantly, I am still a coastal person that is born on the Coast and bred on the Coast. My grandfather and uncles were the people who taught us to fish. In my case, my parents would go to work and our grandparents would look after us together with our uncles. My first fishing experience was through "line fishing" which I would just throw into the ocean and catch fish. The interesting thing happened when stories were told of how our great-great parents were fishing and when we were invited in 2018 by President Zuma to be on the harbour itself and experience the walk on the harbour that was amazing!

You know, the seawater calms you and helps you connect with your ancestors. Listening to the ocean, it is a spiritual experience and each time when I am at the ocean I feel quite happy as I relax and meditate and talk to my ancestors. Where I live there is no ocean. Exclusion started apartheid and it went on for decades with the laws that were exclusive up until now. We do not see a new South Africa because we are still excluded. There is no transformation for us yet, except the Government saying we must be in the cooperatives, something which we also did not know about until recently.

How the coops started and how those that are part of it is not clear. We hear that so and so are part of those coop or that coop, but you do not get to know the criteria. So how can we say we are free? Worse still, those that are in coops are also excluding us and making sure we stay away from the process of being part of the coops. While being happy for my sisters and brothers that are in cooperatives I want the Government to think of us in Uitenhage (officially renamed Kariega in post-apartheid South Africa). We were robbed of self-sustainability, our traditions and customs. Fishing was a traditional way of feeding our families and it was taken away from us by the apartheid government and now by the current regime. Oppression has moved from one regime to the next without our coastal voices being heard – this pains me.

When I was growing up fishermen would catch fish and share it with the whole village without any discrimination, that is how beautiful it was then. You would catch fish to feed your family and to share with the neighbours; all that is gone! The government need to engage with us to correct this. "Nothing about us without us!" My biggest hope is that all people of every race will benefit equally from the ocean without any restrictions. Also, I want to emphasise the restoration of the ocean – please restore what you have taken back from us – include everyone because we would like to be economically empowered! Exclusion must come to an end!

Gogo Jolene

My connectivity to the ocean that I was taught by my parents and grandparents, is the most important thing. My dad passed away when I was five months old, so I lost that aspect of father-to-daughter mentorship. Therefore, my mother raised me with the help of my grandparents and their focus was mainly on the healing power of the ocean. I was taught to listen to the ocean and hear its communication and interpret what it says and communicate with me. Nothing beats that! For me, the ocean offers more than the food; it feeds my spirit. I was taught to take what one needs, not more!

There is a special shell that my mother showed me and taught me to use in a very special way. My parents were displaced and forcefully removed from their traditional place/home and relocated to a further place from the ocean. When we moved away, this shell would bring me closer to the ocean when I put it close to my ear. My 88-year-old mother talks about the mermaid which was taken from the ocean and it was of such significant importance to her and the history of the Khoi people. We are of the Khoi origins and it is there in the history of our people. So, the specific shell is the most important thing as it brings me closer to the ocean – having learnt about it is amazing! It is our tradition! You cannot just find it anywhere …

During apartheid, we were not allowed to come to beaches like these at Summerstrand (a beach in Gqeberha, an Eastern Cape coastal city) – ours were those at St Georges Strand beach (also in Gqeberha) – so coming here for the first time after apartheid was the best thing that ever happened to me as we also experienced the best beaches ever and generally the movement to be closer to the ocean. We are always excluded and they forget that they found us here! We are the people that should have a say in everything but it is not the case. We have been stripped of everything! This exclusion emerged when we were punished by the colonialist rulers for speaking our mother language. It was a way to make sure that we lose our mother language because if you were caught talking/speaking in your mother language, your four teeth would be removed. The youngsters do not know this.

History must be rewritten so that all the lies and wrongdoings are told truthfully and corrected. It is upsetting that we are not part of any decision-making in this country. Nobody tells us of anything and it pains me so much. We now need permits to access the ocean and we also hear about the permits. When we ask to join these Coops, we are kept away and told that it is full and they want us to work under them. We have been stripped of our rights.

One day, I will buy a house near the ocean so I can fulfil the ancestral rights to be near the ocean because I believe in the ocean … I belong to the ocean.

We were taught to take what we need, but the big commercial companies are allowed to do as they please and sadly the Government is supporting and in agreement with them. They are plundering the ocean resources and over-harvesting and the impacts are felt by us the excluded. The Government cannot come to tell us that we cannot fish here or there because it is reserved for MPAs without consulting us because it is our livelihood at stake here. Restore what you took from us! Nothing about us without us!

Discussion

These powerful descriptions of lives lived with the sea, and the struggles to continue to live well with the sea are deeply inspiring and harrowing. From these accounts, there are common thematic threads: (1) A gendered division of labour which begins as children and is carried on to adult-hood, whereby relationality to the ocean is inherently gendered. (2) All experienced dispossession geographically from the ocean due to the apartheid Group Areas Act, and subsequent forced removals, but more recently the legislative control of ocean access through permits, the establishment of cooperatives, and their slow and sluggish approvals, checks and balances associated with both, keep the Grandmothers from the sea. (3) The women all derive not only an important livelihood from the sea, but a deep spiritual and emotional relationship, which cannot be easily separated, yet these same livelihoods can be easily exploited by governments and big business. (4) All the women speak of generational learning connected with the sustainable and customary use as well as the cultural relationality that is associated with the sea. The sea connects them to memories of their grandparents and parents. (5) Finally, all the women collaborate and articulate with careful political rigour (Borrás & Edquist, 2013) how their voice and knowledge(s) are silenced, excluded and sidelined by government and big business, and explore ways in which this should be amended. Finally, (6) the Grandmothers express how they are part of the ocean, that the ocean speaks with them, and is the conduit to their ancestors, their history and their identity.

The Grandmothers' stories and their personal analysis of the ocean space and their place in it, resonates with a global turn towards transformation in the governance and sustainable use of our fragile marine resources (Gissi et al., 2018). The Grandmothers clearly articulate their desire for inclusivity in the way the oceans are managed both economically and in finding more robust and participative approaches to marine protection and use. The value of the ocean is described in nuanced poetic ways, as Gogo Nofoto Demise says: "To me the ocean is 'HONEY' it is my pot of honey. Honey is nice but once spoiled it becomes undesirable!" She concludes by saying "we are suppose to be free, but we are still not free" this is in reference to lack of freeedom to participate in the ocean space. For Gogo Charlotte, seawater calms her and connects her with ancestors. For Gogo Jolene, a shell her mother gave her, kept the sea close within her imagination during forced removals, and for all the Grandmothers, it is clear that the ocean encounters they have while harvesting, fishing or even within their imagination brings them peace, freedom and creativity. This experience is, at the same time, painfully contrasted with the many ways their lives are cut off from the sea, denied access to decision making and robbed of many other freedoms. The contrast between these realities is distinct.

The Grandmothers reveal that their ocean livelihoods are driven and inspired well beyond economic benefits, but are rooted in rich and nuanced relationality with the ocean. Indeed it is an oversight of most marine resource management policies and practices to ignore spiritual, cultural and emotional relationships that women have with the ocean.

Speaking and listening to the ocean is important in their lives, with the Grandmothers reflecting on the ways they communicate and make meaning with the sea. There is an intimacy in and relationality with the sea that cannot be fully described or defined and manifests in the tone and languaging in Xhosa, which exists beyond the confines of any existing policy or permit as evident in Gogo Margaret's story.

By far, the majority of the Grandmothers concerns surround struggles with accessibility to the ocean and to decision making. Not only do they offer clear critiques of the systems in place, they also have clear suggestions for ways forward. Such as improved seasonal permit regulations, more inclusive policies in permit allocations, removing 'middle-men' from the value chain, to alternative management of protected areas and harvesting schedules that align more with the moon and weather cycles, than arbitrary calendar and financial dates. They also articulate how improved legislation that protects the rights of women to access selected coastal and ocean areas would have a powerful impact on their livelihoods and wellbeing. They argue for their indigenous local ecological knowledge and other practical wisdoms to be included in decision making and management, and for genocide and epistemicide to be acknowledged.

In our experience, and with the insights of these Grandmothers we argue that the consultation of coastal communities (especially women, who often lead households) is included in ocean decision making, and their inclusion is key and beneficial in resetting the balance in human and more-than-human flourishing in and with the ocean.

The majority of coastal economies research has shown that there has been a gradual bias in appreciating the role of traditional or those from marginalised structures and the management of the ocean resources only in cases where these drive the broader corporate economic agenda (Mnguni, 2014). As Nofoto, Demise & Magaret describe, an unfair advantage, power and freedom is awarded to large companies or industries, yet their access to these resources, which are theirs constitutionally remain out of reach.

In the majority of cases, coastal communities are driven out to the peripheral economic activities of the benefits that were initially promised at the inception of major projects (Andrews, et al., 2021; Erwin & Marks, 2021). In South Africa, these economic expansions are tied up with the legacy of apartheid policies, and leaves communities impoverished and excluded from ocean benefits (Sowman & Sunde, 2018). In some situations, coastal communities in the Eastern Cape and other provinces have to travel extremely long distances to access traditionally accessible coastal areas, where they once lived and thrived (Kalina et al., 2019).

Conclusion

In their own language, context and idiomatic analysis the Eastern Cape Grandmothers articulate and argue clearly their critique of ocean exclusions, and the value of their knowledge and their livelihoods for future sustainable ocean use and local economies. As Gogo Charlotte says: "Nothing about us without us!". We have heard this often, and alongside her rallying call we have heard in meetings and conversations over the past few years – *'Wathinta' abafazi, wathinta' imbokodo'* (You Strike a woman, You Strike a Rock). In this case, the rock is covered in shellfish and seaweed, and can withstand the tidal changes and the stormy waves with such grace and steadfastness. While we reject the archetypal narrative of the 'resilient African women', we honour this phrase more as a figuration or metaphor for 'foundation' or 'bedrock' – the substrate that their practical wisdoms offer for building inclusive, participatory and dynamic ocean governance. Their powerful contributions to human and more-than-human flourishing, care practices, livelihood expansion, heritage education must no longer be violently neglected, sidelined, silenced, excluded and patronised in a myriad of ways that it currently is by ocean decision makers (Thomas et al., 2021). As Poltera (2019) argues, women's strength should not be ignored in the exploitation of ocean resources and issues of guardianship; indeed, it should be celebrated and listened to, and acted upon. While we are cautious, and do not intend to romanticise the extremely difficult and complex reality, burden and domestic labour held by these Grandmothers, we take guidance from Chazan (2008, p. 935) who calls for more nuanced and forward-looking analyses and interventions for how we might support rural Grandmothers in South Africa, analyses that recognise Grandmothers as central to the society's thin safety net and precarious and tangled realities of older women's complex and diverse vulnerabilities. We hope that this chapter shifts for a moment our attention away from what from scientists and sociologists have to say, and rather gifts our attention to these elders who embody and live all the qualities and practical wisdoms needed for care and custodianship practices, policies and principles of ocean governance. More still, they offer the field of Hydrofeminism a rich, unique and politically rigorous feminist analysis of the ocean decision making space, one that expands and includes Xhosa Grandmothers in all their luminiferous wisdom.

Acknowledgements

The Coastal Justice Network is funded and supported by the One Ocean Hub, which is a collaborative research for sustainable development project funded by UK Research and Innovation (UKRI) through the Global Challenges Research

Fund (GCRF) (Grant Ref: NE/S008950/1). We are grateful for their generous support for this work. We would also like to express our gratitude to Coastal Justice Network colleagues, namely; Anna James, Danel Janse van Rensburg, Kira Erwin, Irna Senekal, Jackie Sunde and Taryn Pereira-Kaplan, who contributed in many meaningful ways towards the work put into this book chapter. Also, we are eternally grateful to the members of the editorial board and reviewers, for their care and diligence in handling and reviewing our work.

Notes

1 www.coastaljusticenetwork.co.za
2 Xhosa Cattle – Killings refer to a prophet – diviner who advised the Xhosa people to kill all their cattle, destroy their crops and not to farm, if they did so, the ancestors would arise, the living restored to youth, the whites would be swept into the sea, the land will be free from diseases and grain pits would overflow (Zarwan, 1976, p. 519).
3 This business woman sells the seaweed she collects from the Grandmothers, to a large pharmaceutical and cosmetics company for overseas trade.

References

Andrews, N., Bennett, N., Le Billon, P., Green, S., Cisneros-Montemayor, A., Amongin, S., & Sumaila, U. (2021). Oil, fisheries and coastal communities: A review of impacts on the environment, livelihoods, space and governance. *Energy Research & Social Science, 75*, 102009.

Bank, L. (2002). Beyond red and school: Gender, tradition and identity in the rural Eastern Cape. *Journal of Southern African Studies, 28*(3), 631–649.

Bantwini, B. (2010). How teachers perceive the new curriculum reform: Lessons from a school district in the Eastern Cape Province, South Africa. *International Journal Educational Development, 30*(1), 83–90.

Borrás, S., & Edquist, C. (2013). The choice of innovation policy instruments. *Technological Forecasting and Social Change, 80*(8), 1513–1522.

Chazan, M. (2008). Seven 'deadly' assumptions: Unravelling the implications of HIV/AIDS among grandmothers in South Africa and beyond. *Ageing & Society, 28*(7), 935–958.

Erwin, K., & Marks, M. (2021). The economic lives of migrant women in a South African city: informal work, gender, and transformative possibilities. *Third World Thematics: A TWQ Journal,* 1–21.

Gissi, E., Portman, M., & Hornidge, A. (2018). Un-gendering the ocean: Why women matter in ocean governance for sustainability. *Marine Policy, 94*, 215–219.

Kalina, M., Mbereko, A., Maharaj, B., & Botes, A. (2019). Subsistence marine fishing in a neoliberal city: a political ecology analysis of securitization and exclusion in Durban, South Africa. *Journal of Political Ecology, 26*(1), 363–380.

Le Guin, U. K. (2020, original edition 1996). *The carrier bag theory of fiction.* Ignota Books.

Mahlatsi, M. L. (2018). The peasants' revolt: Analysing the role of the democratic state in the struggle for land and environmental justice in Xolobeni, Eastern Cape, South Africa. *Journal of Public Administration, 53*(2), 615–631.

Mnguni, E. (2014). The role of traditional leaders in the promotion of cultural tourism in the south coast of Kwazulu-Natal: A case study of Umzumbe Municipality. *Journal of Educational and Social Research, 4*(6), 265–270.

Neimanis, A. (2012). Hydrofeminism: Or, on becoming a body of water. In H. Henriette Gunkel, C. Nigianni, & F. Söderbäck (Eds.), *Undutiful daughters: Mobilizing future concepts, bodies and subjectivities in feminist thought and practice* (pp. 96–115). Palgrave Macmillan.

Poltera, J. (2019). Exploring examples of women's leadership in African contexts. *Agenda, 33*(1), 3–8.

Sowman, J., & Sunde, J. (2018). Social impacts of marine protected areas in South Africa on coastal fishing communities. *Ocean and Coastal Management, 157*, 168–179.

Thomas, A., Mangubhai, S., Fox, M., Meo, S., Miller, K., Naisilisili, W., Veitayaki, J., & Waqairatu, S. (2021). Why they must be counted: Significant contributions of Fijian women fishers to food security and livelihoods. *Ocean & Coastal Management, 205*, 105571.

Zarwan, J. (1976). The Xhosa Cattle Killings, 1856–57. *Cahiers d'etudes Africaines, 16*(63), 519–539.

13

RE-IMAGINING TROUBLED SPACES OF ACADEMIA WHILE THINKING WITH AND THROUGH OCEANS

Black feet white sand – A photo essay

Cheri Hugo

I explore the use of the ocean as a metaphor to navigate difficult spaces within academia for womxn of colour. In addition, the ocean and my personal swimming adventure are intertwined. That is the visual tale of how I used swimming and the water metaphorically to guide me through two challenging environments – the sea and academia. Using autoethnographic methodology and drawing on hydrofeminism and Black feminist theories, I share personal narratives from my experiences with and through the water in Cape Town, South Africa, as a womxn of colour. The chapter highlights two strategies that emerge through this journey: resilience and empathy. Through a poem and narratives, I unpack and explain the significance of these strategies in supporting my survival and thriving in both the ocean and academia. I foreground the need for re-imagining troubled spaces in academia and for using creative and personal narratives as a means to highlight social justice perspectives in the design of higher education.

My work focuses on strategies for womxn of colour in academia to navigate postgraduate education, and move from surviving to thriving. Who am I, and what challenges do womxn of colour face? I am interested in the experiences of womxn of colour, who navigate whiteness and patriarchy, while juggling an often-overwhelming teaching load and attempting postgraduate degrees. I engage autoethnography to examine my experiences as a Black womxn academic and doctoral student teaching in the University of Technology's Design Department. I use autoethnography to present a first-person narrative of prejudice and address injustice. To conduct the autoethnography, I combined theory and narrative to connect analysis with action, bridge material and ethical practice, and illuminate methods to embody change. I collected data through various methods, including original poetry, journaling, drawings, self-timed photography, and mixed media. I also use methodologies that focus on embodiment and affect to move past traditional logics of study (Figures 13.1 and 13.2).

DOI: 10.4324/9781003355199-13

FIGURE 13.1   Cheri Hugo, Black feet 1. Photo: Verity FitzGerald.

FIGURE 13.2   Cheri Hugo, Sacred. Photo: Verity FitzGerald.

As I look back on my childhood in Cape Town, I am struck by how much the experiences of exclusion and discrimination have stayed with me. From a young age, I knew that some beaches were not meant for people like me.

And even now, as I move through the city's beaches, I can still feel that sense of unease and uncertainty. These childhood experiences have influenced the way I approach other spaces as well, including the classroom where I now teach. As a drawing instructor in a design course, I am constantly aware of the need to reassure both myself and my students that we belong here. It can be challenging, but I know it is important work.

Lately, I have been immersed in a PhD study on the strategies that womxn of colour in design can use to thrive in academia. This research has led me to explore my own embodied experiences with rage, race, and respectability politics. Using autoethnography, supported by decolonised feminist theory and methodologies, I hope to tell a story that can help others navigate these complex issues. However, I am more than just a PhD student and teacher. I am also a mother, a designer, a writer, and a creator. I carry with me the legacy of my ancestors who were enslaved, displaced, and forcibly removed from their homes. These experiences continue to haunt me, but they also drive me to push for change and to be a force for good in the world.

In 2020, as the world was grappling with the COVID-19 pandemic, I found solace in the ocean. I had read that swimming could help with COVID-19 lungs, and I was drawn to the water in a way I had not been before. Despite feeling like an outsider in the ocean, much like I do in academia, I felt a sense of freedom and release (Figures 13.3, 13.4, 13.5, 13.6, 13.7, 13.8, 13.9, 13.10, and 13.11).

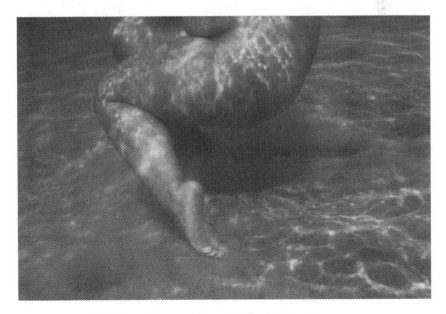

FIGURE 13.3   Cheri Hugo, Homage. Photo: Verity FitzGerald.

FIGURE 13.4   Cheri Hugo, White sand 1: plunge. Photo: Verity FitzGerald.

FIGURE 13.5   Cheri Hugo, White sand 2: step. Photo: Verity FitzGerald.

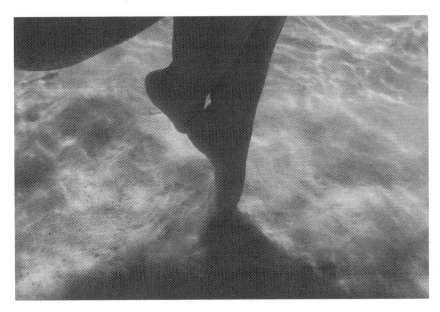

FIGURE 13.6   Cheri Hugo, White sand 3: tippy toe. Photo: Verity FitzGerald.

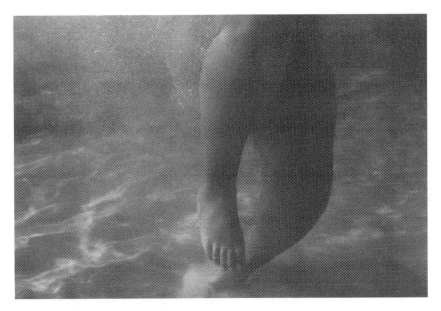

FIGURE 13.7   Cheri Hugo, White sand 4: defend. Photo: Verity FitzGerald.

FIGURE 13.8   Cheri Hugo, Black feet 1: play. Photo: Verity FitzGerald.

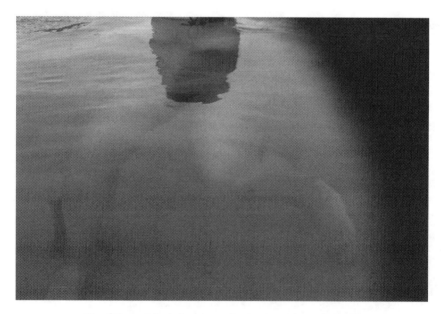

FIGURE 13.9   Cheri Hugo, Black feet 2: perform. Photo: Verity FitzGerald.

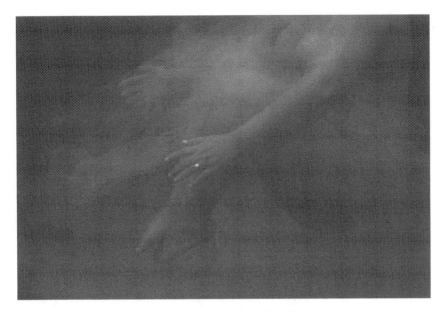

FIGURE 13.10   Cheri Hugo, Black feet 3: prepare. Photo: Verity FitzGerald.

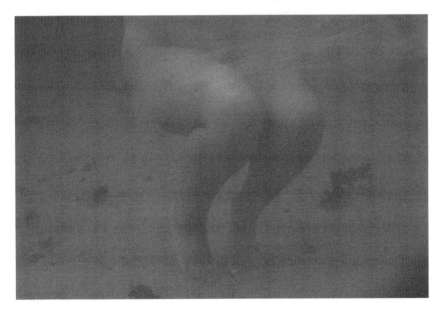

FIGURE 13.11   Cheri Hugo, Black feet 4: pray. Photo: Verity FitzGerald.

Black feet, white sand

Black feet through this white gate
Black feet on the mountainside, high
Black feet overlooking the white sands and oceans deep
Black feet on white tiles
Black feet all over this lady's white sheets

Black feet in black adidas slippers Adidas branding all over this white
  neighbourhood and cobbled sidewalk
Black feet tippy toe over the railway line
Black feet over the rocks and creepy crawly goedetjies
Black feet on the white sands
Black feet sinking deep
Black feet wet with salty water

Black feet slow and steady deep we go
Black feet respect we must show, the highest honour is bestowed
Black feet I can hear them fret
Black feet tippy toe on the ocean floor
Black feet glide, slide, step and gently push up

Black feet pointed, glide, Grand Jete and Pirouette
Black feet with ancient one's dance all over the ocean floors
Black feet stand firm in the ocean waves
Black feet remember you are on the front line
Black feet must be ready steady against the tide
Black feet with teeny tiny white sands, on this white lady's garden table high
Black feet performing, remember who you a r e.

During my stay near the sea in Simons Town, on the Kalk Bay side of Cape Town, I was eager to participate in an early morning swimming event with a community I had recently joined. However, I had to stay at a bed and breakfast, a predominantly white space, and I could not help but reflect on the labour and sacrifices I had to make to be there. As I gazed at my black feet on the white sheets, I reflected on the added burden that womxn of colour face when enjoying beach days – the financial cost, the responsibility of caring for their families, and the extra effort required to access the ocean. All of these thoughts made me feel like an impostor, performing for a white audience (Figure 13.12, 13.13, 13.14, 13.15, 13.16, 13.17, 13.18, 13.19, 13.20, 13.21, 13.22, 13.23, and 13.24).

FIGURE 13.12   Reflection on a poem. Photo: Cheri Hugo.

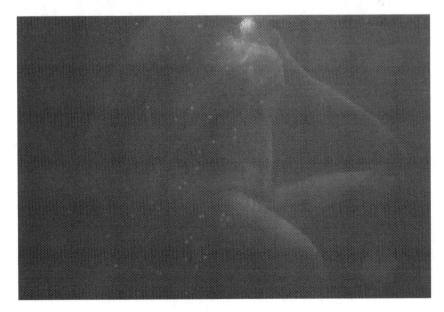

FIGURE 13.13   Cheri Hugo, Venus. Still from an Mp3 video in which the poem is read
while the figure dances. Photo: Verity FitzGerald.

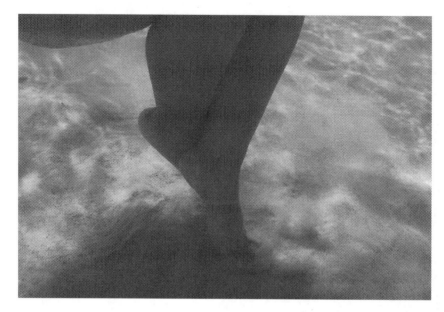

FIGURE 13.14 Cheri Hugo, Ancient voices 1: Honour. Photo: Verity FitzGerald.

FIGURE 13.15 Cheri Hugo. Ancient voices 2: Acknowledge. Photo: Verity FitzGerald.

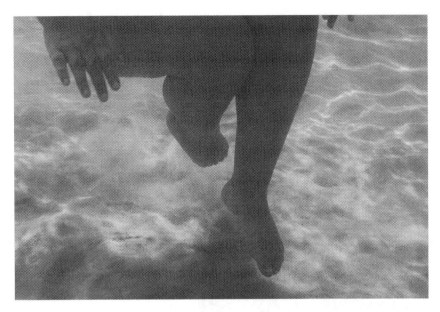

FIGURE 13.16   Cheri Hugo, Ancient voices 3: Communion. Photo: Verity FitzGerald.

FIGURE 13.17   Ancient voices 4: Action. Photo: Verity FitzGerald.

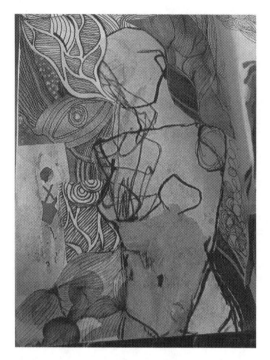

FIGURE 13.18 Cheri Hugo, Creating with ocean 1: See. Photo: Cheri Hugo.

FIGURE 13.19 Cheri Hugo, Creating with ocean 2: Feel. Photo: Cheri Hugo.

FIGURE 13.20   Cheri Hugo, Creating with ocean 3: Write. Photo: Cheri Hugo.

FIGURE 13.21   Cheri Hugo, Creating with ocean 4: Entangled. Photo: Cheri Hugo.

FIGURE 13.22 Cheri Hugo, Creating with ocean 5: Grow. Photo: Cheri Hugo.

FIGURE 13.23 Cheri Hugo, Creating with oceans 6: Become/(un)become. Photo: Cheri Hugo.

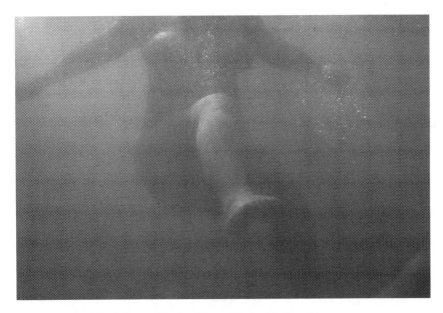

FIGURE 13.24   Cheri Hugo, Warrior. Photo: Verity FitzGerald.

I advocate for the re-imagining of troubled spaces in academia by thinking with and through the ocean. Womxn of colour in academia have learned to negotiate and survive by being resilient, offering care to ourselves and others, and making difficult sacrifices as we navigate spaces that are often unwelcoming. By drawing on embodied, affective, situated, and autoethnographic methodology, we can disrupt the colonial, patriarchal, capitalist, anthropocentric logics that continue to shape hegemonic practices in the academy.

Contributors:

Verity FitzGerald (Photography)

Cheri Hugo Poems (artwork, figure, art direction, journal entries and photography)

Year: 2022

AFTERWORD

Between spin and drift, or overviews and undercurrents

Meghan Judge

In August 2022, I was invited to present a response to the conference *Hydrofeminism and wild engagements with ocean/s: Towards a justice-to-come in South African contexts* (which has since expanded into this book) under the theme "what bubbles up". As a scholar of the Oceanic Humanities and an artist and curator who has participated in and facilitated cultural exchanges between islands in the Western Indian Ocean region and Eastern and Southern continental Africa, I have drawn on my ever-expanding and varied reception of the complex material-affective and socio-political oceanic frequencies transmitted across the region. Sounding within this are the always already entangled histories of interconnectivity, situated knowledges, migration, forced labour, mythology, spirituality, modernity, terra-biases, power, resistance, amphibious technologies and cosmologies, all of which thicken the present with the settled and unsettled presence of the past. Being of varied settler and migratory descent in the region,[1] I also take up and grapple with (post)colonial legacies that continue to divide eco-socio relations today. I pay specific attention to limits of knowability, taking up an in/corporeal openness (Alaimo, 2010; Grosz, 2017) that allows for adjustments to epistemological frameworks that are brittle and corroding.

Paying attention to histories in this context asks of the artist-researcher in me to congeal a praxis for rupturing the linearity of time-as-progress that has been largely asserted through modernity. This praxis notices the past that has been silenced by narratives of power. It listens to where the past has become stuck in the present – a noisy excess that refuses to disappear (Dayan, 2008; Trouillot, 1995). At its core, this rupture reshapes imaginaries of human figurations from the overdetermined figure benefiting from the Anthropocene to those that live in more harmonious ecological relations. While centring the human in this inquiry poses problems for noticing planetary imaginaries of more-than-human plurality,

DOI: 10.4324/9781003355199-14

staying with the trouble (Haraway, 2016) of such imagined figurations is essential to the project of deconstructing the active power that exercises agency over what is possible. Further, finding ways for *how to experience* is an important part of modular change towards an ethics of relational care. I thus cannot do away with the human entirely. This praxis is always moving towards potentials and possibilities for sensing and making sense of life outside of exceptionalism. It finds amphibious hydro-figurations where the socio-eco divide is less prominent (Neimanis, 2019), expanding and dissolving imaginaries where necessary.

This book works with the past to locate a thicker present (Barad, 2017), understanding this now-time as something to be sensitised towards. The book acts at the unruly edges (Tsing, 2015) of in/abilities to perceive what is here, congealing through the corporeal complexities of histories and presence in South Africa. As a person with varying ancestral lines that knot and ring through the apparatus of the whiteness project active here,[2] I understand the imaginary that the book grapples with as one of fullness and emptiness constructed by what counts as human (and is central to who benefits) and also what is pushed outside of this figuration – the less-than-human. Civilised Man is full and centred/those outside of this figuration are empty and othered; the land is full and ready for extraction/the ocean is empty and a backdrop for voyage. This imaginary asserts a dialectics for hierarchies of being, granting permission for dominance and control. As this book demonstrates, this imaginary extends into and through colonial technologies for erasing nature–human relations on lands and oceans, dividing bodies that once coexisted. The forwarding of hydrobodies as an alternative to this imaginary is a move away from the terra-bound centres of exceptionalism, recognising bodies as different, watery and mixing with the potential for what they might become – a future on its way, yet also remembered.

Engaging with the materialities of the ocean, especially in relation to the sonic that I work mostly with, I am reminded that some frequencies are beyond the hearing range of the hegemonic constructions of an over-terra-centric determined (Wynter, 2003; da Silva, 2007, McKittick, 2015) and exceptionalised human listener. This reminder calls two points together: the specifically constructed figurations of the human and the material activities of the ocean itself. These two points open a productive tension for inquiring into the ocean–human relations; the material and immaterial touch, move and become through the undercurrents that are driven by positions, density, winds and force. In this, it is possible to learn how to drift: to be moved by that which moves. Realising temporalities of matter active within planetary activities allows for reorienting outside of narrative construction – a before space where power over narrative construction is necessarily relinquished so that stories shape through encounters and relations.

The chapters in this book work through the present as a movement as it dips and splashes along the surface of undercurrents and atmospheres, bubbles spinning around differing bodies that plunge between past and future, above and below the waterline. Stories are shaped through skin and salt. These bubbles act around bodies in oceanic relations, churning in a temporality that diverges from the linear assertions of colonial spacetime. The South African context offers a scaling of attention through frequency ranges that are too often silenced by dominant narratives of historiography, yet always corrode into their edges.

The book moves towards justice, towards rest, but is not quite there yet. As such, the chapters do not sound in harmony, but instead perform through differences that noise together. This book rings through such noise, it rings with the release of ghosts that haunt an amnesiac climate, shaking the scaffoldings of colonial apparatuses. In this ringing the air is smudged and the smog of racialised structures cleans towards clearer breathability. Below, I move through the chapters without order, responding instead to the ways that they well up and rumble together in mixed temperature, generating movements in their shared activity.

I begin in the middle of the book with Zayaan Khan's chapter, *Listening with the ocean through deep time and ancient futures: sea/shore sound piece* that draws us into the cyclic movement of the ocean. Khan draws our attention towards a final outbreath, a resting place, the exhale that we give to the ocean after an inhale that the ocean gives to us. In this, the work takes up rituals for death that draws the reader into a cycle that is born and dies in the ocean. Her work is a reminder of the ocean as an ancestor, a womb, a breeder of bacterial multi-species climate-changers that give and take life. In times of such anthropocentric climate precariousness, it may be wise to recall ways, as Khan does, to breathe in the deep time of photosynthetic activities. That is, to remember beyond a single lifespan and sense what already exists. The work presented by Khan shapes the imaginable by listening and responding to the sounds of consciousness submerged. What sounds is from the inside, an already-present and already-there frequency below hearing range that asks for a different perceptive attunement. Khan's proposed attention shift activates through oceanic memory, funnelling down to the depths, where, in the ocean, deeper mixed layers contain greater heat content that confer more thermal inertia. Khan's rituals rise through such heat, drawing up and transmogrifying the nutrients and gasses that are released into the thick uppermost memory surface layers for dissemination and spread.

Oceanic rituals continue in the book through grandmothers whose technologies of relations already exist. The presence of these rituals store memory and refuse cultures of amnesia built into colonialism and capitalism that erase shared eco-socio-sentience. For Gogo Nomalibongwe, Gogo Margaret, Gogo Nomalibongwe, Gogo Charlotte and Gogo Jolene, the grandmothers in Buhle Francis and Dylan McGarry's *Grandmothers of the Sea: Stories and lessons from five Xhosa ocean elders*, time has become stuck between their embodied knowledge recalled through ritual and systematic erasure. They spin in the present unable to move forward, pulled by the past and pushed by the future, a tension in unproductive disturbance. Buhle and McGarry listen to the clash of these epistemic and ontological oceanic relations in the present and seek out how they can create divergent currents for hierarchical, socio-political knowledge through ocean policy that can release the past into the future. They seek ways to align with the yearnings of these grandmothers for a state of relations that rests in its past in ways that are present, accessible and felt.

The care demonstrated in such listening extends in McGarry's *When ancestors are included in ocean decision & meaning making* and is joined by Aaniyah Martin's *Collaborative innovations into pedagogies of care for South African hydrocommons*, Adrienne Van Eden-Wharton's *Restless Remains and Untimely Returns: on walking and Wading* and Barry Lewis' *Diffracting forests: Making home in the (Post)Apartheid city*. These authors propose various practices that encompass embodied caring at intersectional edges. In this, community-making at the edges of difference congeals through empathy. Here, empathy becomes a glutinous mode for perceiving inter-species justice through embodied practices. These chapters work through different sensibilities that are evoked through story-making and the narration of storytelling, where unusual parts are allowed to come together like chimeric worlds of the ecotones. The chapters pose that opening through empathic sensing across worlds of difference allows for necessary becoming-through-community that moves across multi-species zones of contact.

The potential for thinking through embodied encounters with the ocean have been dived further into by Cheri Hugo's photo-essay *Re-imagining troubled spaces of academia while thinking with and through oceans*: *Black feet white sand,* Karen Graaff's *Surfing as a space for activism and change: What could surfing be(come)?,* Tamara Shefer, Nike Romano and Vivienne Bozalek's *Oceanic swimming-writing-thinking for justice-to-come scholarship*. Here, the sea becomes both a place for fugitive escape from the overdetermined pressures of terra-centric life in the South African context, as well as a place for reckoning with the tension that pushes these bodies below water. The chapters from these authors grant permissions for being with the ocean by mixing; becoming rearranged within the ocean's material activities offers a necessarily affective rearrangement from the overburdening grooves of work and life on land. In their writing, an underwater breath of calm is drawn so that the inevitable return to the doldrums and atmospheric pressures on land can be somehow survived. A common thread here is the finding of a practice for return that, again and again, dips and threads through the disrupting and caring surface line as it holds both above and below together in a potential for existing through and with both.

In storying, this book draws attention to the notion of aesthetics which is raised by the works of Delphi Carsten's and Mer Roberts' *Octopus Aesthetics*, Joanne Peers' *Relational bodies of memory, time and place: Hauntings in salty waters* and Kristy Stone's *Affect in the Archives and Object Refusals: Toward an Oceanic Aesthetic*. The aesthetics here are drenched in the researchers' implicit involvement with and in their oceanic work, wherein the researcher inquires open-endedly finding themselves within their work. The projects in these chapters slow down to notice the mutations of researcher in relation to the storying process, and how the image that the story holds adjusts through the inquiry into it. The affective aesthetics gathered in these works seep towards the reader, offering pools for slipping into the research that is itself opened and shaped by movements, creatures and temporalities of the oceanic.

The practices that pulse through the chapters mentioned above materialise within an utterly unjust landscape, demonstrating different attentions and abilities to attend. The works dive into and rise from the very core of the imaginaries that perpetuate the unjust, remaking this core from multiple directions and discourses. And yet, it does not feel like this is enough. The justice never feels enough, it is on its way there but not there yet – as Derrida points out, justice is never here: it is yet to come.

The rage of this unrest bubbles up in Hugo's photo essay *Black feet on white sand*, where she dunks the build-up of heat, the fever, into the chaotic ocean. This acts as a re-orientation with and in the waters, accompanied by a mass of bubbles from land that spin around her body. Hugo self-dunks, again and again. This is a practice towards cooling, towards becoming amphibious. Her story is with and through the restless past that is stuck in and haunts the present. Here, the ocean is a space for processing what it means to swirl between rage and "spots of enjoyment". Such spots echo the acupuncture points for reconciliation that McGarry's locates in a messy chorus of voices, pierced and piercing through the sinews of now. Finding such points requires slowing to the rupturing prick of disruption, then sinking into the opened hole at the surface to allow the linear progression of time to rush overhead so that alternative and wayward temporalities might be sensed.

Doing this, Shefer, Romano and Bozalek's storytelling "hiccups" like a breath within a breath. Their storied bubbles pop into the continuously moving background from submerged under spaces. Each bubble holds its own anxious terra-bound breath, yet their thinning edges exist in a threshold of oceanic encounters, transparent and quivering between bodies and touching worlds. This touching together and apart offers a staying-place to sense the in-between – a useful analogy for the notion of slowing down and listening in order to "re-navigate", as Stone forwards in her writings. Navigating relies on orientation, noticing what is already present and moving and what is moved by that which moves. Finding drift within this Van Eeden-Wharton delineates from overdetermined "atlases", calling for slow returns that iteratively orient a different sort of "being-with". These atlases are sensory openings that leak towards colours and emotions of multispecies decay, holding affective potentials for (joining Stone again) "attuning" towards a palette of entangled sensitivity. Such palettes of entanglement also well up in Peers' configuring of the colour brown that mixes and sounds in her porous skin as she swims with salty ghosts.

The poetic patterning that occurs throughout the chapters brings together importantly overwhelming terrains, where the excess of what can be is sensed. Carstens and Roberts, Peers, Hugo and Stone's aesthetics of unbecoming and becoming reveal the oftentimes overwhelming sensations of slow reconfiguration in the world. In part, the discomfort politicised here is an opening to Graaff's notion of making the unusual usual, and goes some way to responding to the need for better, more just narration about different bodies set in states of trauma and unrest, configured through colonial, apartheid, capitalist and anthropocentric frameworks that materialise varied and situated positionalities. The now-time that this book presents communicates within pasts and futures, sounding within the frequencies of the hydro-relational, at times rising, like Shamier Magmoet's film about coming into a relationship with the ocean from the nearby but historically segregated "Cape Flats",[3] as if to lift off the sea floor and fly with the marine creatures towards a something that is "more" – "more-than" the violence that grips so much of the lived daily experiences that seep through unsettled pasts. Martin proposes that, if we are to clean up and repair damaged spaces for co-existence, this can only happen with and through the presence of hauntologies in acts of community that are relational. Shefer, Romano and Bozalek open to being permeated by hauntologies where porous relations make and re-make bodies that are malleable, like Carstens and Roberts *Octopus Aesthetics*, which propose a shifting of perception towards a different kind of alive.

Such aliveness found in the amphibious potentials of hydrobodies are critical to troubling the scaffolding of hydroviolences that affect the social and the ecological. Hydrobodies slip through the binary lines that slice up scattered littoral cultures and livelihoods co-existing within oceanic relations. As Graaff points out, these binaries can be queered by tracing the unevenness of what they divide and weigh. The authors in this book critically play along the surface of these binary lines, rising and sinking between tensions of terra and ocean to recall amphibious atmospheres across social and ecological constructs. Playing here takes up being and becoming along varying wet-dry lifelines, offering differing vantage points for considering the ocean itself, oceanic relations and situated geographies, where social and ecological justices are drawn together.

Toni Giselle Stuart's opening poem, *Ocean Home*, is perhaps a good ending place for this overview, as it seems to scatter any attempt at universalising and "higher vision" that the very word overview suggests. In the poem, the reader is swept through the cyclic activity of the tides, along with the many parts moved within it, including the tides of history and an imaginary of time itself. The heaving inhale and exhale of her poetic utterances release a sense of now-time, of presence where past and future act together, felt most acutely before the tide comes in and before the daily preparations of labour at the harbour begin. Dawn marks a new return. Her words generate a hum of presence that she describes as both yesterday and tomorrow, yet tilting all the same towards what is to come. There is an offering here, a pause for reorientation within and amongst the movements of the ongoing beginning again.

Notes

1 Some of which come through: the adoption of a baby girl (my grandmother) during the depression of the inter-war years of coastal Scotland; a few sailors working for fleets in the Indian ocean trade who found opportunities for their families during a climate crisis in Norway on an island in the Western Indian Ocean but landed up in South Africa following the lure of the opportunities set up in the whiteness project at the time; and a somewhat reluctant move from a musician escaping "the troubles" in Ireland (my father), who fell in love with a South African woman (my mother) in London and subsequently moved here for a period of time to raise us children, despite his disdain for Apartheid rule. As oral knowledge fades, so does broader knowledge of my ancestral lines, notably on my great grandmother's side.
2 This project exceptionalised and bloated the white population through carefully constructed racial binaries that, in the face of much resistance, violently othered and extracted from black and brown bodies, as well as lands, animals and oceans essentially building the (post)colonial Anthropocene (Yusoff, 2018).
3 www.myhero.com/rise-from-the-cape-flats

References

Alaimo, S. (2010). *Bodily natures: science, environment, and the material self*. Indiana University Press.

Barad, K. (2017). What Flashes Up: Theological-Political-Scientific Fragments. In Keller, C. & Rubenstein, J. (Eds), *Entangled Worlds: Religion Science and New Materialisms* (pp. 21-28).Fordham University Press.

Da Silva, D.F. (2007). *Toward a global idea of race*. University of Minnesota Press.

Dayan, J. (2008). *Haiti, history, and the gods*. Berkeley University of California Press.Grosz, E. (2017). *The incorporeal ontology, ethics, and the limits of materialism*. Columbia University Press.

Haraway, D. (2016). *Staying with the trouble: Making kin in the Chthulucene*. Duke University Press.

Neimanis, A. (2019). *Bodies of water: posthuman feminist phenomenology*. Bloomsbury Academic.

Trouillot, M. (1995). *Silencing the past: Power and the production of history*. Beacon Press.

Tsing, A. (2015). *The mushroom at the end of the world: On the possibility of life in capitalist ruins*. Princeton University Press.

Wynter, S. (2003). Unsettling the coloniality of being/power/truth/freedom: Towards the human, after man, its overrepresentation—An argument. *CR: The New Centennial Review*, 3(3), 257–337. https://doi.org/10.1353/ncr.2004.0015.

Yusoff, K. (2018). *A billion black anthropocenes or none*. University of Minnesota Press.

INDEX